WILLIAM McKINLEY

THE AMERICAN NATION: A HISTORY

VOLUME 25

AMERICA AS A WORLD POWER

1897–1907

BY

JOHN HOLLADAY LATANÉ, Ph.D.

PROFESSOR OF HISTORY, WASHINGTON AND LEE UNIVERSITY

WITH MAPS

NEW YORK AND LONDON
HARPER & BROTHERS PUBLISHERS
Republished, 1970
Scholarly Press, 22929 Industrial Drive East
St. Clair Shores, Michigan 48080

Library of Congress Catalog Card Number: 79-145131
Standard Book Number 403-01064-0

TO THE
MEMORY OF MY BROTHER
HENRY WARING LATANÉ
THE HERO OF MY CHILDHOOD AND THE
INSPIRATION OF MY YOUTH
A STRONG AND NOBLE LIFE CUT SHORT IN A
CAREER FULL OF EARLY ACHIEVEMENT
AND OF BRILLIANT PROMISE

60984 81800

CONTENTS

MAPS

EDITOR'S INTRODUCTION

THIS, the last volume of narrative text in *The American Nation*, takes up the story where it is left off by Professor Dewey's *National Problems* (Vol. XXIV.), at the point where, after the election of 1896, the country began to take an absorbing interest in the insurrection in Cuba. The main field of the volume is therefore the Spanish War of 1898 and its consequences on the spirit and policy of the American people; but it also includes the great administrative and economic questions which have pressed for a solution.

The first four chapters are wholly devoted to the preliminaries of intervention in Cuba, the war with Spain and the following Peace of Paris; with a fifth chapter on the Philippine insurrection. The perplexing questions as to the status of the new dependencies is treated in chapter viii., (which includes Porto Rico), and in chapter ix. on the progress of government in the Philippines. Another phase of the outcome of the Spanish War is the history of the Republic of Cuba (chapter x.). On the other side of the world the possession of the Philippines

brought the United States into new relations with
the Orient, and into the Chinese Boxer movement
of 1900, described in chapter vi.   The latest phases
of the silver agitation are the currency standard bill
of 1900 described in chapter vii., and the election
of 1904 in chapter xiii.   Five other questions of
foreign policy: the Alaskan Boundary, Panama
Canal, International Arbitration, the Monroe Doctrine, and the collection of public debts in Latin
America, are the subjects of chapters xi.–xii., and
xiv.–xvi.   The volume closes with a study of the
immigration problem (chapter xvii.), and of the
economic problems of the time, particularly the
regulation of corporations (chapter xviii.)

The special importance of this volume in the
series is that it brings almost to the date of publication, and in many cases to a conclusion, questions
which have arisen within the fields of other volumes.
It rounds out the political and particularly the diplomatic history of the last half-century.   Professor
Latané's treatment is objective, and as far removed
from prejudgment as is possible on questions so
instant and so absorbing.   The special service of
the volume is to bring out clearly how the Spanish
War and its results set the nation in a strong position among the world's great powers, and gave to
the American people a new set of interests and
purposes.

AUTHOR'S PREFACE

THE difficulties of writing contemporary history can be fully appreciated only by those who have essayed the task. In employing a method, which, while progressive, is topical rather than strictly chronological, the first problem is the selection of those topics which best illustrate the progress and tendency of events and the exclusion of those that would unnecessarily burden or obscure the narrative. Many interesting and some important subjects have been omitted for lack of space. Another problem is that of proportion—the relative emphasis which each subject should receive. As the title of this volume would indicate, special attention has been given to questions of international and colonial policy, and the space devoted to internal affairs has been correspondingly reduced. A third and still more difficult problem is the treatment of the personal element, which enters as a prime factor into the history of every age. It is impossible to pass anything approximating final judgment on living men, for the real motives underlying their acts are rarely, if ever, fully revealed during their lifetime.   The personal element has therefore been somewhat subordinated.

In collecting material for this volume I have had occasion to work in a number of different libraries. I wish here to express my appreciation of the courtesies extended me by the authorities and attendants of the libraries of Congress, of the Department of State, of Harvard University, and of the University and State Historical Society of Wisconsin.   I wish also to express my obligations to Senator Thomas S. Martin and Representative Henry D. Flood, of Virginia, and to Hon. James B. Scott, Solicitor of the Department of State, for copies of valuable government publications, which, through their courtesy, I was able to secure in advance of distribution through the usual channels.   In the preparation of maps I have had the valuable assistance of Mr. David M. Matteson, of the Harvard Library.

Finally, to the editor of this series, whose friendship and sympathetic interest have long been a great stimulus to me, I wish to express my gratitude for the suggestions and criticisms he has so generously bestowed on this work at every stage of its preparation.

JOHN HOLLADAY LATANÉ.

AMERICA
AS A WORLD POWER

AMERICA

AS A WORLD POWER

CHAPTER I

INTERVENTION IN CUBA

(1895–1898)

A NATION rarely achieves in war precisely what it has in mind to achieve when the appeal to arms is made. The issue of battles imposes its burdens on the victor no less than on the vanquished. Our victory over Spain forced upon us unforeseen tasks of colonial government, and afforded a new point of departure in our national history. So vast have been the changes wrought, and so complex the questions that have arisen, that nine years afterwards it is difficult to recall with what singleness of purpose war was begun. The sole aim was to put a stop to a condition of affairs in the island of Cuba that had become intolerable. The blowing up of the *Maine* was an incident merely, but it came, when feelings were tense, as the climax in a long series of acts which served to illustrate the governmental incompetency of Spain.

When we consider the commercial importance of Cuba, its unique strategic position, and the chronic discontent of its inhabitants, occasioned by Spain's policy of systematic exploitation, the wonder is that the island should have remained so long a dependency of the mother country. For a century Cuba had been an object of peculiar interest and concern to the United States. Jefferson coveted it, and declared that its possession by Great Britain would be a great calamity to us; John Quincy Adams asserted that there were laws of political gravitation which would inevitably draw it towards the American Union; Henry Clay, as secretary of state, declared in 1825 that we could not consent to the occupation of Cuba or Porto Rico "by any other European power than Spain under any contingency whatever"; and Daniel Webster in 1843, while occupying the same post, assured Spain that in any attempt to wrest Cuba from her, "she might securely rely upon the whole naval and military resources of this country to aid her in preserving or recovering it." [1] During this early period the fear was that Cuba might be acquired by France or Great Britain, and the policy of the United States was to guarantee the island to Spain. With the consciousness of national expansion, and the growing conviction of "manifest destiny" that came with the Mexican

[1] Turner, *New West* (*Am. Nation*, XIV.), chap. xii.

War, American foreign policy assumed a much more aggressive character, and Cuba became an object of desire in the eyes not only of the slave-holding population of the South, as an accession to slave territory, but of a large part of the nation, on account of its strategic position commanding the proposed isthmian canal routes; for these routes were beginning to assume new importance as the most available line of communication with the rapidly developing interests in California. Consequently various attempts were made to annex Cuba to the United States, both by purchase from Spain and forcibly by filibustering expeditions.[1]

After the Civil War the main object of Cuban diplomacy was the extension of commercial relations with the island and the protection of American interests. The "Ten Years' War," from 1868 to 1878, was characterized by great cruelty, destruction of property, and irregular methods of warfare, and imposed grave responsibilities upon the United States. President Grant seriously considered, and even threatened intervention, and intervention at this time would probably have meant annexation; but such action was postponed, and peace was finally restored as a result of the exhaustion of both parties and the promise of definite reforms by Spain. The promised reforms were not carried out in good faith, and the old policy of exploitation was continued.[2]

[1] Latané, *Dipl. Relations of the U. S. and Spanish America*, 89 et seq.   [2] Dunning, *Reconstruction (Am. Nation*, XXII.), chap. x.

Finally, in February, 1895, the last insurrection against Spanish rule began, and soon developed the same features as the "Ten Years' War": both sides were guilty of outrages. The policy of the insurrectionary chief, Maximo Gomez, a man of great ability and tenacity of purpose, was to fight no pitched battles, but to keep up incessant skirmishes, to devastate the country, and to destroy every possible source of revenue, with the end in view of either exhausting Spain or forcing the intervention of the United States. He ordered first the suspension of work on all plantations; and later, in his proclamation of November 6, 1895, he ordered the destruction of all plantation buildings and their railroad connections. All laborers who continued at work in connection with any sugar factories were to be considered as traitors to their country and shot.[1] General Weyler arrived in Havana February 10, 1896, as governor and captain-general of Cuba, and six days later inaugurated a "reconcentration" policy: all the inhabitants of the island outside the garrisoned towns were directed by proclamation to "reconcentrate themselves" immediately in the towns occupied by troops. Any individual who should be found outside of these towns after the expiration of eight days was to be considered a rebel and tried as such.[2]

The United States was not a disinterested spec-

---

[1] *Senate Docs.*, 58 Cong., 2 Sess., No. 25, p. 125.
[2] *Foreign Relations*, 1898, p. 739.

tator to the execution of policies which paralyzed
the industries of Cuba and destroyed its commerce,
for American citizens owned at least fifty millions
of property in the island, and American commerce
at the beginning of the insurrection amounted to a
hundred millions annually. By the close of 1897
the claims on file in the state department against
Spain for the destruction of property amounted to
sixteen million dollars.[1] Aside from these special
pecuniary considerations the American people as a
whole felt a traditional interest in the Cubans and
generously extended to them the hearty sympathy
which they have been so quick to bestow since the
days of Henry Clay upon the Latin-American races
in their struggles for freedom.

From the beginning of the insurrection the authorities in Washington were seriously embarrassed
by numbers of Cubans who had sought naturalization in the United States, only to return to their
native isle and there to claim a privileged status
under the protection of the American government.
Between February 24, 1895, and January 22, 1897,
seventy-four persons claiming to be citizens of the
United States were arrested by the Spanish authorities on various charges, cast into prison, and in some
cases very harshly treated. Fully three-fourths of
those arrested were Cubans, or sons of Cubans, who
had been naturalized in the United States. Some

---

[1] Senate Com. on For. Rels., *Compilation of Reports*, VII., 339;
Moore, *Digest of Int. Law*. VI.. 121.

were released as the result of investigations that showed the charges to be groundless; others were expelled from the island; and the rest, including some who had been sentenced to long terms of imprisonment or death, were released as a concession to the United States when Weyler was recalled.[1]

Other Cubans, including many who were still Spanish subjects, worked out their revolutionary schemes on American soil and furnished the insurrectionists with military supplies. In order to meet this situation President Cleveland issued a proclamation June 12, 1895, in which he warned all persons within the jurisdiction of the United States against taking part in the insurrection against the established government of Spain, by doing any of the acts prohibited by American neutrality laws.[2] Notwithstanding this proclamation illegal expeditions were constantly being fitted out in the United States by Cubans or Cuban agents, and while the great majority of them were stopped by port officials or intercepted by the navy, a number did succeed in reaching the coasts of Cuba. When it is remembered that the United States had to watch more than five thousand miles of coast, from New York to Texas, and that Spain made very inadequate provision for the patrolling of Cuban waters, the number of successful expeditions was surprisingly small.[3]

---

[1] Senate Com. on For. Rels., *Compilation of Reports*, VII., 581–585.   [2] Richardson, *Messages and Papers*, IX., 591.
[3] Moore, *Digest of Int. Law*, VII., 1024.

In addition to the efforts of the naval and port officials several cases were successfully prosecuted in the courts at great expense. So far from Spain having any ground for complaint, the efforts put forth by the United States were very unusual for a contest in which belligerency had not been recognized. President Cleveland's proclamation recognized insurgency as a status distinct from belligerency; it merely put into effect municipal statutes; it did not bring into operation any of the rules of neutrality under international law, for such a result could be brought about only by the recognition of belligerency, and President Cleveland consistently refused to recognize the Cubans as belligerents.[1] Congress, however, attempted to force his hand: a concurrent resolution recognizing a state of war in Cuba, and offering Spain the good offices of the United States for the recognition of Cuban independence, passed the Senate February 28, 1896, by a vote of 64 to 6; and on April 6 the same resolution passed the House by a vote of 246 to 27. The president was not bound by this resolution, and, in spite of the overwhelming majority which it had received, he ignored it; it amounted simply to an expression of opinion by Congress; and no evidence of a responsible Cuban government was forthcoming.[2]

Meanwhile the president was following another

---

[1] Moore, *Digest of Int. Law*, I., 242, 243.

[2] *Senate Journal*, 54 Cong., 1 Sess., 158; *House Journal*, 54 Cong., 1 Sess., 372.

line of action. Secretary Olney addressed a note to
the Spanish minister April 4, 1896, in which the
United States offered to mediate between Spain and
the insurgents for the restoration of peace on the
basis of a more complete autonomy. To this note
Spain replied under date of May 22, rejecting the
offer and claiming that Cuba already enjoyed "one
of the most liberal political systems in the world."
The note concluded with the suggestion that the
United States could contribute greatly to the pacification of the island by prosecuting "the unlawful
expeditions of some of its citizens to Cuba with more
vigor than in the past." [1] In his annual message,
December 7, 1896, President Cleveland discussed
the Cuban situation at length. After rejecting as
inexpedient the recognition of either belligerency or
independence, and holding the purchase of the island
to be impracticable, he declared: "When the inability
of Spain to deal successfully with the insurgents has
become manifest and it is demonstrated that her
sovereignty is extinct in Cuba for all purposes of its
rightful existence, and when a hopeless struggle for
its reestablishment has degenerated into a strife
which means nothing more than the useless sacrifice
of human life and the utter destruction of the very
subject-matter of the conflict, a situation will be
presented in which our obligations to the sovereignty
of Spain will be superseded by higher obligations,
which we can hardly hesitate to recognize and dis-

[1] *Spanish Dipl. Corresp. and Docs.*, 7, 8.

charge." [1] No further action was taken by the Cleveland administration, which was rapidly drawing to a close.

The McKinley administration, which began March 4, 1897, was not long in addressing itself to the task of securing peace and independence for Cuba, a policy to which it stood committed in the party platform. Unfortunately at this critical juncture a political deal placed the management of the state department in feeble hands. Marcus A. Hanna, who had managed the McKinley campaign with consummate ability, claimed as a reward a seat in the United States Senate, and in order to make a place for him at once, President McKinley induced John Sherman, the veteran statesman of Ohio, to resign the seat he had so long and so ably filled and to accept the post of secretary of state. Sherman's mind was beginning to show the weaknesses of age, and in spite of the fact that he had in Judge William R. Day a very able assistant secretary, the conduct of the department was very far from satisfactory.

The attitude of the new administration was first officially communicated to Spain in Secretary Sherman's note of June 27, 1897, in which he protested in the name of humanity and the interests of the United States against the decrees and acts of General Weyler, particularly his reconcentration order.[2] To this protest the Spanish government, pursuing

---

[1] Richardson, *Messages and Papers*, IX., 722.
[2] *Spanish Dipl. Corresp. and Docs.*, 25.

its usual tactics of delay, replied August 4, asserting
that the situation in Cuba was not as bad as de-
picted; that at the date of Sherman's note only
six thousand dollars of the fifty thousand dollars
appropriated by Congress for the relief of American
citizens in Cuba had been spent, because there were
no more to be found who needed it; that General
Weyler's orders were not unusual, and were no more
severe than the measures adopted by Hunter and
Sheridan in the Valley of Virginia, or by Sherman
in Georgia.   In conclusion attention was called to
the operations of the Cuban Junta in New York and
to the assistance the insurgents were receiving from
the United States.[1]

General Woodford succeeded Hannis Taylor as
minister to Spain September 13, 1897; and ten days
later he presented a note setting forth at length the
views of the McKinley administration, and again
tendering the good offices of the United States for
the adjustment of Cuban affairs, presumably on a
basis of independence.   He called attention to the
resolution passed by Congress the year before [2] and
to the fact that Congress was shortly to convene
again.   He requested therefore an early answer to
the tender of good offices.[3]   Six days later the Spanish ministry resigned, and on October 14 the liberal
ministry of Sagasta took the oath of office.   On the
17th of the same month General Blanco was ap-

---

[1] *Spanish Dipl. Corresp. and Docs.*, 28.
[2] See p. 9 above.   [3] *Foreign Relations*, 1898, p. 568.

pointed to succeed General Weyler as governor and captain-general of Cuba.

October 23 General Woodford received the answer to the tender of good offices. The new ministry promised to grant autonomy to Cuba, and again urged the United States to enforce with more vigor its neutrality laws.[1] The autonomy decree was published in Madrid November 27, and a summary of its contents was at once cabled to Washington in time for the president's message. In his annual message of December 6, 1897, President McKinley reviewed the Cuban situation at length, dwelling particularly on the possibility of intervention; but he concluded that it was only fair to Spain to give the new government of Sagasta time to test its policy of autonomy. He added that Weyler had been recalled, the order of concentration modified, some specified prisoners released; and that "not a single American citizen is now in arrest or confinement in Cuba of whom this government has any knowledge."[2]

It was soon evident that the grant of autonomy had come too late. The condition of affairs was pitiable in the extreme: Consul-General Fitzhugh Lee reported December 14, 1897, that in the province of Havana alone there had been 101,000 "reconcentrados," and that of this number 52,000 had died. He declared that the "reconcentrado order" of Wey-

---

[1] *Foreign Relations*, 1898, p. 582.
[2] Richardson, *Messages and Papers*, X., 131.

ler had "transformed about 400,000 self-supporting
people, principally women and children, into a multi-
tude to be sustained by the contributions of others
or die of starvation or of fevers." January 13, 1898,
serious riots occurred in Havana which were intended
as a popular demonstration against the autonomy
scheme. General Lee expressed doubt as to whether
Blanco could control the situation, and declared his
belief that autonomy would prove a failure.

While the autonomy plan was under trial Senator
Proctor, of Vermont, visited Cuba, and on his return
delivered a speech in the United States Senate,
March 17, 1898, which made a profound impression
not only on Congress but on the whole country.
"Outside of Havana," said he, "all is changed. It
is not peace nor is it war. It is desolation and distress, misery and starvation. Every town and village is surrounded by a 'trocha,' a sort of rifle-pit,
but constructed on a plan new to me, the dirt being
thrown up on the inside and a barbed-wire fence on
the outer side of the trench. These trochas have at
every corner, and at frequent intervals along the
sides, what are there called forts, but which are
really small block-houses, many of them more like
large sentry-boxes, loopholed for musketry, and
with a guard of from two to ten soldiers in each. . . .
I saw no house or hut in the four hundred miles of
railroad rides from Pinar del Rio Province in the
west across the full width of Habana and Matanzas
provinces, and to Sagua La Grande on the north

shore, and to Cienfuegos on the south shore of Santa
Clara, except within the Spanish trochas." Senator
Proctor found that the Spanish scheme of autonomy
had practically no supporters on either side: "There
is no doubt that General Blanco is acting in entire
good faith; that he desires to give the Cubans a fair
measure of autonomy, as Campos did at the close of
the ten-year war. He has, of course, a few personal
followers, but the army and the Spanish citizens do
not want genuine autonomy, for that means government by the Cuban people. And it is not strange
that the Cubans say it comes too late." [1]

Upon the occasion of the riots of January 13,
General Lee advised his government that the presence of war-ships might be necessary later on, but
not then. January 24 he received the following
despatch from Assistant-Secretary Day: "It is the
purpose of this Government to resume friendly naval
visits at Cuban ports. In that view the *Maine* will
call at the port of Havana in a day or two. Please
arrange for a friendly interchange of calls with authorities." General Lee at once advised that the
visit be postponed six or seven days so as to give
the last excitement more time to disappear, but his
despatch arrived too late. The *Maine* had already
sailed for Havana, where she arrived January 25, at
11 A.M., without any demonstration on the part of
the populace.[2] Here she continued until her de-

[1] *Cong. Record*, 55 Cong., 2 Sess., p. 2916.
[2] *Foreign Relations*, 1898, p. 1025.

struction three weeks later.   This action on the part
of the United States was openly resented by Spanish
adherents in Cuba, and is said to have been freely
criticised by Señor de Lôme, the Spanish minister at
Washington, in private conversations; officially,
however, the Spanish government declared its intention of returning the compliment by sending a battle-
ship to an American port.   Three days after the destruction of the *Maine* the *Vizcaya* arrived in New
York harbor and remained there for a week closely
guarded by the United States authorities.

While the *Maine* was anchored in Havana harbor
attention was diverted from Cuba to Washington by
an incident which led to the retirement of the Spanish
minister, Señor Dupuy de Lôme.   February 9, 1898,
the *New York Journal* published the facsimile of a
letter surreptitiously acquired, written by the minister about the middle of December to a friend in
Havana, which reflected on President McKinley.
It referred to him as "a bidder for the admiration of
the crowd" and "a would-be politician who tries to
leave a door open behind him while keeping on good
terms with the jingoes of his party."   In addition
to this the letter revealed the bad faith of the minister in the negotiations for a commercial treaty in
progress at the time.   The letter was of such a character that it could not be overlooked, and Mr. Day,
who was now practically in charge of the state department, at once called on Señor de Lôme and
asked him if it was genuine.   The latter admitted

having written such a letter, but was disposed at first to question the accuracy of the words ascribed to him; but on being shown the original he confirmed its genuineness, and without retracting in terms the offensive utterances, contended that the English translation had intensified certain phrases which he claimed were permissible under the seal of private correspondence. In accordance with instructions from the department, Woodford had an interview with the Spanish minister of foreign affairs February 10, at which he stated that the president expected the immediate recall of Señor de Lôme. The minister replied that his government sincerely regretted the *indiscretion* of their minister, and that his resignation had already been accepted by cable. Four days later, under instructions from the department, Woodford addressed a note to the foreign minister enclosing the exact language of the objectionable passages and requesting a formal disavowal of the sentiments expressed; but when the Spanish government replied that they considered the tender and acceptance of Señor de Lôme's resignation as sufficient amend, the department instructed Woodford to consider the incident closed.[1]

Before the excitement of the De Lôme incident had subsided, the whole world was startled by the news of the catastrophe that befell the *Maine* in Havana harbor. On February 15, at 9.40 P.M.,

---

[1] *Foreign Relations*, 1898, pp. 1007-1020; *Spanish Dipl. Corresp. and Docs.*, 80-85.

while this ship was lying quietly moored to the buoy
to which she had been taken on her arrival, an
explosion occurred which utterly wrecked her and
killed two of her officers and two hundred and fifty-
eight of her crew.[1]   Brief despatches telling of the
disaster were at once sent to Washington by Consul-
General Lee and Captain Sigsbee, the commander of
the ill-fated ship, the latter asking that the American
people suspend judgment until an investigation could
be made.   A naval court of inquiry was at once organized in the regular manner, which, aided by a
strong force of wreckers and divers, proceeded to
make a thorough investigation on the spot.

After twenty-three days of continuous labor, the
report was completed March 21 and transmitted to
the president.[2]   The testimony showed that there
were two explosions, the first like the report of a
gun, the second more open, prolonged, and of greater
volume.   It was further found that a part of the
outer shell of the ship had been forced up thirty-four
feet above where it would have been had the ship
sunk uninjured.   The findings of the court were that
the *Maine* was destroyed by the explosion of a sub-
marine mine, which caused the partial explosion of
two or more of the forward magazines.   The court
was unable to obtain evidence tending to fix the
responsibility upon any person or persons.   A Spanish board of inquiry, after examining a number of

---

[1] Richardson, *Messages and Papers*, X., 153.
[2] *Senate Docs.*, 55 Cong., 2 Sess., No. 207.

Witnesses who had seen or heard the explosion, made a report, March 22, stating their conclusion that the destruction of the ship was due to an explosion in the forward magazine.[1] The real responsibility for the mine has never been disclosed: it is not believed by those in a position to judge that the Spanish government either plotted or countenanced the destruction of the *Maine*. It may have been the work of Cuban insurgents, whose object was to bring on war.[2]

In spite of the clamorings of the "yellow" press, the American public had acted on Sigsbee's advice and suspended judgment until the investigation was over; but when the court of inquiry reported that the explosion was caused by a mine, all restraint was thrown aside and the demand for war was overwhelming. Flags were unfurled everywhere; "Remember the Maine" became a watchword; and the country witnessed an outburst of popular feeling such as had not been seen since 1861. The movement was not confined to any one section, though it was stronger in the South and West than in New England.

Apart from the destruction of the *Maine*, the failure of autonomy meant intervention by the United States, and it had been evident since the Havana riots in January that autonomy was doomed to failure. Still the president determined to give Spain one more chance to retreat peaceably from an im-

[1] Senate Com. on For. Rels., *Compilation of Reports*, VII., 900.
[2] Long, *New Am. Navy*, I., 144.

possible position. The Spanish ministry were engaged in the perilous attempt to steer a course between revolution at home and war with the United
States. They desired peace; but they recognized
the fact that public opinion in Spain would not
countenance such concessions as the Cubans demanded, and that any ministry which conceded too
much would be discredited and driven from office.[1]
At a personal interview with Minister Gullon, Señor
Sagasta, president of the council, and Señor Moret,
minister for the colonies, March 29, General Woodford presented the ultimatum of the United States
in the following terms: "The president instructs me
to say that we do not want Cuba. He also instructs
me to say, with equal clearness, that we do wish
immediate peace in Cuba. He suggests an armistice,
lasting until October 1, negotiations in the meantime
being had looking to peace between Spain and the
insurgents, through the friendly offices of the President of the United States." An informal discussion
followed in which Sagasta said that if the insurgents
asked for an armistice it would be at once granted,
but that it would not be possible under any circumstances for Spain to offer it. Woodford urged the
necessity for a speedy reply, and requested that he
be granted an interview two days later for the purpose of receiving it. To this the Spanish ministers
reluctantly agreed.[2]

[1] Hannis Taylor, in *North Am. Rev.*, CLXV., 628.
[2] *Foreign Relations*, 1898, p. 719.

At the appointed interview, March 31, 1898, the president of the council handed General Woodford certain counter-propositions to the effect that the differences arising out of the destruction of the *Maine* should be submitted to arbitration; that the reconcentration order having already been revoked by General Blanco, the Spanish government would assist the country people to return to their labors, although this measure could not be fully carried out until military operations terminated; that the pacification of the island should be left to a Cuban parliament which was to convene May 4; that in the meantime the governor-general would be authorized to accept a suspension of hostilities if asked for by the insurgents.[1]

In transmitting these proposals to his government General Woodford, who was earnestly striving to avoid war, said that they did not mean peace, but a "continuation of this destructive, cruel, and now needless war." He further said that the ministry had gone as far as they could, for "I am told confidentially that the offer of an armistice by the Spanish government would cause revolution here." [2] Again, April 2, Woodford cabled the department: "I have worked hard for peace. I am hoping against hope, and still I cannot bring myself to the final belief that in these closing years of the nineteenth century Spain will finally refuse, on a mere

---

[1] *Foreign Relations*, 1898, p. 726; *Spanish Dipl. Corresp. and Docs.*, 107.   [2] *Foreign Relations*, 1898, p. 727.

question of punctilio, to offer immediate and effective armistice." [1]

While these lengthy negotiations were going on in Spain, public feeling in America was at the highest pitch of excitement; the "yellow" press was clamoring for war; and it was only with the greatest difficulty that the president, who really wanted peace, could hold Congress in check. Had Spain agreed to an armistice, the war might at least have been postponed, but Spain tried again to temporize. At eleven o'clock Monday night, April 4, the following despatch was sent to Woodford: "We have received to-day from the Spanish minister a copy of the manifesto of the autonomy government. It is not armistice. It proves to be an appeal by the autonomy government of Cuba urging the insurgents to lay down their arms and to join with the autonomy party in building up the new scheme of home rule. It is simply an invitation to the insurgents to submit, in which event the autonomy government, likewise suspending hostilities, is prepared to consider what expansion if any of the decreed home-rule scheme is needed or practicable. It need scarcely be pointed out that this is a very different thing from an offered armistice. The president's message will go in Wednesday afternoon." [2]

Congress was now completely dominated by public opinion, and a reference of the question to Congress meant war; but after the rejection of his ultimatum

[1] *Foreign Relations*, 1898, p. 731.   [2] *Ibid.*, p. 733.

President McKinley had no further pretext for delay; he decided therefore with reluctance to shift the responsibility to Congress. With that decision the die was cast. Meanwhile, Archbishop Ireland had come to Washington at the direction of the Pope to work for peace, and reported that the president earnestly desired peace; and, he thought, would accept the good offices of the Pope.[1] The Spanish government expressed itself as willing to grant a suspension of hostilities at the request of the Pope, provided the truce should be accompanied by the withdrawal of the American squadron from Cuban waters.[2]

Finally Wednesday, April 6, arrived, and no word from Spain that hostilities had been suspended. On that day, however, the representatives of Germany, Austria-Hungary, France, Great Britain, Italy, and Russia made a formal appeal to the president for peace.[3] The president suddenly decided to withhold his message until the following Monday, not on account of the representations of the powers, as was supposed by some at the time, or in the hope that Spain would make concessions, but as the result of a telegram from General Lee, who urged that he be given that much time to get Americans safely out of Havana.[4] The president regarded matters as closed with Spain. On Saturday the representatives

[1] *Spanish Dipl. Corresp. and Docs.*, 111.
[2] *Ibid.*, 110; *Foreign Relations*, 1898, p. 732.
[3] *Foreign Relations*, 1898, p. 740.   [4] *Ibid.*, p. 743.

of the powers at Madrid called on the minister of state and urged Spain to accede to the solicitations of the Holy See and grant an armistice.[1]   The next day, Sunday, April 10, the Spanish minister at Washington informed the secretary of state that the queen had yielded to the wishes of the Pope and had directed General Blanco to suspend hostilities; that after May 4, the date when the Cuban parliament was to convene, the Cubans would have all the liberty they could expect.   These concessions did not meet fully the American ultimatum and seemed too much like another play for time.   The Spanish minister was, therefore, simply informed that the president would in his message notify Congress of this latest communication.[2]

President McKinley has been severely criticised for not giving greater consideration to this communication and for merely alluding to it in his message, instead of transmitting it in full; it was, it is claimed, a complete surrender on the part of Spain, and should have paved the way for peace.[3] The facts do not bear out this view: Spanish concessions to Cuba have always had strings attached to them, and in this case the string was the statement that the duration and details of the suspension of hostilities would be left to General Blanco; and the indefinite promise that after May 4 the Cubans

[1] *Spanish Dipl. Corresp. and Docs.*, 114
[2] *Foreign Relations*, 1898, pp. 747-749
[3] *The Nation*, LXXIII., 4.

would have all the liberty they could reasonably
desire.   War might have been delayed six months,
but it would not have been averted, for Spain was
not willing to make concessions that would satisfy
the Cubans.

In the message of April 11, 1898, President McKinley reviewed the question at length and came to the
conclusion that forcible intervention was the only
solution of the difficulty, and was justified on grounds
of humanity, for the protection of the lives and property of American citizens in Cuba, and for the purpose of putting a stop to a conflict which was a constant menace to our peace and which entailed an
enormous expense on our government.   He referred
to the *Maine* only incidentally as "a patent and im-
pressive proof of a state of things in Cuba that is
intolerable." [1]

Two days later the House passed a resolution, by
a vote of 324 to 19, authorizing and directing the
president to intervene at once to stop the war in
Cuba, with the purpose of "establishing by the free
action of the people thereof a stable and independent
government of their own in the island."   On the
same day the Senate committee on foreign relations
made a report, dwelling at length on the *Maine*
disaster, and directing the president to demand the
immediate withdrawal of Spain from the island. [2]

[1] Richardson, *Messages and Papers*, X., 147
[2] Senate Com. on For. Rels., *Compilation of Reports*, VII.,
321–340.

The minority report, however, urging in addition the immediate recognition of the Cuban Republic as then organized, was finally embodied in the Senate resolution, April 16, by a vote of 67 to 21. The two Houses were thus brought into conflict over the question of recognition of the Cuban republic so-called. After two days of heated controversy the Senate gave way, and on April 19, the anniversary of the battle of Lexington, and of the first bloodshed of the Civil War on the streets of Baltimore, the fateful resolution was adopted in the following terms:

"Resolved by the Senate and House of Representatives of the United States in Congress assembled,

"First, That the people of the island of Cuba are, and of right ought to be, free and independent.

"Second, That it is the duty of the United States to demand, and the Government of the United States does hereby demand, that the Government of Spain at once relinquish its authority and government in the island of Cuba, and withdraw its land and naval forces from Cuban waters.

"Third, That the President of the United States be, and he hereby is, directed and empowered to use the entire land and naval forces of the United States, and to call into the actual service of the United States the militia of the several States to such extent as may be necessary to carry these resolutions into effect

"Fourth, That the United States hereby disclaims any disposition or intention to exercise sovereignty, jurisdiction, or control over said island except for the pacification thereof, and asserts its determination, when that is accomplished, to leave the government and control of the island to its people."[1]

These resolutions were, of course, equivalent to a declaration of war. As soon as they were approved by the president, April 20, the Spanish minister asked for his passports, thus severing diplomatic relations, and Woodford left Madrid the following day. The American people entered on this war with enthusiasm, eager to test the national strength. Every movement of army and navy was closely watched, and the public was almost hourly informed by the newspapers, through special editions, of what was going on. A special interest was felt in the navy, which, as was well known, had, through the efforts of Assistant-Secretary Roosevelt, been for months engaged in target practice. Even with this practice only 123 out of about 8000 projectiles hit the Spanish ships at Santiago.

There has been much discussion as to the validity of the grounds on which the United States based its right of intervention in Cuba. Most writers sanction intervention for the enforcement of treaty rights, for the preservation of the balance of power, and for self-preservation. "Interventions for the purpose of self-preservation," according to Hall, "naturally

[1] U. S. *Statutes at Large*, XXX., 738.

include all those which are grounded upon danger
to the institutions, to the good order, or to the
external safety of the intervening state." [1]   As to
humanitarian intervention, there is a wide difference of opinion among modern jurists; [2] some sanc-
tioning it and others denying that it is ever legal;
while still others approve it only when undertaken
by the body of states, or by representatives of the
body of states acting jointly.   Most of the discussions of this subject are specially applicable to the
situation in Europe, and can be applied only by
analogy to America, where the United States has
to undertake many things alone which in Europe
would require concerted action. [3]

[1] Hall, *Int. Law* (5th ed.), 285.
[2] *Ibid.*, 291, note.
[3] Moore, *Digest of Int. Law*, VI., 8.

CHAPTER II

FIRST PERIOD OF THE SPANISH WAR
(April–May, 1898)

PRESIDENT ROOSEVELT has said that the most striking thing about the war with Spain was the preparedness of the navy, and the unpreparedness of the army. For fifteen years we had been building up a navy, and for months preceding the war every effort was made, with the resources at the command of the navy department, to put it in a state of first-class efficiency. As early as January 11, 1898, instructions were sent to the commanders of the several squadrons to retain in the service men whose terms of enlistment were about to expire. As the Cuban situation grew more threatening, the North Atlantic Squadron and a torpedo - boat flotilla were rapidly assembled in Florida waters; and immediately after the destruction of the *Maine* the ships on the European and South Atlantic stations were ordered to Key West.

Commodore Dewey assumed command of the Asiatic station January 3, 1898, succeeding Rear-Admiral McNair. The ships were at the time scattered along the coasts of China and Korea. On

February 25 the following secret orders were cabled to Dewey: "Order squadron, except *Monocacy*, to Hong-Kong. Keep full of coal. In event of declaration of war Spain, your duty will be to see that the Spanish squadron does not leave the Asiatic coast, and then offensive operations in Philippine Islands. Keep *Olympia* until further orders." This despatch was signed "Roosevelt," then assistant secretary of the navy. On the following day another despatch was sent to Dewey, and also to the commanders of all our squadrons: "Keep full of coal, the best that can be had."[1] The *Olympia*, Dewey's flag-ship, had been ordered home for repairs, but this order was revoked in view of the seriousness of the situation. The *Mohican* was ordered to proceed at once from Mare Island to Honolulu with a large supply of ammunition, to be transferred to the *Baltimore* and conveyed by that ship to Dewey at Hong-Kong.

The battle-ship *Oregon*, which was at Bremerton, on the coast of Washington, was ordered early in March to proceed to San Francisco and prepare for a long voyage. After receiving a supply of ammunition at the latter port, she started, March 19, on the voyage around the Horn that was to make her name immortal in naval history. The *Marietta*, then at San José, Guatemala, was ordered to precede the *Oregon* and arrange for coaling.

Both from a political and a military point of view,

[1] Sec. of the Navy, *Report*, 1898, App., p. 23.

the blockade of Cuba was the first step for the
American government to take, and the surest and
quickest means of bringing things to an issue. Cuba
was the point in dispute between the United States
and Spain, and a blockade would result in one of
two things—the surrender of the island, or the despatch of a Spanish naval force to its relief. The
navy department had very little apprehension of an
attack on our coast, as no squadron could hope to
be in condition after crossing the Atlantic for offensive operations without coaling, and the only places
where Spain could coal were in the West Indies.
The public, however, took a different view of the
situation and no little alarm was felt in the eastern
cities. A few coast-defence guns of modern pattern
would have relieved the department of the necessity
of protecting the coast, and enabled it to concentrate
the whole fighting force around Cuba. To meet
popular demands, however, a Northern Patrol
Squadron was organized April 20, under command
of Commodore Howell, to cover the New England
coast; and a more formidable Flying Squadron, under Commodore Schley, was assembled at Hampton
Roads, and kept there until the appearance of the
Spanish fleet in the West Indies. The main squadron was stationed at Key West under Rear-Admiral
William T. Sampson, who had just been promoted
to that grade, and given command of the entire
naval force in North Atlantic waters. His appointment over the heads of Schley and other officers of

superior rank and longer service created a great deal
of criticism, although he was everywhere conceded
to be one of the most efficient and progressive officers of the new navy.[1]

A great effort was made before the outbreak of
hostilities to purchase war-ships abroad, but with
only partial success. It was not so important to
add such ships as were for sale to our navy as to
keep them from being purchased by Spain. Ninety-
seven steam merchantmen, however, were procured
at home and abroad, and became cruisers, gun-boats,
and colliers. The department also chartered with
their crews five ocean liners, the *City of Pekin* from
the Pacific Mail Steamship Company, and the
St. Paul, *St. Louis*, *New York*, and *Paris* (the two
latter renamed *Harvard* and *Yale*) from the International Navigation Company. One ice-boat and two
yachts were loaned, and a number of revenue-cutters
and light-house tenders were transferred to the navy
department. One hundred and twenty-eight ships
were thus added to the navy, and the government
yards were kept busy transforming them. To man
these ships the number of enlisted men was raised
from 12,500 to 24,123, and a number of new officers appointed.[2] The heavy fighting force consisted
of four first-class battle-ships, the *Indiana*, *Iowa*,
Massachusetts, and *Oregon;* one second-class battle-
ship, the *Texas;* and two armored cruisers, the

[1] Long, *New Am. Navy*, I., 209.
[2] *Message and Docs.*, Abridgment, 1898–1899, II., 921.

Brooklyn and the *New York*. As against these seven
armored ships Spain had five armored cruisers of
modern construction and of greater reputed speed
than any of ours except the *Brooklyn* and the *New
York*, and one battle-ship of the *Indiana* type.
Spain had further a type of vessel unknown to
our navy and greatly feared by us—namely, torpedo-boat destroyers, such as the *Furor*, *Pluton*,
and *Terror*. It was popularly supposed that the
Spanish navy was somewhat superior to the American.

As soon as the Spanish minister withdrew from
Washington, a despatch was sent to Sampson at Key
West directing him to blockade the coast of Cuba
immediately from Cardenas to Bahia Honda, and to
blockade Cienfuegos if it was considered advisable.
On April 29, Admiral Cervera's division of the
Spanish fleet left the Cape de Verde Islands for
an unknown destination, and disappeared for two
weeks from the knowledge of the American authorities. This fleet was composed of four armored
cruisers, the *Infanta Maria Teresa*, *Cristobal Colon*,
Oquendo, and *Vizcaya*, and three torpedo-boat destroyers. Its appearance in American waters was
eagerly looked for, and interest in the war became
intense.

While this fleet was on its way across the Atlantic,
a great battle was fought across the Pacific all unknown to the American people, which was destined to
open up a new world to them. Admiral Dewey was

at Hong-Kong where his ships had been gathered. On April 7 he was ordered to land all woodwork and stores not necessary for operations; and on April 21 he was informed that the naval forces on the Atlantic were blockading Cuba and that war might be declared at any moment. His ships were at once painted slate-color. On the 24th, the day that Spain declared war, Great Britain issued a proclamation of neutrality, and Dewey at once prepared to leave for Mirs Bay, about thirty miles north of Hong-Kong. On the same day the now celebrated cablegram was sent him by the secretary of the navy: "War has commenced between the United States and Spain. Proceed at once to Philippine Islands. Commence operations at once, particularly against Spanish fleet. You must capture vessels or destroy. Use utmost endeavors." These were the last instructions Dewey received. His squadron left Mirs Bay, April 27, for the Philippines, and three days later Luzon was sighted. As Dewey had heard that the Spanish admiral proposed to take position at Subig Bay, a few miles north of the entrance to Manila Bay, he directed his course thither, but no signs of the enemy were to be seen. Admiral Montojo had indeed taken his squadron to Subig Bay, but, finding that the modern guns provided for its defence had not been mounted, he left twenty-four hours before Dewey arrived, and returned to Manila Bay, where he stationed his ships under the guns of Cavité. Dewey's squadron was superior

to that of Montojo, but the Spanish fleet had the
support of the shore batteries. Dewey's fighting
force was four cruisers and two gun-boats, while
the Spanish admiral had two cruisers, eleven gun-
boats of antiquated type, and a number of smaller
craft.

At 11.30 P.M., April 30, 1898, the American squadron entered the Boca Grande, or south channel,
leading into the Bay of Manila, steaming at eight
knots, the flag-ship *Olympia* in the lead. When
about half through the shore batteries opened fire,
but none of the ships was hit; the fire was returned
by the *Boston* and the *McCulloch*. The squadron
continued its even course across the bay, and at day-
break was off Manila, near enough to see the ship-
ping. At 5.15 A.M. they were fired upon by three
batteries at Manila and two at Cavité and by the
Spanish fleet, which was anchored on a line running
almost due east from Cavité. Dewey's squadron
quickly turned to the south and proceeded to the
attack, the *Olympia* in the lead, followed at distance by the *Baltimore*, *Raleigh*, *Petrel*, *Concord*, and
Boston. When they had arrived within fifty-six
hundred yards, Dewey turned to the captain of the
Olympia and said, coolly, "You may fire when you're
ready, Gridley." With quick response one of the
eight-inch guns in the forward turret sent forth its
charge, and the battle of Manila Bay had begun.
Three times Dewey led his ships to the westward
and twice to the eastward in front of the Spanish

line and shore batteries, keeping up a continuous
and destructive fire at ranges varying from five thousand to two thousand yards.   The Spanish ships and
batteries returned the fire vigorously but ineffec-
tively.

At 7.35 A.M. the squadron ceased firing and stood
out into the bay.   When out of range, Dewey ordered, "Let the people go to breakfast."   This
movement was made under the erroneous impression
that the ammunition was getting low in some of the
batteries.   The opportunity was taken to let the
men, who had had nothing but coffee at 4 A.M., re-
fresh themselves.   The batteries at Manila had kept
up a steady fire, but at this point Dewey sent a
message to the governor-general to the effect that if
this was continued the city would be shelled; where-
upon the Manila batteries ceased firing.   At 11.16
A.M. the squadron returned to complete its work,
the *Baltimore* leading the column.   The duel that
followed between the *Baltimore* and the shore batteries is described as the most picturesque scene of
the battle.   The American fire was overwhelming,
and the Spanish flag-ship and most of the fleet were
soon in flames.   At 12.40 the squadron withdrew
and anchored off Manila, leaving the *Petrel* to complete the destruction of the smaller gun-boats which
were behind the point of Cavité.   In this remarkable
battle the American ships escaped all but slight injury, and only seven men were slightly wounded.
On the Spanish side ten ships were destroyed, three

batteries silenced, and 381 men killed, besides numbers wounded.[1]

The *McCulloch* was sent post-haste to Hong-Kong to cable the news to Washington, where it was received early on the morning of May 6. The public had known little of Dewey's movements or instructions, and the suddenness and unexpected character of the news greatly heightened the enthusiasm with which it was received. The eyes of the nation were at once turned to the Orient, and people who had to search closely on their maps in order to find the Philippine Islands were soon discussing glibly the commercial and strategic importance of the group. President McKinley at once appointed Dewey acting rear-admiral, and recommended that he be promoted to the grade of admiral and receive the thanks of Congress.

In spite of his great victory, Dewey's position was critical. A few days after the battle he cabled the department that he could take Manila at any time, but did not have the men to occupy it. Ammunition and men were forwarded as soon as possible, but with the utmost endeavors they did not leave San Francisco before May 21. For more than two months Dewey was left without reinforcements. The most serious cause for embarrassment was the presence in Manila Bay of the war-ships of European powers, which were assigned to duty there after

[1] Sec. of the Navy, *Annual Report*, 1898, App. pp., 63–93; Long, *New Am. Navy*, I., 165–200.

the destruction of the Spanish fleet. Germany, whose interests in the Philippines were very slight, sent five men-of-war, Great Britain three, France one, and Japan one.[1] The German force was stronger than Dewey's, and displayed open sympathy for the Spaniards, committing breaches of international and naval etiquette. They undertook to disregard the blockade and to land provisions. Dewey promptly sent his flag-lieutenant, Brumby, to present his compliments to Rear-Admiral Diederichs, to inform him of his "extraordinary disregard of the usual courtesies of naval intercourse," and to tell him that "if he wants a fight he can have it right now."[2] The German admiral at once disavowed the act, and thereafter treated the Americans with more consideration. No satisfactory explanation of Admiral Diederichs' conduct has ever been given; he was ordered to Manila in answer to an appeal for protection from the German residents, who anticipated trouble from the insurgents, it seems, and not from the Americans. The German admiral, however, not understanding the situation, took his instructions to mean that he was to hold the Americans in check. The state department evidently saw that there was a mistake somewhere, for Andrew D. White, ambassador to Germany at the time, has stated that no explanations were sought from the German government.[3]

---

[1] Sec. of the Navy, *Annual Report*, 1898, App., p. 109.
[2] Long, *New Am. Navy*, II., 111, 112.
[3] *Washington Post*, April 17, 1907.

The interest of the American people was soon diverted from Dewey and his remarkable achievement and centred once more on the movements of the Atlantic squadron and its efforts to locate the fleet of Admiral Cervera. It will be remembered that the latter left the Cape de Verde Islands, April 29, destination unknown, though rightly believed by our department to be the West Indies. A natural surmise was that he would go to Porto Rico; but if coal enough remained he might push straight ahead to Cuba. That he could get to the coast of the United States without first coaling at some point in the West Indies, whence he would be reported, seemed most improbable. On May 5 Sampson proceeded eastward towards the Windward Passage (between Cuba and Haiti), with the *Iowa, Indiana, New York*, and a number of lighter ships, so as to be in a position to intercept or pursue Cervera in case he should make a dash for the American coast from Porto Rico. This movement was greatly delayed by the presence of two monitors, which, on account of their inferior speed, had to be towed.[1] North of Cape Haitien, shortly before midnight of May 7, he heard from the department that no information had been received as to Cervera's movements. Two American liners, the *St. Louis* and the *Harvard*, had been sent out April 30 to cruise along a north and south line eighty miles eastward of Guadeloupe and Martinique. They met at the middle of the course

[1] Mahan, *Lessons of the War with Spain*, 111.

once a day, communicated, and then went back in opposite directions. In case the enemy was discovered, word was to be sent from the nearest cable station to Sampson and to the department. If by May 10 no information was received, the *Harvard* was to touch at Martinique and the *St. Louis* at Guadeloupe, cable the department and Sampson, wait twenty-four hours for orders, and, if none were received, proceed with all haste to Hampton Roads.[1]

Sampson continued east as far as San Juan, Porto Rico, arriving off that point early on the morning of May 12, having taken eight days instead of five, as he had expected. After satisfying himself that the Spanish fleet was not there, and rather aimlessly shelling the forts for a couple of hours, he sailed off to the northeast until out of sight, then, turning west, hastened back towards Havana.[2] From the log of the *Cristobal Colon* it appears that Cervera's division at noon of May 10, the day the *Harvard* and *St. Louis* were to abandon their patrol, reached a point one hundred and thirty miles east of Martinique, reduced its speed, and sent the *Terror* ahead to reconnoitre. That day the *Harvard*, according to orders, left its patrol station: her commander afterwards stated that he believed another stretch to the south would have revealed the Spanish squadron. On May 11 Cervera's fleet came within sight of Martinique, and that night remained practically

[1] Sec. of the Navy, *Annual Report*, 1898, App., pp. 360–362.
[2] *Ibid.*, App., p. 368.

motionless. The next morning he probably heard
that Sampson was off San Juan, for he put his
squadron in motion and started for Curaçao just
about the time that Sampson started back for Key
West.[1]

News of Cervera's appearance off Martinique was
first received at the navy department about midnight, May 12–13, nearly thirty-six hours after the
fact. Schley was ordered at once to proceed with
the Flying Squadron from Hampton Roads to
Charleston, there to receive further orders. When
Sampson left Porto Rico he was, of course, in igno-
rance of Cervera's appearance in the West Indies.
The following night he heard from a passing ship the
rumor that Cervera was back at Cadiz, and this he
cabled to the department. Early Sunday morning,
May 15, he received a despatch from Washington
telling him that Cervera was at Curaçao the day
before, that the Flying Squadron was on its way to
Key West, and ordering him to proceed with all
possible despatch to the same point.[2] The problem
now was to locate Cervera the moment he entered
one of his own ports and blockade him, or to pounce
on him in case he advanced north from the Caribbean
Sea.

The presence of the Spanish fleet at Curaçao
caused serious apprehensions as to the fate of the
Oregon. The last news of her was that she had

---

[1] Mahan, *Lessons of the War with Spain*, 123.
[2] Sec. of the Navy, *Annual Report*, 1898, App., p. 387.

left Bahia, Brazil, May 9. Her movements were unknown to the navy department, for the question of
prescribing her route and sending a detachment to
meet her had been carefully considered but abandoned. She was left to shift for herself, and was
considered safer if not so closely watched. She
reached Barbadoes May 18, and turned up safely
off Jupiter Inlet, Florida, on the 24th, ready for
service, after a voyage of fourteen thousand miles,
one of the most remarkable recorded in history.[1]

Sampson reached Key West at 4 P.M., May 18,
several hours after the arrival of Schley. The department had heard that Cervera had munitions of
war essential to the defence of Havana, and that
his orders were to reach Havana, Cienfuegos, or a
port connected with Havana by rail. As Cienfuegos seemed the only place he would be likely to
choose, Schley was ordered there with the *Brooklyn*,
Massachusetts, and *Texas*, May 19. He was joined
later by the *Iowa*, under Captain Evans, and by
several cruisers. The Spanish squadron slipped into
Santiago, unobserved by the cruisers on scouting
duty, May 19, two days before Schley arrived at
Cienfuegos, so that had Cervera known the conditions
he could easily have made the latter port. On the
same day the department received from spies in
Havana probable information, conveyed by the cable which had been allowed to remain in operation,
that Cervera had entered Santiago. As we now

---

[1] Mahan, *Lessons of the War with Spain*, 135.

know, he had entered early that morning. Several auxiliary cruisers were immediately ordered to assemble before Santiago in order to watch Cervera and follow him in case he should leave.

At the same time the department "strongly advised" Sampson to send Schley to Santiago at once with his whole command. Sampson replied that he had decided to hold Schley at Cienfuegos until it was certain that the Spanish fleet was in Santiago. Later he sent a despatch to Schley, received May 23, ordering him to proceed to Santiago if satisfied that the enemy were not at Cienfuegos.[1] The next day Schley started, encountering on the run much rain and rough weather, which seriously delayed the squadron. At 5.30 P.M., May 26, he reached a point twenty-two miles south of Santiago, where he was joined by several of the auxiliary cruisers on scouting duty. Captain Sigsbee, of the *St. Paul*, informed him that the scouts knew nothing positively about the Spanish fleet. The collier *Merrimac* had been disabled, which increased the difficulty of coaling. At 7.45 P.M., a little over two hours after his arrival, Schley without explanation signalled to the squadron: "Destination, Key West, *via* south side of Cuba and Yucatan Channel, as soon as collier is ready; speed nine knots." Thus began the much-discussed retrograde movement, which occupied two days. Admiral Schley states in his book that Sigsbee's report and other evidence led him to con-

[1] Sec. of the Navy, *Annual Report*, 1898, App., pp. 465, 466.

clude that the Spanish squadron was not in Santiago; hence the retrograde movement to protect
the passage west of Cuba.[1]   But he has never yet
given any satisfactory explanation why he did not
definitely ascertain the facts before turning back.
Fortunately the squadron did not proceed very far;
the lines towing the collier parted and other delays
occurred.   The next morning Schley received a despatch from the department stating that all the information at hand indicated that Cervera was in
Santiago, but he continued on his westward course
slowly and at times drifting while some of the ships
coaled.   The next day, May 28, Schley returned to
Santiago, arriving before that port about dusk, and
established a blockade.[2]

[1] Schley, *Forty-five Years Under the Flag*, 276.
[2] Sec. of the Navy, *Annual Report*, 1898, App., p. 402; Long,
New Am. Navy, I., 258–287.

CHAPTER III

SECOND PERIOD OF THE SPANISH WAR
(June–August, 1898)

ADMIRAL SAMPSON arrived off Santiago June 1, and assumed direct command of the squadron. The blockade, which lasted for over a month, was eagerly watched by the whole American people. The most thrilling incident was the daring but unsuccessful attempt made by Lieutenant Richmond Pearson Hobson to sink the collier *Merrimac* across the entrance to Santiago harbor, undertaken by direction of Admiral Sampson. Electric torpedoes were attached to the hull of the ship, sea-valves were cut, and anchor chains arranged on deck so that she could be brought to a sudden stop. Early on the morning of June 3, Hobson, assisted by a crew of seven seamen, took the collier into the entrance of the harbor under heavy fire and sunk her. The unfortunate shooting away of her steering-gear and the failure of some of the torpedoes to explode kept the ship from sinking at the place selected, so that the plan miscarried. Hobson and his men escaped death as by a miracle, but fell into the hands of the Spaniards.[1]

[1] Sec. of the Navy, *Annual Report*, 1898, App., p. 437.

As soon as Cervera was blockaded in Santiago and the government was satisfied that all his ships were with him, it was decided to send an army to co-operate with the navy.   Hitherto the war had been a naval war exclusively, and the two hundred thousand volunteers who had responded to the calls of the president in May had been kept in camp in different parts of the country.   Most of the reg-ular infantry and cavalry, together with several volunteer regiments, had been assembled at Tampa and organized as the Fifth Army Corps, in readiness to land in Cuba as soon as the navy had cleared the way.   Conspicuous among these troops was the First Volunteer Cavalry, popularly known as Roosevelt's Rough Riders, a regiment which through the energetic efforts of Dr. Leonard Wood, an army surgeon, who became its colonel, and Theodore Roosevelt, who resigned the position of assistant secretary of the navy to become its lieutenant-colonel, had been enlisted, officered, and equipped in fifty days.   It was recruited largely from Arizona, New Mexico, and Oklahoma, and had in its ranks cowboys, hunters, ranchmen, and more than one hundred and sixty full-blooded Indians, together with a few graduates of Harvard, Yale, and other eastern colleges.

Tampa was ill-suited for an instruction camp, and the preparations made by the department for the accommodation and provisioning of such large bod-ies of men were wholly inadequate.   One of the

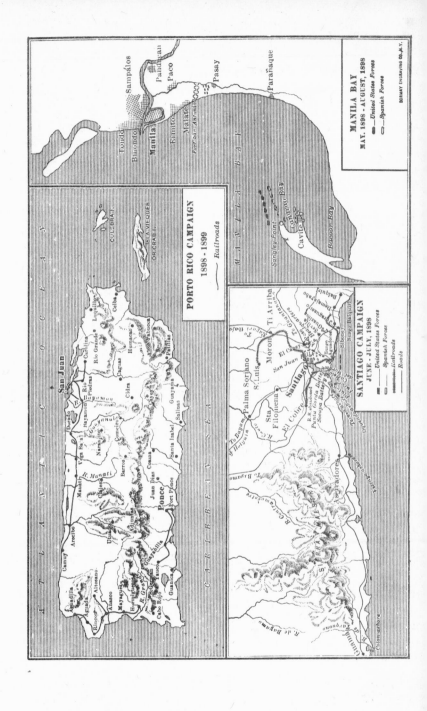

MANILA BAY
MAY, 1898 - AUGUST, 1898
━━ *United States Forces*
━○ *Spanish Forces*

BORMAY ENGRAVING CO., N.Y.

PORTO RICO CAMPAIGN
1898 - 1899
━━ Railroads

SANTIAGO CAMPAIGN
JUNE - JULY, 1898
━━ United States Forces
━━ Spanish Forces
━━━ Railroads
━━━ Roads

main difficulties was the inability of the commissary and quartermaster departments, hampered by red tape, senseless regulations, and political appointees, to distribute the train-loads of supplies which blocked the tracks leading to Tampa; so great was the congestion that the soldiers could not even get their mail. This condition continued for weeks. The great majority of the troops were finally sent to Santiago to fight under a tropical sun in heavy woollen clothes; lighter clothing was not supplied to them until they were ready to return to Montauk Point, where they needed the woollen. The sanitation of the camp was poor and the water supply bad; dysentery, malaria, and typhoid soon made their appearance. Similar conditions prevailed at the other camps. The administrative inefficiency of the war department was everywhere revealed in striking contrast with the fine record of the navy department. Secretary Alger had been too much occupied with questions of patronage to look after the real needs of the service. Although war had been regarded for months as inevitable, when it finally came the department was found to be utterly unprepared to equip troops for service in Cuba. As the result of this neglect, for which it should be said Congress was partly responsible, it was necessary to improvise an army, a rather serious undertaking!

It had been the original intention to land the Fifth Army Corps at Mariel, near Havana, and begin operations against the capital city under the direct

supervision of General Miles; but the bottling-up of
Cervera at Santiago caused a change of plan, and
General Miles, who still expected the heavy fighting to
take place at Havana, selected Major-General William R. Shafter for the movement against Santiago.
By June 1 the battle-ship *Indiana*, under Captain
Henry C. Taylor, with a dozen smaller vessels, was
ready to convoy the expedition. The army was very
slow in embarking, and it was not until June 8 that
the force was ready to depart. Further delay was
caused by the unfounded rumor that a Spanish cruiser
and two torpedo-boat destroyers had been sighted off
the north coast of Cuba.[1] In order to ascertain whether all the Spanish ships were at Santiago, Lieutenant
Victor Blue, of the navy, landed, and by personal ob-
servation from the hills back of the city located Cervera's entire division in the harbor. On June 14 the
transports, about thirty in number, sailed from
Tampa with their convoy. They were crowded and
ill-provided with supplies, the whole movement showing lack of experience in handling large bodies of men.
The expedition consisted of 815 officers and 16,072 enlisted men, regulars with the exception of the Seventy
first New York, the Second Massachusetts, and the
First Volunteer Cavalry.[2]

While the expedition was *en route* for Santiago
the state department received information that the
Spanish reserve fleet under Admiral Camara was

[1] Sec. of the Navy, *Annual Report*, 1898, App., p. 667.
[2] Major-General commanding the Army, *Report*, 1898, p. 149.

on its way to the Philippines. Commodore John C. Watson was, therefore, detached from the command of the blockading squadron at Havana and placed in command of a squadron consisting of the *Iowa*, *Oregon*, and four cruisers, which it was widely announced would sail for the coast of Spain immediately. The real intention was that Watson should follow Camara through the Suez Canal and form a junction with Dewey. Camara arrived at Port Saïd June 26, but his actions here led to some doubt as to his intentions, and Watson's squadron was held pending developments. On June 30 the Egyptian government forced Camara to leave; the ships began their passage through the canal, some of them on July 2, and others on the 5th and 6th. Meanwhile Cervera's ships had been destroyed and Camara was recalled.[1]

The expedition under Shafter began disembarking at Daiquiri on the morning of June 22, and by night 6000 men had with great difficulty been put ashore. No lighters or launches had been provided, and the only wharf, a small wooden one, had been stripped of its flooring: the war department expected the navy to look after these matters. In addition, the troops had been crowded into the transports without any reference to order, officers separated from their commands, artillery-pieces on one transport, horses on another, harness on a third, and no means of finding out where any of them were.

[1] Long, *New Am. Navy*, II., 17.

By the aid of a few launches borrowed from the
battle-ships, the men were put ashore, or near
enough to wade through the surf, but the animals
had to be thrown into the sea, where many of them
perished, some in their bewilderment swimming out
to sea instead of to shore.

General Lawton advanced and seized Siboney next
day, and Kent's division landed here, eight miles
nearer Santiago.   General Wheeler pushed on with
part of Young's brigade, and on the morning of
the 24th defeated the Spanish force at La Guasima,
with a loss of 1 officer and 15 men killed, 6 officers
and 46 men wounded.[1] During the next week the
army, including Garcia's Cuban command, was concentrated at Sevilla.   These were trying days.   The
troops suffered from the heavy rains, poor rations,
and bad camp accommodations.   No adequate provision had been made for landing supplies or for
transporting them to the camps, so that with an
abundance, such as they were, aboard the transports, the soldiers were in actual want.

On June 30 it was decided to advance.   San
Juan Hill, a strategic point on the direct road to
Santiago, could not be taken or held while the
Spaniards occupied El Caney, on the right of the
American advance.   The country was a jungle, and
the roads from the coast little more than bridle-
paths.   Lawton moved out to a position south of
El Caney that afternoon, so as to begin the at-

[1] Major-General commanding the Army, *Report*, 1898, p. 162.

tack early next morning.   Wheeler's division of dis-
mounted cavalry and Kent's division of infantry advanced towards El Poso, accompanied by Grimes's
battery, which was to take position early in the
morning and open the way for the advance towards
San Juan.   The attack at this point was to be delayed until Lawton's infantry fire was heard at El
Caney.   After forcing the enemy from this position,
Lawton was to move towards Santiago and take
position on Wheeler's right.   Little was known of
the ground over which the troops were to move or
the position and strength of the forces they were to
meet, consequently they went into battle without
knowing what they were about and fought without
any generalship being displayed.   General Shafter
was too ill to leave his headquarters in the rear.

At El Caney, which was surrounded by trenches
and block-houses, the Spaniards developed unexpected strength, and held Lawton in check until
late in the afternoon, when he finally carried the
position.   In this fight about 3500 Americans were
engaged and not more than 600 or 1000 Spaniards.
The American loss was 4 officers and 77 men killed,
and 25 officers and 335 men wounded.   About 150
Spaniards were captured, and between 300 and 400
killed and wounded.[1]

Meanwhile there had been a desperate fight at
San Juan Hill.   As soon as Lawton's musket-fire

[1] Major-General commanding the Army, *Report*, 1898, pp. 152,
169, 171, 319, 366, 381.

was heard at El Caney, Grimes's battery opened fire from El Poso on the San Juan block-house. This fire was immediately returned by the enemy's artillery, who had the range, and a number of men were killed. The Spaniards used smokeless powder, which made it difficult to locate them, while some of the Americans had black powder, which quickly indicated their position. The road along which the troops had to advance was so narrow and rough that at times they had to proceed in column of twos. The progress made was very slow, and the long-range guns of the enemy killed numbers of men before they could get into position to return the fire. By the middle of the day the advance had crossed the river, the cavalry division under Sumner deploying to the right in front of Kettle Hill, and Kent's division of infantry deploying to the left directly in front of San Juan Hill. During this movement the troops were exposed to a galling artillery and rifle fire, and suffered greatly, especially the third brigade of Kent's division, which lost three commanders in fifteen minutes, General Wikoff being killed and Colonels Worth and Liscum disabled. The suffering of the wounded, many of whom lay in the brush for hours without succor, was the most terrible feature of the situation.

Finally the long-expected order to advance was given. The First Regular Cavalry, the Rough Riders, and the Negro troopers of the Ninth and a part of the Tenth advanced up Kettle Hill and

drove the Spaniards from the ranch-house, while the
infantry division with the Sixth and Sixteenth regiments under Hawkins in the lead charged up
San Juan Hill in the face of a destructive fire and
captured the block-house. Then the cavalry under Sumner and Roosevelt advanced from Kettle
Hill and occupied the trenches on San Juan Hill
north of the block - house. The Spaniards fled
to their second line of trenches, six or eight hundred yards in the rear.[1]

After occupying San Juan Hill the cavalry were
still exposed to a constant fire, and many were dis-
couraged and wanted to retire, but General Wheeler,
who, though ill, had come to the front early in the
afternoon, put a stop to this and set the men to work
fortifying themselves. The next day Lawton came
up and advanced to a strong position on Wheeler's
right. The fighting was resumed on the two following days, but about noon, July 3, the Spaniards
ceased firing. The losses in the three days' fight
were 18 officers and 127 men killed, 65 officers and
849 men wounded, and 72 men missing.[2] The condition of the troops after the battle was very bad;
many of them were down with fever, and all were
suffering from lack of suitable equipment and supplies. General Shafter cabled to the secretary of
war, July 3, that it would be impossible to take
Santiago by storm with the forces he then had,

---

[1] Major-General commanding the Army, *Report*, 1898, pp. 147,
164, 172, 305, 340, 341, 371, 391, 445, 590.　　[2] *Ibid.*, pp. 167, 173

and that he was "seriously considering withdrawing about five miles and taking up a new position on the high ground between the San Juan River and Siboney."[1] The destruction of Cervera's fleet the same day materially changed the situation.

The advance made by the American troops around Santiago on July 1 and 2 forced the Spanish authorities to come to a decision in regard to Cervera's fleet. Captain-General Blanco insisted that the fleet should not be captured or destroyed without a fight. Cervera refused to assume the responsibility of leaving the harbor, and when ordered to do so went out with consummate bravery, knowing that he was leading a forlorn hope. Sampson seems to have been under the impression all along that the Spanish squadron would attempt to escape at night, but the American ships kept in so close to the shore, with dazzling search-lights directed against the entrance of the harbor, as to render it almost impossible to steer a ship out. On the morning of July 3, at 8.55, Sampson started east to meet General Shafter in conference at Siboney, signalling to the fleet as he left: "Disregard movements commander-in-chief." The *Massachusetts* had also left her place in the blockade to go to Guantanamo for coal. The remaining ships formed a semicircle around the entrance of the harbor, the *Brooklyn* to the west, holding the left of the line, then the *Texas*, next the *Iowa* in the centre and at the south of the curve, then, as the line

---

[1] *Message and Docs., Abridgment*, 1898–1899, I., 270.

curved in to the coast on the right, the *Oregon* and
the *Indiana*. The *Brooklyn* and the *Indiana*, holding the left and the right of the line, were about
two miles and one and a half miles respectively from
the shore, and near them, closer in, lay the converted gun-boats *Vixen* and *Gloucester*.

At 9.35 A.M., while most of the men were at
Sunday inspection, the enemy's ships were discovered slowly steaming down the narrow channel
of the harbor. In the lead was the *Maria Teresa*,
followed by the *Vizcaya*, the *Colon*, the *Oquendo*,
and the two torpedo-boat destroyers. The *Iowa*
was the first to signal that the enemy were escaping,
though the fact was noted on several ships at almost
the same moment, and no orders were necessary.
The American ships at once closed in and directed
their fire against the *Teresa*. For a moment there
was doubt as to whether the Spanish ships would
separate and try to scatter the fire of our fleet or
whether they would stick together. This was quickly settled when Cervera turned west, followed by
the remainder of his command. At this point Commodore Schley's flag-ship, the *Brooklyn*, which was
farthest west, turned to the eastward, away from the
hostile fleet, making a loop, at the end of which
she again steamed westward farther out to sea but
still ahead of any of the American vessels. The sudden and unexpected turn of the *Brooklyn* caused
the *Texas*, which was behind her, to reverse her en-
gines in order to avoid a collision and to come to

a stand-still, thus losing position, the *Oregon* and the *Iowa* both passing her. The two destroyers, which came out last, were attacked by the *Indiana* and the *Gloucester*, the commander of the latter, Wainwright, dashing towards them in utter disregard of the fragile character of his vessel. The *Furor* was sunk and the *Pluton* was run ashore. The *Teresa*, struck by several shells which exploded and set her on fire, turned to the shore at 10.15 and was beached about six miles west of the Morro. The *Oquendo* was riddled by shell and likewise soon on fire. She was beached about half a mile west of the *Teresa* at 10.20. The *Vizcaya* and *Colon* were now left to bear the fire of the pursuing American ships, which were practically uninjured. In this running fight the *Indiana* dropped behind, owing to the defective condition of her machinery, but kept up her fire. At 11.05 the *Vizcaya* turned to run ashore about fifteen miles west of the Morro. The *Brooklyn* and the *Oregon*, followed at some distance by the *Texas*, continued the chase of the *Colon*. The *Indiana* and the *Iowa*, at the order of Sampson, who had come up, went back to guard the transports. At 1.15 P.M. the *Colon* turned to shore thirty miles west of the *Vizcaya* and surrendered.[1]

The fight was over, one of the most remarkable naval battles on record. On the American side, though the ships were struck many times, only one

[1] Sec. of the Navy, *Annual Report*, 1898, App., pp. 505-602; Long, *New Am. Navy*, II., 28-42.

man was killed and one wounded. These casualties both occurred on Commodore Schley's flag-ship, the *Brooklyn*. The Spaniards lost about six hundred in killed and wounded. The American sailors took an active part in the rescue of the officers and crews of the burning Spanish ships.

On July 3, General Shafter demanded the surrender of the Spanish forces in Santiago. This being refused, he notified General Toral that the bombardment of Santiago would begin at noon of the 5th, thus giving two days for the women and children to leave the city. Nearly twenty thousand people came out and filled the villages and roads around. They were in an utterly destitute condition, and had to be taken care of largely by the American army, a great drain on their supplies. On the 10th and 11th the city was bombarded by the squadron. At this point General Miles arrived off Santiago with additional troops intended for Porto Rico. He and Shafter met General Toral under a flag of truce and arranged terms for the surrender, which took place on the 17th. Shafter's command was by this time in a serious state of health and anxious to return home. Malarial fevers had so weakened the men that an epidemic of yellow-fever, which had appeared sporadically throughout the command, was greatly feared. The situation was desperate and the war department apparently deaf to all representations of the case. Under these circumstances the division and brigade commanders and the surgeons met at

General Shafter's headquarters early in August and signed a round-robin addressed to the secretary of war urging the immediate removal of the corps to the United States. This action was much criticised at the time, but it had the desired effect, and on August 4 orders were given to remove the command to Montauk Point, Long Island. The movement was begun at once and completed before the end of the month.

The surrender of Santiago left General Miles free to carry out plans already matured for the invasion of Porto Rico. He left Guantanamo, July 21, with 3415 men, mostly volunteers, convoyed by a fleet under the command of Captain Higginson, and landed at Guanica on the 25th. Early next morning General Garretson pushed forward with part of his brigade and drove the Spanish forces from Yauco, thus getting possession of the railroad to Ponce. General Miles was reinforced in a few days by the commands of Generals Wilson, Brooke, and Schwan, raising his entire force to 16,973 officers and men. In about two weeks they had gained control of all the southern and western portions of the island, but hostilities were suspended by the peace protocol before the conquest of Porto Rico was completed. The American losses in this campaign were three killed and forty wounded.[1]

The last engagement of the war was the assault on

[1] Major-General commanding the Army, *Report*, 1898, pp. 138–147, 226–243, 246–266.

Manila, which was captured August 13, 1898, by the forces under General Merritt, assisted by Admiral Dewey's squadron. This occurred the day after the signing of the peace protocol, the news of which did not reach the Philippines until several days later.[1]

Two controversies growing out of the war with Spain assumed such importance that they cannot be passed by. The first related to the conduct of the war department, which was charged with inefficiency resulting from political appointments and corruption in the purchase of supplies. The most serious charge was that made by Major-General Miles, commanding the army, who declared that much of the refrigerated beef furnished the troops was "embalmed beef," preserved with secret chemicals of an injurious character. In September, 1898, President McKinley appointed a commission to investigate these charges, and the hearings held were sensational in the extreme. Commissary-General Eagan read a statement before the commission which was so violent in its abuse of the commanding general that he was later court-martialled and sentenced to dismissal for conduct unbecoming an officer and a gentleman, though this sentence was commuted by the president to suspension from rank and duty, but without loss of pay. The report of the commission[2] failed to substantiate General Miles's charges, but it was not satisfactory or con-

---

[1] See chap. iv., below.
[2] *Senate Docs.*, 56 Cong., 1 Sess., No. 221, 8 vols.

vincing.   In spite of its efforts to whitewash things,
the commission had to report that the secretary of
war had failed to "grasp the situation."   Many
leading newspapers demanded Alger's resignation,
but President McKinley feared to discredit the
administration by dismissing him.   Nevertheless, a
coolness sprang up between them; and several months
later, when Alger became a candidate for the Michigan senatorship, with the open support of elements
distinctly hostile to the administration, the president asked for his resignation, which was tendered
July 19, 1899.[1]   He was succeeded by Elihu Root,
a very able and distinguished lawyer of New
York.

The other controversy, which waged in the papers
for months, was as to whether Sampson or Schley
was in command at the battle of Santiago.   As a
reward for their work on that day, the president advanced Sampson eight numbers, Schley six, Captain
Clark of the *Oregon* six, and the other captains five.
These promotions were all confirmed by the Senate
save those of Sampson and Schley, a number of
senators holding that Schley should have received
at least equal recognition with Sampson.   The controversy was waged inside and outside of Congress
for three years.   The officials of the navy department were for the most part stanch supporters of
Sampson, while a large part of the public, under the
impression that the department was trying to dis-

[1] *Nation*, LXIX., 61.

credit Schley, eagerly championed his cause. Finally, at the request of Admiral Schley, who was charged in certain publications with inefficiency and even cowardice, a court of inquiry was appointed July 26, 1901, with Admiral Dewey as president, for the purpose of inquiring into the conduct of Schley during the war with Spain. The opinion of the court was that his service prior to June 1 was "characterized by vacillation, dilatoriness, and lack of enterprise." Admiral Dewey differed from the opinions of his colleagues on certain points, and delivered a separate opinion, in the course of which he took up the question as to who was in command at Santiago, a point which had not been considered by the court. His conclusion was that Schley "was in absolute command and is entitled to the credit due to such commanding officer for the glorious victory which resulted in the total destruction of the Spanish ships." This made matters worse than ever. Secretary Long approved the findings of the majority of the court and disapproved Dewey's separate opinion. Schley appealed from the findings of the court to the president. February 18, 1902, President Roosevelt's memorandum, in which he reviewed the whole controversy, was made public. He declared that the court had done substantial justice to Schley. As regards the question of command at Santiago, he said that technically Sampson commanded the fleet, and Schley the western division, but that after the battle began not a ship took orders from either

Sampson or Schley, except their own two vessels.
" It was a captains' fight." [1]

The Spanish War revealed many serious defects in
our military system, some of which have been reme-
died by the reorganization of the army and the creation of a general staff.[2] It demonstrated the necessity of military evolutions on a large scale in time
of peace, so as to give the general officers experience
in handling and the quartermaster and commissary
departments experience in equipping and supplying
large bodies of troops; it showed the folly and danger
of appointing men from civil life through political
influence to positions of responsibility in any branch
of the military or naval service; it showed the value
of field artillery, of smokeless powder, and of high-
power rifles of the latest model; it also showed the
necessity of having on hand a large supply of the
best war material ready for use. While every
American is proud of the magnificent record of the
navy, it must not be imagined that the war with
Spain was a conclusive test of its invincibility, for,
however formidable the Spanish cruisers appeared
at the time, later information revealed the fact that
through the neglect of the Spanish government they
were very far from being in a state of first-class efficiency.

[1] Proceedings of the Schley Court of Inquiry, *House Docs.*, 57
Cong., 1 Sess., No. 485.
[2] Act of February 14, 1903, *U. S. Statutes at Large*, XXXII.,
pt. i., p. 830.

CHAPTER IV

PEACE NEGOTIATIONS

(1898–1899)

THE tone of the European press prior to the Spanish War undoubtedly encouraged Spain in her determination to reject the proposals of the United States for the adjustment of the Cuban question. Outside of England, foreign public opinion was distinctly hostile to the United States; but before the war was over this sentiment had undergone a marked change, and Spain abandoned whatever hope she had cherished of European intervention. The question as to who were our friends in 1898 has been much discussed, and when revived by the press upon the occasion of the visit of Prince Henry of Prussia to the United States in February, 1902, even the cabinets of Europe could not refrain from taking part in the controversy. In order to diminish the enthusiasm over the prince's visit, the British press circulated the story that Lord Pauncefote had checked a movement of the European powers to prevent the intervention of the United States in Cuba; while the German papers asserted that Lord Pauncefote had taken the initiative in proposing such action.   On the eve of Prince Henry's departure, Emperor William said to Ambassador White: "My brother's mission has no political character whatever, save in one contingency.   If the efforts made in certain parts of Europe to show that the German government sought to bring about a European combination against the United States during your Spanish war are persisted in, I have authorized him to lay before the president certain papers which will put that slander at rest forever." [1] These papers were despatches of 1898 from the German ambassador at Washington containing Lord Pauncefote's proposals, with the marginal comment by Emperor William that they were "completely futile and purposeless."   An official statement by Lord Cranborne in the House of Commons, February 11, 1902, denying emphatically that the British ambassador had ever made "any declaration adverse to the action of the United States in Cuba," caused the German emperor to make public the following day the despatches he had intrusted to his brother. [2]

Whatever the precise nature of Lord Pauncefote's proposal, it is certain that the attitude of the British government, as well as of the British people, from the outbreak of hostilities to the close of the war, was friendly.   As for Germany, while the conduct of the government was at all times officially correct, public sentiment expressed itself with great violence against

---

[1] Andrew D. White, *Autobiography*, II., 204.
[2] *Review of Reviews*, XXV., 270.

the United States.[1]   Even this sentiment gradually melted away in the face of the overwhelming triumph of the American navy.   The rest of Europe experienced the same change of heart, and by the end of July, 1898, the American as well as the European press was beginning to ask why the war should not be brought to a close, a consummation earnestly desired by the business interests of both hemispheres.

There was a still more cogent reason why Spain should sue for peace: the despatch of troops to the Philippines and to Porto Rico served to show that, although the war had been undertaken for the liberation of Cuba, the American government did not feel under any obligation to confine its military operations to that island, and that the occupation of other territory would almost certainly be made the basis of a war indemnity.   Having met all the demands of honor, Spain asked the French government, July 18, 1898, to authorize the French ambassador at Washington to arrange with the president of the United States the preliminary terms of peace.[2]   On July 26, Ambassador Cambon presented to President McKinley a note in which the Spanish government frankly acknowledged the futility of further resistance, and requested to know on what basis the Cuban question might be settled.   The president expressed his gratification at receiving the message, and requested the ambassador to return to

[1] Andrew D. White, *Autobiography*, II., 170.
[2] *Spanish Dipl. Corresp. and Docs.*, 200.

the White House later in order to discuss the question.[1]

In the formal reply, which was given July 30, the president reviewed briefly the causes of the war, expressed regret that the United States had been forced to act, and outlined the following terms of peace: first, the immediate evacuation of Cuba and the relinquishment of Spanish sovereignty; second, the cession of Porto Rico and one of the Ladrones by way of indemnity; and third, the occupation by the United States of "the city, bay, and harbor of Manila pending the conclusion of a treaty of peace which shall determine the control, disposition, and government of the Philippines."[2]   It should be remembered that these terms were proposed a few days after General Miles landed in Porto Rico and nearly two weeks before the capture of Manila.

As the war had been fought for Cuba, Spain endeavored to limit the negotiations so far as possible to the adjustment of the Cuban question, suggesting even that, if a money indemnity were insisted on for the expenses of the war, it should be assessed on Cuba, in whose behalf the war had been waged. She was especially anxious to retain Porto Rico, "the last memory of a glorious past," and asked that if her suggestion of saddling the debt on Cuba should be rejected, some other form of territorial com-

Spanish Dipl. Corresp. and Docs., 206; *Foreign Relations*, 1898, p. 819.   [2] *Ibid.*, p. 820.

pensation might be substituted.[1] In regard to the third condition, the disposition of the Philippine Islands, the Spanish government said, in its communication of August 7, that the language was quite indefinite; taking it to mean that Spain did not thereby renounce her sovereignty over the archipelago, but would agree to institute certain reforms there, she accepted it.[2]

This note was presented at the White House by Ambassador Cambon, August 10, and he reported that the president was visibly annoyed at its contents. The result was that Secretary Day drew up a formal protocol, embodying the demands of the United States, and presented it to M. Cambon practically as an ultimatum. Two days later the French ambassador was authorized by the Spanish government to sign this protocol, which he accordingly did August 12. The language of the protocol in regard to the Philippines was identically the same as that originally suggested: it left that question open. The protocol contained further provisions for the appointment within ten days of commissioners to arrange for the evacuation of Cuba and Porto Rico; for the appointment of peace commissioners to meet at Paris not later than October 1; and for the immediate suspension of hostilities.[3] The designation of Paris as the place of meeting was considered propitious for Spain.

[1] *Spanish Dipl. Corresp. and Docs.*, 214.
[2] *Foreign Relations*, 1898, p. 822.   [3] *Ibid.*, p. 824.

No sooner had the commissioners met to arrange for the evacuation of Cuba and Porto Rico than differences developed as to the interpretation of the protocol. The Spanish government advanced the view that evacuation meant simply military evacuation; that it did not mean the withdrawal of civil authorities or the abandonment of sovereignty until the conclusion of a treaty of peace. The United States finally carried its point, however, that the complete evacuation of these islands was a condition precedent to the negotiation of a treaty.[1]

The peace commission met at Paris October 1. The United States delegation was composed of William R. Day, who resigned the office of secretary of state to head this mission; Cushman K. Davis, chairman of the senate committee on foreign relations; William P. Frye, president *pro tem.* of the Senate; Senator George Gray, of Delaware; and Whitelaw Reid, editor of the New York *Tribune;* with John Bassett Moore, assistant secretary of state, as secretary. At the first meeting the Spanish commissioners demanded a restoration of the *status quo* of August 12 in the Philippines, Manila having been taken the day after the signing of the protocol.[2] The American commissioners refused to consider this question, on the ground that it had already been discussed in the notes that had passed between M. Cambon and the department of state, and was not

[1] *Spanish Dipl. Corresp. and Docs.*, 251.
[2] *Senate Docs.*, 55 Cong., 3 Sess., No. 62, pt. ii., p. 15.

properly within their powers.[1] The Spanish commissioners waived the point for the time being, but
reserved the right to bring it up later. The discussion in regard to the cession of Cuba occupied almost
the entire month of October, the difficulty being the
arrangement of the Cuban debt. The American commissioners proposed an article embodying the language of the protocol, that Spain should relinquish
her sovereignty over Cuba; but the Spanish commissioners proposed as a substitute that Spain should
cede Cuba to the United States, to be transferred
later to the Cuban people, Spain relinquishing and
transferring all prerogatives and rights, and "all
charges and obligations of every kind in existence
at the time of the ratification of this treaty." This
was an effort to saddle on the United States the
Cuban debt, the greater part of which had been
incurred by Spain in trying to suppress the Cuban
insurrection. The American commissioners emphatically declined to assume the burden of the so-called
Cuban debt, either in behalf of the United States or
of Cuba. The Spanish commissioners then accepted
the American draught provisionally, subject to the
conclusion of a treaty.[2]

The Philippine question was taken up October 31,
and occupied most of the time of the commissioners
during the month of November. Meetings were
held two or three times a week, at which proposals

[1] *Senate Docs.*, 55 Cong., 3 Sess., No. 62, pt. ii.. p. 21.
[2] *Ibid.*, 27, 52, 62.

and counter-proposals were presented. When the American commissioners had set out for Paris the mind of President McKinley was not made up on this important subject, and the matter was left, to a certain extent, open. In his letter of instructions to the commissioners, September 16, he said: "Without any original thought of complete or even partial acquisition, the presence and success of our arms at Manila imposes upon us obligations which we cannot disregard. The march of events rules and overrules human action. Avowing unreservedly the purpose which has animated all our effort, and still solicitous to adhere to it, we cannot be unmindful that, without any desire or design on our part, the war has brought us new duties and responsibilities which we must meet and discharge as becomes a great nation on whose growth and career from the beginning the Ruler of Nations has plainly written the high command and pledge of civilization. Incidental to our tenure in the Philippines is the commercial opportunity to which American statesmanship cannot be indifferent. It is just to use every legitimate means for the enlargement of American trade; but we seek no advantages in the Orient which are not common to all. Asking only the open door for ourselves, we are ready to accord the open door to others. The commercial opportunity which is naturally and inevitably associated with this new opening depends less on large territorial possession than upon an adequate commercial

basis and upon broad and equal privileges." Hence
he concludes: "The United States cannot accept
less than the cession in full right and sovereignty
of the island of Luzon." [1]

General Merritt was sent from Manila to Paris
to advise with the commissioners on this subject.
Several other army and navy officers, as well as
writers and travellers familiar with the subject,
were also heard by the American commissioners.
Decided differences of opinion having developed in
the commission, they submitted their views to the
president by cable, October 25, and asked for ex-
plicit instructions. Davis, Frye, and Reid were of
the opinion that it was not feasible to divide the
group, and that therefore the United States ought
to acquire all the islands; Day favored taking
Luzon, and possibly other islands of strategic importance; while Gray was opposed to taking any
part of the group, on the ground that there was no
place for colonial administration or government of
subject people in the American system. [2]

Secretary Hay replied the following day: "The
information which has come to the president since
your departure convinces him that the acceptance
of the cession of Luzon alone, leaving the rest of
the islands subject to Spanish rule, or to be the
subject of future contention, cannot be justified
on political, commercial, or humanitarian grounds.
The cession must be of the whole archipelago or

[1] *Foreign Relations*, 1898, p. 907.   [2] *Ibid.*, p. 932.

none. The latter is wholly inadmissible, and the former must therefore be required." [1]   Senator Hoar states in his *Autobiography* that the enthusiastic reception accorded the president on his trip through the South and West to California, when he discussed the issues of the war and the problems presented by Dewey's victory at Manila, had a great deal to do with changing his mind on the Philippine question.[2]   The situation just at this time in China, which was on the point apparently of being partitioned out among the European powers to the exclusion of the United States, undoubtedly made a profound impression on the president and his cabinet; and the acquisition of the Philippines seemed to afford a good opportunity to secure a foothold in the East.[3]   This idea also dominated the larger business and commercial interests of the country, which were beginning to feel the reactionary effects of the Dingley tariff in the retaliatory measures adopted by Germany, France, and other countries of Europe; and no mere abstract theory of government could be allowed to stand in the way of the opening of new markets in the Orient. Added to this was the religious motive: many clergymen and editors of religious papers agreed with the idea expressed by President McKinley that Providence had opened a way for the spread of American civilization in the East.   For one reason or another the American peo-

[1] *Foreign Relations*, 1898, p. 935.
[2] Hoar, *Autobiography*, II., 311.   [3] See chap. vi., below.

ple were gradually drifting into a current of sentiment which was soon overwhelmingly in favor of retaining the entire Philippine group.

When the American commissioners, acting on the above instructions, demanded the cession of the whole Philippine group, the Spaniards expressed great surprise, claiming that the demand was a violation of the protocol, which in express terms contemplated only the provisional occupation of Manila, and did not impair Spanish sovereignty over the islands.[1] The American commissioners had already warned the president that this demand would very likely lead to a rupture, and that a majority of them were clearly of the opinion that the demand could not be based on conquest. In reply the president insisted that the claim by right of conquest be not yielded, that "the destruction of the Spanish fleet on May 1 was the conquest of Manila, the capital of the Philippines."[2] On November 11 the commissioners again cabled to Washington expressing their individual views, urging the necessity of paying for the Philippines, and asking for definite instructions. On the 13th they were authorized to offer Spain $10,000,000 to $20,000,000.[3] An offer of $20,000,000 was made on the 21st, and a reply was requested by the 28th. The Spanish commissioners recognized this as an ultimatum, and, after consulting their government, on the date set yielded

---

[1] *Senate Docs.*, 55 Cong., 3 Sess., No. 62, pt. ii., pp. 107, 119.
[2] *Foreign Relations*, 1898, p. 940.   [3] *Ibid.*, p. 945.

under protest.[1] The draughting of the articles occupied some days, but on December 10, 1898, the
treaty was signed.[2]

By the terms of this treaty Spain relinquished all
claim of sovereignty over Cuba, and the United
States undertook to discharge during its occupation
of the island the obligations that might result from
such occupation for the protection of life and property; Spain ceded to the United States Porto Rico,
Guam, and the Philippines, the United States undertaking to pay twenty million dollars for the latter;
the United States agreed to admit Spanish ships
and merchandise to the ports of the Philippines for
a period of ten years, on the same terms as American ships and merchandise; the United States and
Spain each relinquished the claims of its citizens
against the other, and the United States agreed
to adjudicate and settle the claims of its citizens
against Spain; the treaty also provided that
"the civil rights and political status of the native
inhabitants of the territories hereby ceded to the
United States shall be determined by the Congress."

The president transmitted the treaty to the Senate
January 4, 1899, together with the protocols and
accompanying papers.[3] From that date until February 6 it was the main subject of debate, and
attracted the close attention of the entire country.

[1] *Senate Docs.*, 55 Cong., 3 Sess., No. 62, pt. ii., pp. 196, 210,
213.   [2] *Ibid.*, 260.   [3] *Ibid.*, pts. i.–iii.

A strong opposition to the treaty developed and the debate took a wide range, involving a discussion of the fundamental principles underlying the American constitutional system. The discussion really began December 6, when Senator Vest, knowing the instructions that had been sent to the commissioners at Paris, introduced a resolution declaring "That under the Constitution of the United States no power is given to the federal government to acquire territory to be held and governed permanently as colonies." This resolution was the centre of much of the debate during the weeks that followed. Senator Platt, of Connecticut, who spoke in opposition to this resolution, expressed the extreme views on one side of the question when he said: "I propose to maintain that the United States is a nation; that as a nation it possesses every sovereign power not reserved in its Constitution to the states or the people; that the right to acquire territory was not reserved, and is therefore an inherent sovereign right." This was a rather startling reversal of the fundamental principle of the Constitution that the powers of the federal government are delegated, and the powers of the states are inherent or reserved.

Senator Hoar, of Massachusetts, delivered a constitutional argument which attracted much attention, declaring that the proposal to acquire and hold the Philippine Islands was in violation of the Declaration of Independence, the Constitution, and

the whole spirit of American institutions.   The op-
portunist view, which ultimately prevailed, was
voiced by the junior senator from Massachusetts,
Mr. Lodge, who said: "Suppose we ratify the treaty!
The islands pass from the possession of Spain into
our possession without committing us to any policy.
I believe we can be trusted as a people to deal hon-
estly and justly with the islands and their inhabitants thus given to our care.   What our precise
policy shall be I do not know, because I for one am
not sufficiently informed as to the conditions there
to be able to say what it will be best to do, nor, I
may add, do I think any one is."   A great many
senators felt as Senator Spooner, when he said:
"This Philippine proposition is one of the fruits of
the war.   To me it is one of the bitter fruits of the
war.   I wish with all my heart we were honorably
quit of it."   He held, however, that the United
States had the absolute right to acquire territory,
and while as a matter of expediency he did not think
that the best interests of the United States would
be subserved by "permanent dominion over far-
distant lands and people," yet he thought it better
to vote for the treaty than to continue the war.
Many resolutions were introduced defining the future
policy in regard to the Philippines, but they were
all voted down.

The treaty could not be ratified without the assistance of Democrats, since the Senate contained
46 Republicans, 34 Democrats, 5 Populists, 2 Silver-

ites, and 3 Independents. While the discussion was at a white heat, Mr. Bryan went to Washington and advised his followers to vote for ratification in order to end the war, saying that the status of the Philippines could be determined in the next presidential campaign.[1] Just at this juncture an event occurred which materially affected the situation — the outbreak of an insurrection on February 4 against the American troops in the Philippines. The Senate had already agreed by unanimous consent that the vote should be taken February 6, and the outbreak of the insurrection against the United States removed the last doubt in the minds of many, who now felt that the national honor was involved and that the country could not withdraw from the islands in the face of an uprising. When the vote was taken it stood 57 for the treaty and 27 against.[2] Of those who voted yea, 40 were Republicans, 10 Democrats, 3 Populists, 2 Silverites, and 2 Independents. Of those who voted nay, 22 were Democrats, 3 Republicans, and 2 Populists. Immediately after its ratification the Senate passed, by a vote of 26 to 22, a resolution introduced by Senator McEnery, of Louisiana, one of the Democrats who had supported the treaty, to the effect that the action on the treaty was not to be deemed a final determination of our attitude towards the islands. This resolution, passed by a mere ma-

---

[1] Hoar, *Autobiography*, II., 322.
[2] *Senate Journal*, 55 Cong., 3 Sess., 216.

jority of the Senate, had no validity as an act of
the treaty-making power, and did not receive the
sanction of the House or the approval of the
president.

The question has often been asked, who was responsible for the treaty of 1899, particularly for the
acquisition of the Philippine Islands? Attempts
have been made to fix the responsibility on Admiral
Dewey, on the peace commissioners, on the Senate,
and on the American people; but the responsibility
must, of course, rest on President McKinley. He
professed, it is true, to follow public opinion, but he
had no right to evade the responsibility when he
had it in his power to bring about an entirely different result. Dewey has been criticised for not
sailing out of Manila Bay as soon as he had destroyed the Spanish fleet. Aside from the fact that
his instructions contemplated offensive operations in
the Philippines, such a course was out of the question. Where was he to go? The United States
had no naval station in the East, and modern international law does not permit a belligerent to use a
neutral port as a base. It was necessary for him
to remain in Manila Bay, and he could have remained there indefinitely, with Cavité as a base,
without the aid of a single regiment from the United
States. In fact, he got on better before the arrival
of Anderson and Merritt than he did afterwards, for
the presence of troops without the announcement
of a clearly defined policy necessarily caused trouble

with the insurgents. The parting of the ways was
when President McKinley sent the first expedition
from San Francisco to Manila.

Of the islands acquired from Spain by the treaty,
Guam, in the Ladrones, is important mainly as a
coaling station. It is about thirty miles long, six
broad, and has a population of between nine and
ten thousand. Porto Rico, the fourth island in size
in the West Indies, has an area of about thirty-
six hundred square miles. According to the census
taken in 1899, the total population was 953,243:
589,426 white, 304,352 mestizos, 59,390 negroes, and
75 Chinese. The Philippine Archipelago contains
3141 islands, of which only 1668 are listed by name,
and only 342 are populated. The total area of the
archipelago is 115,000 square miles, of which Luzon
makes 40,969, and Mindanao 36,292; while the area
of 2775 islands is less than a square mile each. The
islands are for the most part of volcanic origin,
mountainous or hilly. In Luzon, Negros, and Mindanao there are broad plains and valleys, but in
general there is comparatively little level land.
Tropic vegetation extends high up on the slopes
and covers the lesser mountains. The coast is
broken and affords numerous harbors. The entire
population, according to the census of 1903, was
7,635,426. Of these 6,987,686 were classed as civilized, and 647,740 as wild. The civilized native
inhabitants are practically all adherents of the
Roman Catholic Church. Of the wild tribes, two-

fifths are Mohammedan Moros. With the exception
of the aboriginal Negritos, who are widely dispersed
through the mountain regions, all the natives are
believed to be Malays.[1]

One subject remains to be finally disposed of.
By the treaty the United States assumed the payment of all claims of its citizens against Spain
which had arisen since the beginning of the Cuban
insurrection. These claims, sixteen million dollars
of which were on file in the state department at the
close of 1897, were one of the principal grievances
urged by the American government against Spain.[2]
When the "Spanish Treaty Claims Commission"
was organized in pursuance of an act of Congress
of March 2, 1901,[3] there were submitted to it 542
claims amounting to $61,672,077.78. Soon after its
organization the commission announced as one of
the principles guiding its action that, although the
Cuban insurgents were never recognized by either
Spain or the United States as belligerents, nevertheless the insurrection had from the first passed
beyond the control of Spain; and therefore, in order
to establish a claim, it would be necessary for the
claimant to show "that the Spanish authorities by
the exercise of due diligence might have prevented
the damages done." The result of this ruling was
that by the close of 1905 only eighteen claimants

---

[1] U. S. Census Bureau, *Census of the Philippine Islands.*
[2] See p. 7 above.
[3] *U. S. Statutes at Large*, XXXI., 877.

had succeeded in establishing the validity of their claims, and these eighteen had been awarded only $362,252, out of $2,387,429.26 claimed by them.[1] It would be useless to attempt to reconcile the position here assumed by the claims commission with that taken by the state department five years before, but consistency is not a diplomatic virtue!

[1] *Senate Docs.*, 59 Cong., 1 Sess., No. 308.

CHAPTER V

THE PHILIPPINE INSURRECTION
(1898–1902)

OF the frequent attempts at revolution during the last hundred years of Spanish rule in the Philippines, the most serious was organized among the tribe of the Tagalogs, in Luzon, by the "Katipunan," or patriots' league, in 1896. The object of this movement was not independence, but the correction of abuses in the local administration, which was almost entirely in the hands of the friars. With the exception of the Mohammedan Moros and the wild pagan tribes, the Philippine people belonged to the Roman Catholic Church, the church registry in 1898 showing a total of 6,559,998 Catholics. All but one hundred and fifty of the regular parishes were administered by Spanish monks of the Dominican, Augustinian, or Franciscan orders. In most of the parishes the priest was the only representative of the Spanish government: he was inspector of primary schools, president of the health board and board of charities, president of the board of taxation, and honorary president of the board of public works. He was not only the spiritual guide, but the

municipal ruler as well. Charges of gross immo-
rality were made against the friars, which in many
cases were undoubtedly true, but the real ground
of opposition was the immense power they wielded
in all the affairs of life. There was also in this opposition an element of agrarianism.[1] During the
insurrections of 1896 and 1898 a general attack was
made against the friars: forty were killed and over
four hundred imprisoned; the rest took refuge in
Manila, and many of them subsequently left the
islands. This expulsion of the friars was the overthrow of Spanish government throughout the greater
part of the archipelago.[2]

Aguinaldo, the youthful leader of the revolution
of 1896, had left the islands in December, 1897, in
pursuance of an agreement, known as the treaty of
Briac-na-bato, by which Governor-General Primo de
Rivera bound himself to introduce certain reforms
and to pay the leaders of the revolution one million
dollars to forego their efforts and withdraw from the
islands. Only four hundred thousand dollars of the
amount was ever paid, and the reforms were not
carried out. While Admiral Dewey was at Hong-
Kong preparing to leave for Manila, he was informed
by the American consul at Singapore that Aguinaldo was there and was willing to come to Hong-
Kong to arrange for a general co-operation between
the insurgents and the American forces, if desired.

---

[1] See p. 171 below.
[2] Philippine Commission, *Reports*, 1900–1903 (collected), 39–49.

Dewey replied: "Tell Aguinaldo come soon as possible." The American squadron left, however, before he arrived, and after the battle of Manila Bay he was brought over with thirteen of his staff on board the United States gun-boat *McCulloch*.

After a conference with Dewey, Aguinaldo was allowed to land at Cavité, organize his forces, and furnish them with guns from the Spanish arsenal.[1] He also established a revolutionary government, and on July 3 proclaimed the Filipino republic. The following day General T. M. Anderson, who at that time commanded the land forces of the United States, sent the following communication to Aguinaldo: "General: I have the honor to inform you that the United States of America, whose land forces I have the honor to command in this vicinity, being at war with the Kingdom of Spain, has entire sympathy and most friendly sentiments for the native people of the Philippine Islands. For these reasons I desire to have the most amicable relations with you, and to have you and your people co-operate with us in military operations against the Spanish forces." [2]

Meanwhile General Merritt had embarked from San Francisco, June 29, with instructions not to recognize Aguinaldo but to organize a provisional government. These instructions were cabled to

---

[1] Memorandum furnished by Dewey, *Report of* [Schurman] *Philippine Commission*, I., 171.

[2] *Senate Docs.*, 56 Cong., 1 Sess., No. 208.

Manila before the arrival of Merritt, and caused General Anderson to reply at once that, in his opinion, the establishment of a provisional government by the United States would bring about a conflict with the insurgents. When General Merritt arrived in Manila Bay on July 25, he found that Aguinaldo's forces encircled the city and extended on the south between the Spanish and American lines. When the American troops were preparing to advance against the city, Merritt requested Aguinaldo to withdraw his forces from this part of the line so as to allow General Greene to advance and occupy the position. This request was granted, and on the morning of August 13 everything was ready for the assault. The insurgents naturally wanted to advance simultaneously with the Americans, and Anderson, who was in command of the attacking forces, telegraphed to Aguinaldo asking him to try to prevent trouble, and saying: "Your forces should not force themselves in the city until we have received the full surrender. Then we will negotiate with you."

Dewey and Merritt had made a formal demand for the surrender of Manila, but the governor-general replied that he could not do this without consulting his government. He agreed, however, not to use his batteries on the fleet, provided Dewey would refrain from shelling the walled city. This limitation did not apply to the trenches south of the city, from which Dewey drove the Spaniards early on the morning of the 13th. The brigades of Greene and MacArthur then advanced through Malate, where there was sharp fighting, and occupied all of Manila except the walled city. A flag was then displayed from the walls, and after the usual formalities General Merritt, who had remained aboard the fleet, went ashore and immediately proceeded to the palace of the governor-general, where the preliminary agreement was soon signed.[1]

Serious trouble now threatened with Aguinaldo, whose troops had followed the Americans into the city and held joint occupation with them over the southern portions. The day after the surrender General Merritt cabled to Washington for instructions on this point, and received a reply that there must be no joint occupation. August 27 Aguinaldo agreed to retire under certain conditions. General Merritt left on the 30th for Paris to confer with the peace commissioners, and was succeeded by General Otis, who replied to Aguinaldo September 8, stating that the United States and Spain were the only recognized belligerents in this war, and that the American troops had forced the Spanish to capitulate. He referred to the unavoidable difficulties of joint occupation, and said that he was compelled by his instructions to direct Aguinaldo to withdraw his armed forces from the entire city of Manila, adding, in conclusion: "I hereby serve notice on

[1] Major-General commanding the Army, *Report*, 1898, p. 39; *Senate Docs.*, 57 Cong., 1 Sess., No. 331, pp. 1406, 2944.

you that unless your troops are withdrawn beyond the line of the city's defences before Thursday, the fifteenth instant, I shall be compelled to resort to forcible action." On the evening of the 15th the insurgents withdrew, marching out in excellent spirits and cheering the American troops, Aguinaldo having kept secret the above ultimatum.[1]

Shortly after the signature of the treaty at Paris, Spain withdrew her troops from most of the posts outside of Luzon and handed them over to the inhabitants. On December 21 the president directed General Otis to extend with all possible despatch to the whole archipelago the military government heretofore maintained in the city, harbor, and bay of Manila. General Miller was sent at once to Iloilo, next to Manila the most important city in the group; but before he arrived it was handed over to the insurgents. He remained in the harbor, but was directed to avoid any act of hostility. Meanwhile the conclusion of the treaty of Paris caused a crisis in the insurgent government. Mabini, Aguinaldo's chief adviser and the leader of the radical element, proposed a declaration of war against the United States, but the more conservative leaders would not consent to it. Any hostile act on the part of the United States at Iloilo would have precipitated war throughout the islands, for Aguinaldo had taken advantage of the uncertain status of affairs to send Tagalog agents throughout the provinces, and their

---

[1] Sec. of War, *Annual Reports.* 1899, I., pt. iv., p. 9.

influence was now dominant over many of the other tribes. They were merely waiting to see what the United States proposed to do with the islands. Early in December Dewey urged President McKinley to define his position in order to allay the spirit of unrest.[1]

The president's proclamation of January 3, 1899, was not calculated to have the desired effect, and therefore General Otis issued it in a modified form, omitting the words "sovereignty," "right of cession," and expressions directing immediate occupation. It was issued by General Miller, without the knowledge of General Otis, in its original form, and copies which soon fell into the hands of Aguinaldo created a bad impression and greatly strengthened the hands of the war faction.[2] There was now little chance of avoiding a conflict. While the Filipinos objected to the term sovereignty, associated in their minds with Spanish oppression, they seem to have had at this time very little idea of national independence. What they wanted was entire freedom from the kind of local control that the priests had exercised. They wanted the protection of the United States in their relations with other powers, but not its control. As for American conceptions of government, such were beyond their comprehension, and they preferred to be left to their own devices rather than to have the best government

[1] *Senate Docs.*, 57 Cong., 1 Sess., No. 331, p. 2745
[2] *Ibid.*, pp. 776, 777.

that was ever devised imposed on them from without.[1]

During the month of January, 1899, the insurgents strengthened their lines around Manila and began to show evident signs of dissatisfaction and restlessness. The conflict, which had been looked for by both parties for some time, came on the night of February 4. It seems to have been entirely unpremeditated. About eight o'clock three or four insurgents approached the lines of the First Nebraska Infantry, and, after being ordered to halt and apparrently disregarding the order, were fired upon. The fight soon became general and was continued on the 5th, 6th, and 10th of February. Admiral Dewey aided the army with a rapid fire from his ships north and south of the city, and the American lines were extended a considerable distance from the city in every direction. During these engagements the American casualties in killed and wounded were about two hundred and fifty, and the insurgent losses probably three thousand. On the 10th General MacArthur advanced north of the city and dislodged about four thousand insurgents who were concentrated south of Caloocan, and occupied the town. On the 11th General Miller, acting under orders from General Otis, captured Iloilo from the insurgents, with the assistance of the *Baltimore* and the *Petrel*. On February 22 the insurgents started fires in various parts of Manila, and a concerted up-

[1] *Senate Docs.*, 57 Cong., 1 Sess., No. 331, pp. 2726–2733.

rising was attempted, but the attempt was suppressed and the city placed under strict military control.[1]

The Eighth Army Corps, under General Otis's command, was composed at this time of 171 officers and 5201 men of the regular army, and 667 officers and 14,831 men of the volunteer army, making an aggregate of 838 officers and 20,032 men. All of the volunteers and 1650 of the regulars were entitled to their discharge upon the exchange of the ratifications of the treaty on April 11, 1899. Practically all of the volunteers, however, consented to remain in the field until their places could be filled by new troops. After the capture of Iloilo the navy took possession of the city of Cebu. In March the "Visayan Military District," including the islands of Panay, Negros, and Cebu, was organized and placed under command of General Miller, with headquarters at Iloilo. On May 19 the Spanish garrison at Jolo, in the Sulu Archipelago, was replaced by American troops. In August General Bates signed an "agreement" with the Sultan of Sulu, covenanting on the part of the United States to pay him and his principal datos monthly stipends, while the latter agreed to acknowledge the sovereignty of the United States. This agreement was much criticised at the time for its incidental recognition of slavery,[2] which could not have been interfered with without precipitating an insurrection. By August 31 the number

[1] Sec. of War, *Annual Reports*, 1899, I., pt. iv., pp. 365 et seq.
[2] *House Docs.*, 56 Cong., 1 Sess., No. 1, pt. ii.

of troops stationed at Jolo and in the Visayan Islands amounted to 4145.

To return to affairs in Luzon, General MacArthur continued his advance northward from Caloocan, and on March 31 entered Malolos, which for several months had been the seat of Aguinaldo's government. The insurgents occupied the swampy country west of Malolos and held a strong position at Calumpit, where the railroad crosses the Rio Grande, which was attacked by MacArthur April 28. After carrying this position MacArthur continued north along the line of the railroad as far as San Miguel, a little town south of Tarlac, while Lawton moved along a parallel line to the east as far as San Isidro. The insurgents evacuated Tarlac, but, as the rainy season was now coming on and many of the volunteers were impatient to return to the United States, the troops were recalled from the north, holding as a base for future operations the line of the railroad as far as San Fernando.[1]

During the summer the process of changing armies was practically completed. By act of March 2, 1899, Congress had authorized an increase of the regular army to 65,000 men and the recruiting of a new volunteer force of 35,000.[2] By the end of August the army in the Philippines numbered 30,963 officers and men, and preparations had been made for a northern advance at the beginning of the dry sea-

---

[1] Sec. of War, *Annual Reports*, 1899, I., pt. iv., pp. 115 et seq.
[2] *U. S. Statutes at Large*, XXX., 977.

son in October.   At this time the American lines in
Luzon included portions of the provinces of Cavité,
Laguna, and Morong, substantially all of the province of Manila, and the southern parts of Bulacan and Pampanga.   North of the American lines
stretched the great plain of central Luzon, over
which Aguinaldo exercised a military dictatorship
from his headquarters at Tarlac.

General Lawton opened the campaign October 12,
1899, by starting up the Rio Grande with a force
of about thirty-five hundred men.   After occupying and garrisoning successively the principal towns
along the river, the column turned west, and by
November 18 Young's cavalry, which formed the
advance, reached a point fifteen or twenty miles
east of San Fabian, on the Gulf of Lingayan.   In
the mean time General Wheaton, with a force of
twenty-five hundred men, had landed at San Fabian
in order to prevent the insurgents from retreating
north along the coast road.   General MacArthur, in
his advance up the railroad, drove the insurgents
from Tarlac, November 12, and reached Dagupan
on the 20th.   The insurgents had retired up the
railroad as far as Bayambang, where they scattered,
most of them escaping west into Zambales; but a
small force, including Aguinaldo, escaped north
through Wheaton's lines.   November 24 General
Otis telegraphed to Washington as follows: "Claim
to government by insurgents can be made no longer
under any fiction.   Its treasurer, secretary of the

interior, and president of congress in our hands; its president and remaining cabinet officers in hiding, evidently in different central Luzon provinces; its generals and troops in small bands scattered through these provinces, acting as banditti, or dispersed, playing the rôle of 'amigos,' with arms concealed." [1]

Meanwhile there was great perplexity as to what had become of Aguinaldo. General Young was given a separate command and started north in pursuit of him. Although he failed to find Aguinaldo, he liberated more than three thousand Spanish and American prisoners. Captain Batchelor was sent to Bayonbong with a battalion of infantry and some Tagalog scouts, with a view of intercepting Aguinaldo; but, not hearing anything of him, he proceeded north on his own authority all the way to Aparri, on the coast, displaying great tact and resourcefulness and receiving the surrender of General Tirona. As we now know, Aguinaldo, after fleeing north, finally sought refuge in the mountains along the eastern coast. [2]

In December General Lawton, after moving down into Bulacan and dispersing a large number of insurgents that infested that province, prepared an expedition against the two thousand insurgents who held the territory northeast of Manila. Through this country, which was easily defended, the insurgents of the north kept up communication with those

---

[1] Sec. of War, *Annual Reports*, 1900, I., pt. iv., pp. 208 et seq.
[2] Diary of Simeon A. Villa, a member of Aguinaldo's staff, *Senate Docs.*, 57 Cong., 1 Sess., No. 331, p. 1986.

of southern Luzon.   On December 18, 1899, while his troops were crossing the Mariquina River at San Mateo, General Lawton was shot and instantly killed by sharp-shooters on the opposite bank: thus fell one of the bravest and most efficient officers in the service.   Operations were continued, and by December 29 all the fortified posts were taken and the line of communication between the insurgents of the north and of the south broken.

During January, 1900, General Bates began an aggressive campaign against the insurgents in Cavité, and in February General Bell sailed from Manila to take possession of the provinces of North and South Camarines and West Albay, in which the insurgent forces had been swelled by individuals from the north.   Similar expeditions were sent to the Visayan group, and in March General Bates established garrisons in Mindanao.   With the successful execution of these movements all formal and open resistance to the Americans ceased for the time being.   Troops were stationed in over four hundred different posts. The casualties during the eight months of active campaigning, from August 31, 1899, to May 1, 1900, were 193 killed; 505 wounded, 65 of whom subsequently died; about 70 missing; and 634 who died from disease.   During this period the average strength of the army was 54,204.[1]

At a council of war held at Bayambang, November 12, 1899, Aguinaldo and his staff adopted a

---

[1] Sec. of War, *Annual Reports*, 1900, I., pt. iv., p. 560.

resolution and issued orders to the effect that the insurgents were incapable of further resistance in the field; that they had decided to disband the army; and that the generals and men were to return to their own provinces with a view to organizing the people for general resistance by means of guerilla warfare.[1] Before MacArthur's advance on Tarlac, Aguinaldo had reorganized his cabinet, dismissing Mabini, his ablest adviser, and causing the assassination of General Luna, whose ability, influence, and following threatened Aguinaldo's supremacy.[2] These men were both extremists and opposed to any pacific compromise with the United States; and it was supposed by some that Aguinaldo, having rid himself of them, might be induced to come to terms. The disbandment of the army was not regarded by the Filipinos as a calamity, but as a transition from one form of action to another, a change regarded by many as a positive advantage. The action was misunderstood by the Americans, and General MacArthur recommended a proclamation of amnesty, which was authorized by the president and issued June 21, 1900. After a period of inactivity, which was necessary for the redistribution of the insurgent forces and their adjustment to the new method of warfare, it became evident that the proclamation had not had the desired effect and

---

[1] Sec. of War, *Annual Reports*, 1900, I., pt. v., p. 59.
[2] *Am. Hist. Rev.*, July, 1906, p. 850; *Senate Docs.*, 57 Cong., 1 Sess., No. 331, pp. 69, 374.

that the insurrection had merely taken on a new form.

The guerilla warfare which the insurgents now began was waged for two years with great cruelty, treachery, and ferocity. It was something wholly new to American experience, and our troops soon learned to retaliate in kind. Murder, rape, torture, and other crimes were too frequently committed by American soldiers and by the native scouts commanded by American officers. The reports of these atrocities which were published in the United States were in many cases exaggerated, but the truth was bad enough. In February, 1902, the Senate committee on the Philippines began an investigation of the conduct of the army and consumed five months in the taking of testimony, including that of Admiral Dewey, General MacArthur, and Governor Taft, as well as that of a number of private soldiers. The printed report of the hearings fills over three thousand pages.[1] While many of the charges were unproven, and it was shown that the great majority of the officers had done what they could to correct abuses, the record is none the less humiliating. The harsh and cruel character of the warfare that was waged during this period may be readily seen from the following figures taken from General MacArthur's report of July 4, 1901. Between May 5, 1900, and June 30, 1901, there were 1026 "contacts" between American troops and insurgents.

[1] *Senate Docs.*, 57 Cong., 1 Sess., No. 331, pts. i.–iii.

The American casualties were 245 killed, 490 wounded, 118 captured, and 20 missing; while the insurgent casualties, as far as ascertained, were 3854 killed, 1193 wounded, 6572 captured, and 23,095 surrendered.[1] The disparity in the numbers killed cannot be attributed to the superior marksmanship of the American soldiers; it was due rather to the fact that the Filipinos were in many cases not armed with rifles, and in some cases, perhaps, to the ruthless slaughter of the wounded.

In February, 1901, it was discovered through despatches that had fallen into the hands of Lieutenant J. D. Taylor that Aguinaldo was at Palanan, in the province of Isabela. General Funston, with a party of eighty-one Macabebe scouts disguised as insurgents, four American officers, and five ex-insurgent officers, started out about the middle of March to capture him. After landing at Casiguran Bay and marching for six days through a very difficult mountainous country, they approached Palanan in the guise of insurgents on their way to join Aguinaldo, the American officers being closely guarded as prisoners. Leaving the Americans in the rear, the Macabebes advanced to Aguinaldo's headquarters and halted in a line opposite a guard of fifty men which had been drawn up to receive them, while the former insurgent officers entered the room where Aguinaldo and his attendants were assembled. Suddenly signalling to the Macabebes

---

[1] Sec. of War, *Annual Reports*, 1901, I., pt. iv., p. 98.

to open fire on the guard, the ex-insurgent officers discharged their pistols at the attendants and seized Aguinaldo. One of his companions was killed, another wounded, and the rest dispersed, as was also the guard.[1]

Contrary to General MacArthur's expectations, Aguinaldo's capture had very little effect of any kind on the insurrection. Open resistance in Luzon was confined mainly to the provinces of Batangas, Tayabas, and Laguna, but outside of Luzon insurgent forces were still operating in the islands of Mindoro, Samar, Cebu, and Bohol. On September 28, 1901, occurred the massacre of Balangiga, on the south coast of Samar: while the members of Company C, Ninth Infantry, were at breakfast, they were surprised by a party of natives, with the result that three officers and about fifty men were cut to pieces with bolos.[2]

In November various campaigns were conducted by General Bell in the Luzon provinces and in Mindoro; by General Smith, popularly known on account of his mode of warfare as "Hell Roaring Jake Smith," in Samar, and by General Hughes in Cebu and Bohol. In the Luzon provinces under his command General Bell adopted a rigid concentration policy. His orders of December 8 and 9 directed all the commanders to establish plainly marked limits around the towns in which they

---

[1] Sec. of War, *Annual Reports*, 1901, I., pt. v., p. 122.
[2] *Ibid.*, pt. vii., p. 9.

were stationed, and to order all the inhabitants outside of such towns to move, with their property and
belongings, within the prescribed limits by December 25.[1] In December peace was restored in Cebu
and Bohol. In February, 1902, General Lukban,
the insurgent leader in Samar, was captured, and in
April his forces all surrendered. General Mulvar,
the last insurgent leader to occupy the field in Luzon,
also surrendered in April. Thus ended the guerilla
warfare which had begun with the dispersion of
Aguinaldo's army more than two years before.

[1] *Senate Docs.*, 57 Cong., 1 Sess., No. 331, p. 1606.

CHAPTER VI

AMERICAN DIPLOMACY IN THE ORIENT
(1897–1905)

THE rivalry of the European powers in the commercial exploitation of China in 1897–1898 served to emphasize more than ever before the fact that commerce has become the greatest of all political interests, and that the prime object of diplomacy is now the extension of trade relations and the maintenance of foreign markets. To the attainment of these ends armies and navies are mere accessories. The downfall of China had been freely predicted after the revelation of her inherent weakness in the war with Japan in 1895; but the suddenness with which she fell a prey to the greed of the western nations was the sensation of the closing years of the nineteenth century. In November, 1897, following the murder of two German missionaries in the province of Shantung, German war-ships appeared at Kiao-chau, demanded the surrender of the city, which was promptly evacuated by the Chinese commander, and landed a body of troops. The next demand was for an indemnity, for the lease of Kiao-chau for ninety-nine years, and for the recognition of a German interest throughout the greater part of the Shantung peninsula. These demands were promptly complied with, and embodied in a treaty signed March 8, 1898.[1]

In the mean time Russia, who already enjoyed extensive railroad franchises in northern Manchuria, despatched five war-ships to Port Arthur, and announced that they would winter there. This occupation was followed by an agreement, signed March 27, 1898, by which China leased to Russia for a period of twenty-five years Port Arthur, Talien-wan, and the adjacent waters as a naval base; and also a rather indefinite extent of territory to the north. This territory was handed over to Russia absolutely for the term of the lease; no Chinese troops were to be allowed within its bounds. The Manchurian Railway Company was furthermore given the right to construct a branch line to Port Arthur.[2]

After protesting in vain against certain features of this agreement, England forced China to sign a lease of Wei-hai-wei, in the province of Shantung, together with the adjacent waters, "for so long a period as Port Arthur shall remain in the occupation of Russia." Prior to this lease, which was signed July 1, 1898, Great Britain had secured an

---

[1] *Foreign Relations*, 1898, p. 187; 1900, p. 383; *Parl. Papers*, 1898, China, No. 1, p. 69.
[2] *Ibid.*, pp. 1–9; 1899, pp. 128, 131; *Foreign Relations*, 1900, p. 383.

extension of the Hong-Kong territory on the mainland so as to include Mirs Bay, and also a definite assurance that China would not "mortgage,
lease, or cede" the Yangtse region to any other
power.[1]

In the mean time France had occupied Kwangchau
Bay in southwestern China under a ninety-nine-year
lease.[2]   In addition to cessions of territory, extensive
concessions for the construction of railways and mining privileges were granted to each power in its
particular "sphere of influence," in utter disregard
of the "most-favored-nation" clauses of existing
treaties.

The movement for the partition of China was well
under way when the United States went to war with
Spain and the Philippine Islands came within its
grasp.   To seize a sphere of influence in China
seemed utterly repugnant to the traditional policy
of the United States, and would not have been
acquiesced in by the Senate; but the occupation of
the Philippines would give a point of vantage from
which the American government could still exercise
a decisive influence in the Orient.   Such considerations were probably the main factor in President
McKinley's decision to retain the Philippines.[3]

In April, 1899, England and Russia reached an
agreement, made effective by an exchange of notes,

---

[1] *Parl. Papers*, 1898, Treaty Series, Nos. 14 and 16; *Ibid.*,
China, No. 2; *Foreign Relations*, 1898, p. 190; 1900, p. 384.
[2] *Ibid.*, p. 191.   [3] See p. 72 above.

that England would not seek on her own behalf or on behalf of her subjects any railway concessions north of the Great Wall of China, and would not obstruct Russian applications for concessions in that territory; similarly Russia agreed to give England a free hand south of the Great Wall.[1] Finally the United States decided to make a formal protest, and on September 6, 1899, Secretary Hay addressed notes to London, Berlin, and St. Petersburg on the subject of the "open door" in China. Each of the powers addressed was requested to give assurances and to make a formal declaration to the effect: (1) that it would not interfere with any treaty port or vested interest in its so-called sphere of influence; (2) that the Chinese tariff should continue in force in such sphere and continue to be collected by Chinese officials; (3) that it would not discriminate against other foreigners in the matter of port dues or railroad rates.[2] Similar notes were later addressed to France, Italy, and Japan. The move was only partially successful. England expressed her willingness to sign such a declaration, but the other powers, while expressing thorough accord with the principles set forth by Mr. Hay, avoided committing themselves and no such declaration was ever made. Mr. Hay made a skilful move, however, to clinch matters by informing each of the powers to whom the note had been addressed that,

[1] *Parl. Papers*, 1899, Treaty Series, No. 11.
[2] *Foreign Relations*, 1899, p. 128.

in view of the favorable replies from the other powers, its acceptance of the proposals of the United States was considered "as final and definitive." [1]

The real intentions of the powers, as contrasted with their professions, became apparent in the discussions that soon arose as to the status of consuls in the various spheres of influence. Japan claimed that sovereignty did not pass with a lease, and that even if China did surrender jurisdiction over her own people the lessee governments could not acquire jurisdiction over foreigners in leased territory. This position was undoubtedly correct, if the territorial integrity of China was really to be preserved; but the United States conceded the whole point, and on February 3, 1900, Mr. Hay wrote to Minister Conger that, "the United States consuls in districts adjacent to the foreign leased territories are to be instructed that they have no authority to exercise extra-territorial consular jurisdiction or to perform ordinary non-judicial consular acts within the leased territory under their present Chinese exequaturs." Application was then made to the European powers for the admission of consuls in the leased territories for the performance of ordinary consular functions; but in no case were they to exercise extra-territorial jurisdiction within a lease, although in some cases

[1] *Foreign Relations*, 1899, p. 142. The evasive French reply to the proposals, and a later British note of April 5, 1900, are both omitted from the *Foreign Relations*, but appear in *Parl. Papers*, 1900, China, No. 2.

they retained this power in the adjacent territory or "sphere of influence." [1]

The rapid exploitation of China, involving as it did the introduction of new ideas and new methods and much that was offensive among the most conservative of all peoples, naturally aroused an intense anti-foreign sentiment. In the provinces of Chili and Shantung an organization, formed ostensibly for the practice of athletics and known as the society of Boxers, began an agitation against foreigners, which rapidly assumed large proportions. The government was unable to stem the tide. The anti-foreign influence soon gained the ascendency under the leadership of Prince Tuan. Organized armies of Boxers, joined by imperial forces, held the territory between Peking and the coast and penetrated into Manchuria. Numbers of foreigners were murdered, and by the end of May, 1900, the situation had become critical. The powers decided to strengthen the legation guards at Peking. June 1 Minister Conger reported the arrival of three hundred and fifty guards, English, Russian, French, Japanese, Italian, and American. The German and Austrian contingents were to follow next day. The American force, consisting of fifty marines and an automatic gun, under Captain McCalla, of the *Newark*, was the first to arrive.

Events now moved with startling rapidity. On the 5th and again on the 8th Minister Conger cabled

[1] *Foreign Relations*, 1900, pp. 382–390.

to Washington, urging that more ships be sent to
Taku.   On the 10th Prince Tuan, who was strongly
anti-foreign in sentiment and a patron of the Boxers,
was appointed head of the foreign office.   A few days
later a relief expedition under Admiral Seymour and
Captain McCalla was driven back with heavy loss.
On June 19, at 4 P.M., each foreign minister at Peking
received a note ordering him to withdraw within
twenty-four hours.   The next day Baron von Ketteler, the German minister, who had an appointment
at the foreign office, started thither to protest; when
he had arrived within a short distance of his destination he was shot and instantly killed by a soldier in
full uniform; his secretary escaped to the legation.
From this date, June 20, until August 14, when the
relief column arrived, the legations were closely besieged by a half-disciplined army of Boxers and
imperial soldiers.   The entire diplomatic corps took
refuge in the British legation, which, with the help
of the native Christians, was converted into a veritable fortress; the lines of defence included at first
all the legations except the Belgian, but after the
burning of the Austrian, Italian, and Dutch legations they had to be greatly shortened.   The Chinese government was completely dominated by the
Boxer movement and, while professing that it was
using every effort to hold them in check, was in
reality encouraging them.[1]

Meanwhile the powers were preparing to take

[1] *Foreign Relations*, 1900, pp. 161–167.

more decisive action. On June 17 the European squadrons shelled the Taku forts and took possession of the place, as a preliminary measure to an advance on Tientsin and Peking. The United States decided to participate in the expedition, and the Ninth Infantry started from Manila June 27, under Colonel Emerson H. Liscum, and on July 1 General Chaffee sailed from San Francisco with the Sixth Cavalry to take command. In another note to the powers July 3, defining the attitude of the United States on the Chinese question, Mr. Hay said: "The policy of the Government of the United States is to seek a solution which may bring about permanent safety and peace to China, preserve Chinese territorial and administrative entity, protect all rights guaranteed to friendly powers by treaty and international law, and safeguard for the world the principle of equal and impartial trade with all parts of the Chinese Empire." In the policy of the United States thus set forth the British government expressed concurrence.[1]

When the report of the murder of Baron von Ketteler reached Tientsin July 9, there were already 20,000 troops ashore, a number which was thought no more than enough to hold the line from Taku to Tientsin; 60,000 in addition were considered necessary for a march to Peking. The proportion assigned to the United States was 10,000, but over 15,000 were soon set in motion for the China cam-

[1] *Foreign Relations*, 1900, p. 345.

paign, of whom between 5000 and 6000 arrived in China before the capture of Peking. A brigade made up of foreign contingents, under command of General Dorward, of the British army, attacked the walled city of Tientsin July 13, and Colonel Liscum, who had with him two battalions of the Ninth Infantry, U. S. A., was killed. The city surrendered on the 14th. At this time most positive and circumstantial accounts were received of the massacre of all the members of the legations at Peking. The general view taken by the civilized world was that the troops were not to rescue the living, but to avenge the dead, and hence preparations for the advance were made with great caution and deliberation. On July 20, however, Secretary Hay, who had been working with great tact and persistency through Minister Wu, received a message in cipher from the United States minister, dated the 16th, and reading as follows: "For one month we have been besieged in British Legation under continued shot and shell from Chinese troops. Quick relief only can prevent general massacre.—Conger."[1] This despatch was received with a certain degree of incredulity, especially in Europe, but an immediate advance was urged without waiting for reinforcements.

The movement was begun August 8 by a force of 8000 Japanese, 4800 Russians, 3000 British, 2500 Americans (joined later by a troop of cavalry), and

[1] *Foreign Relations*, 1900, p. 156.

800 French—an aggregate of 19,100.[1]   They reached Peking August 14, bringing deliverance to the little band of diplomats and missionaries who had struggled with undaunted courage to maintain themselves in the face of an overwhelming tide of lawlessness.

On July 20 Minister Wu presented to the president a cablegram from the emperor of China, reciting the fact that China had incurred "well-nigh universal indignation," and appealing to the United States to aid her in settling her difficulties.   To this appeal President McKinley replied that the United States would use its good offices for China on the following conditions: (1) China to give public assurance whether the foreign ministers were still alive; (2) if so, to put them in immediate and free communication with their governments; (3) to cooperate with the relief expedition.   These conditions were not complied with, and in view of the fact that the state department was still cut off from all communication with Minister Conger, the president appointed W. W. Rockhill special commissioner to China.   He reached Shanghai August 29, and later proceeded to Peking to act as adviser to Mr. Conger. When the latter was granted a well-earned leave of absence and returned to the United States, Rockhill remained to conduct the negotiations with the powers.[2]

As the relief expedition approached Peking the

[1] Sec. of War, *Annual Reports*, 1900, I., pt. i., p. 24.
[2] *Foreign Relations*, 1901, App., Affairs in China, p. 12.

imperial court fled westward, and later appointed
Earl Li Hung Chang to conduct in its behalf the
negotiations with the powers. Having rescued her
minister, Russia seemed disposed to withdraw her
forces from Peking; but the United States urged
the continued occupation of the capital by all the
powers, and joint action rather than individual
protection of individual interests.[1] Throughout the
lengthy negotiations that followed, the United States
adhered closely to the principles laid down in Secretary Hay's note of July 3, 1900; he displayed
great skill in giving to the world at a critical moment a definite expression of policy, and in urging
the powers to observe it. England and Germany
formally adopted this policy by making it the basis
of an agreement signed October 16, 1900, in which
they declared that it was a matter of permanent
international interest that the ports of China should
remain free and open to trade; that neither of them
would take advantage of present conditions to obtain for itself any territorial advantages in China;
that they would direct their policy towards maintaining the territorial integrity of China; and that
in case any other power should attempt to take
advantage of conditions as they then existed, the
contracting powers would take joint action to protect their interests. The adherence of other powers
was invited, and the agreement was accepted fully
by Austria, Italy, and Japan, evasively by Russia

[1] *Foreign Relations*, 1901, App., Affairs in China, 20.

and France, and in part by the United States, which declined to commit itself to the policy of protecting existing interests.[1]

By December 22, 1900, the powers had embodied their demands in a joint note, which was presented to the Chinese government and agreed to by the emperor. These demands, twelve in number, may be classified under four heads: (1) adequate punishment for those who were responsible for and who engaged in the foreign massacres and riots; (2) the adoption of measures to prevent the recurrence of such disorders; (3) indemnifications for losses sustained by foreign states and individuals; (4) the improvement of the relations of foreigners, both official and commercial, with China.[2] Then followed nearly a year of tedious negotiations, spent in putting these demands in definite shape and arranging the details. The final protocol was signed September 7, 1901.[3] During the negotiations the main points of difficulty were the punishment of the chief culprits, the best method of preventing such disturbances in the future, and the amount of the indemnity. In all these matters the United States threw the weight of its influence on the side of moderation, urging the powers not to impose too many burdens on China, and declaring that the

[1] *Parl. Papers*, 1900, China, No. 5; *Foreign Relations*, 1900, p. 354.
[2] *Foreign Relations*, 1901, App., Affairs in China, 59.
[3] *Ibid.*, 312.

only hope for the future lay in a strong, independent, responsible Chinese government. The amount of the indemnity was fixed at 450,000,000 taels ($333,000,000 approximately). The powers agreed that on September 17 they would withdraw from Peking all troops except the legation guards.

Secretary Hay's management of the Chinese imbroglio reflected great credit on himself and on his country. While the other powers looked upon the Chinese government as hostile, the United States insisted on regarding the outrages as, *prima facie*, the work of insurrectionists, and remained on friendly terms with the constituted authorities, thus gaining valuable information, and in all probability saving the lives of the entire diplomatic corps. The amount of the indemnity to be paid the United States for the losses of its citizens during the Boxer disturbances and for the support of the troops in China was fixed by the protocol of September 7, 1901, at over twenty-four million dollars. This was greatly in excess of the actual amount of the losses sustained, which was subsequently found to be about eleven million dollars. In June, 1907, Secretary Root informed the Chinese minister that the president had decided to recommend in his next message to Congress that China be released from all obligation in excess of this amount. This is an act of simple justice, and it remains to be seen whether similar action will be taken by the European powers, who took advantage of China's prostration to demand far heavier indemnities than their claims justified.[1]

Contrary to the terms of the final protocol, Russia retained in Manchuria the troops concentrated there during the Boxer movement, with a view to exacting further concessions from China. The seriousness of the situation led England and Japan to sign a permanent defensive agreement January 30, 1902, recognizing England's interests in China and Japan's in Korea, and providing that if either party should be attacked in defence of its interests the other party would remain neutral, unless a third power joined in, in which event the second party would come to the assistance of the first.[2] A formal protest made by the United States February 1 against some of the demands Russia was making on China, led Russia to conclude that the American government had an understanding with England and Japan; but Mr. Hay gave the assurance that he had known absolutely nothing about the Anglo-Japanese agreement until it was made public. He succeeded in securing from Russia, however, a definite promise to evacuate Manchuria by October 8, 1903, which was the date set in the Russo-Chinese Manchurian convention of April 8, 1902. As the time for withdrawal drew near, Russia began imposing new conditions on China, and deliberately misrepresented to the United States the character of the new proposals.[3]

---

[1] *Washington Post*, June 19, 1907.   [2] *Foreign Relations*, 1902, p. 514.
[3] *Ibid.*, pp. 280, 926, 929; 1903, pp. 54, 56.

In the protocol of September 7, 1901, China had agreed to extend the scope of her commercial treaties with the powers.   When the negotiation of a new treaty was begun by Consul-General Goodnow at Shanghai, the United States demanded that at least two new ports in Manchuria be opened to foreign trade and residence.   The Chinese commissioners declined to discuss this subject, on the alleged ground that they had no instructions to do so.   It was evident that there was secret opposition somewhere, and on May 7, 1903, Mr. Conger reported that it came from the Russian *chargé d'affaires*.   Later he secured a written acknowledgment from the Chinese government that such was the case.   Meanwhile Russia was giving positive assurances at Washington that she was not opposed to open ports and consulates in Manchuria.   Mr. Hay then appealed with the utmost directness to the Russian government, stating that the negotiations with China were substantially terminated, with the exception of the question of the open ports in Manchuria, and that the Chinese government still claimed that it was prevented from coming to an agreement on this point by Russian opposition; he requested to know whether instructions had been sent to the Russian minister at Peking, and, if not, that prompt action be taken.   The Russian government promised to send the necessary instructions, but when Mr. Conger approached the Russian minister at Peking, the latter replied that the matter had been taken out of his hands, and that he had been instructed to await the result of the discussion of the question at Washington.

After this sort of evasion had gone on for a month, on July 14 a definite answer was at length received from Russia, in which she declared that it had never entered into her views to oppose the opening of certain cities in Manchuria to foreign commerce, but that this declaration did not apply to Harbin, one of the cities selected by the United States, which was situated within the railway zone, and therefore was not under the complete jurisdiction of China. A copy of this note was shown to the Chinese government, which finally agreed to insert in the treaty on October 8 (the date on which Russia had agreed to completely withdraw from Manchuria) a provision for the opening of two ports. The United States agreed to this arrangement, and on October 8 the treaty was signed, and Mukden and Antung named as the open ports.[1]   If the United States had had a stronger navy in the Pacific, Mr. Hay's diplomacy might have been more effective.

Japan now took up the Manchurian question. The presence of Russian troops on the soil she had conquered in 1895 and returned to China was more than she could stand. After long negotiations, Japan presented to Russia, on January 16, 1904, an ultimatum, in which she stipulated: (1) that Japan would recognize Manchuria as being outside her sphere of interest, provided Russia would respect

[1] *Foreign Relations*, 1903, pp. 56–77. 91.

the territorial integrity of China in Manchuria; (2)
that Russia would not impede Japan or other powers
in the enjoyment of rights and privileges acquired
by them in Manchuria under existing treaties with
China; (3) that Russia would recognize Korea as
being outside her sphere of interest.   After waiting
for what she considered a reasonable time for a
reply, Japan withdrew her minister from St. Petersburg, and on February 10, 1904, issued a formal
declaration of war.[1]

During the struggle that ensued the status of
China was wholly unique.   Although she was not a
party to the war, most of the military operations
were carried on within her borders.   As soon as war
was declared the United States addressed identic
notes to Russia and Japan, expressing the earnest
desire that "the neutrality of China and in all practicable ways her administrative entity should be
respected by both parties, and that the area of
hostility should be localized and limited as much as
possible."   In reply both powers agreed to respect
Chinese neutrality outside of Manchuria.[2]   The neutral status of China was several times called in question, and Russia and Japan each charged the other
with violating it.   A number of Russian vessels took
refuge in Chinese ports.   In the case of the *Ryeshi-
telni*, at Chefoo, when she continued her stay beyond the twenty-four-hour limit, a Japanese vessel
entered the harbor, captured, and towed her out, in

---

[1] *Foreign Relations*, 1904, pp. 410–413.   [2] *Ibid.*, p. 2.

disregard of Chinese sovereignty.   Japan claimed, of
course, that Chinese neutrality was conditional, and
that Russia had violated it.[1]   In most of the other
cases agreements were finally reached, in accordance
with which the ships were dismantled and their
crews interned at specified places until the close of
the war.[2]   Upon two occasions during this war the
United States felt compelled to interne Russian
ships.   The first case was that of the *Lena*, which
entered San Francisco harbor September 11, 1904,
and the second, that of three vessels of Admiral
Enquist's squadron, which entered Manila harbor
June 3, 1905, and requested permission to repair
injuries received in battle.   In both cases, after ex-
aminations by naval officers of the United States
which showed that the vessels needed a thorough
overhauling, they were disarmed and interned, and
the crews paroled until the close of the war.[3]   Should
the rule of internment thus applied by the United
States continue to be enforced in future wars, it
will tend to limit greatly the area and duration of
maritime contests.

The services of President Roosevelt to the cause
of peace in bringing Russia and Japan to a conference within the United States in 1905 have received universal recognition, and doubtless constitute a notable diplomatic achievement, though how
far the result was due to other influences it is not

[1] *Foreign Relations*, 1904, pp. 139, 424, 425.
[2] *Ibid.*, pp. 136, 138, 140, 323, 426.   [3] *Ibid.*, pp. 428, 785.

yet possible to say. The success of the move was
at any rate a gratifying recognition of the growing
importance of the United States in world politics,
particularly in the affairs of the Pacific Ocean. Not
only did the president appeal with great force and
in the interest of the civilized world to the emperors
of Russia and Japan to open direct negotiations
with each other, but when the commissioners met
he kept in constant touch with them, advising,
restraining, urging, and compromising their differences. The president's appeal was made June 8,
1905; the formal meeting of the envoys took place
aboard the president's yacht August 5; the conference began its regular sessions at Portsmouth, New
Hampshire, August 8; and the treaty was signed
September 5. Russia and Japan agreed to evacuate
Manchuria, with the exception of the Liaotung
peninsula, and to restore it to China; the Russian
leases of Port Arthur, Talienwan, and adjacent
territories and territorial waters were to be transferred, with the consent of China, to Japan.[1]

While the treaty of Portsmouth was being negotiated, England and Japan signed a treaty of alliance
for the protection of England's interests in India and
Japan's interests in Korea, and also for the preservation of Chinese territorial integrity and the principle of commercial equality of all nations.[2]

[1] *Foreign Relations*, 1905, pp. 807-828.
[2] *Am. Journal of Int. Law*, I., No. 1, Document Supplement.
15.

During the war between Russia and Japan the sympathies of the American people were very largely with Japan, partly because her resources were more limited, and partly because the underhand methods of Russian diplomacy had created an unfavorable impression. But no sooner had the Russian pleni-potentiaries set foot on American soil than Count Witte drew to himself the sympathetic interest of the public. This was due in part to his striking personality, and in part to the realization that the odds were greatly against him. Public opinion undoubtedly helped the Russian negotiations. The result was that the Japanese envoys went home somewhat disgruntled, and with at least an out-ward resentment, because they had failed to get any indemnity, and had been forced to relinquish their claims to half of the island of Saghalien. With the great prestige derived from this war, and an absorbing ambition to dominate China, Japan will undoubtedly be a formidable rival of the United States for commercial and naval supremacy in the Pacific.

CHAPTER VII

FREE SILVER *VERSUS* IMPERIALISM
(1900)

WHEN the presidential campaign of 1900 opened, the Republican party had been in undisputed control of all branches of the federal government for over three years. During that time it had passed a new tariff, conducted a war with Spain resulting in the annexation of vast insular dependencies, and passed a gold-standard act. The Dingley tariff was enacted July 24, 1897, by a special session of Congress convened by President McKinley shortly after his inauguration. The duties thus imposed were excessive, but were accompanied by a provision through which it was claimed that many of the higher rates would be greatly reduced and our commerce at the same time proportionately extended: limited reciprocity agreements were authorized with foreign powers, to be entered into by the president and proclaimed without the action of the Senate. Several such agreements were made. In addition, the act provided for reciprocity of a more extended nature: it gave the president power for a period of two years to enter into treaties with foreign countries, providing for a reduction of not more than twenty per cent. of the Dingley rates, in return for concessions in favor of American commerce; or to transfer to the free list articles which were the natural products of such countries, but not of the United States. The reduction offered was no real concession, for the tariff had been raised to a point where with the twenty per cent. off the rates were about normal. Under this provision seven treaties were negotiated within the next two years by John A. Kasson, and submitted by the president to the Senate for ratification; but that body, controlled by special interests, failed to act upon them.[1] This was an act of bad faith to say the least, for the House had agreed to the bill and the president had signed it with the distinct understanding that the rates were to be reduced by reciprocity agreements.

The financial measure known as the gold-standard act[2] was passed by the Fifty-sixth Congress, and signed by the president March 14, 1900.[3] By this act the dollar consisting of 25.8 grains of gold, nine-tenths fine, was made the standard of value, and the duty was imposed on the secretary of the treasury of maintaining at a parity with that standard all forms of money issued or coined. For this purpose the secretary was authorized to set aside

[1] Senate Com. on For. Rels., *Compilation of Reports*, VIII., 474–635.   [2] *U. S. Statutes at Large*, XXXI., 45.
[3] Cf. Dewey, *National Problems* (*Am. Nation*, XXIV.), chap. xx.

$150,000,000 in gold coin and bullion from the general funds of the treasury as a reserve fund with which to redeem United States notes and treasury notes issued under the act of 1890. If at any time this fund falls below $100,000,000 and the secretary is unable to replenish it in the usual manner, he is authorized to borrow money by the issue of bonds until the fund is restored to $150,000,000. The act did not affect the legal-tender quality of the silver dollar, but provided for the retirement of the treasury notes of 1890 as fast as silver bullion should be coined into dollars and silver certificates issued in amounts equal to the treasury notes so retired. The act also amended the national banking law by providing for the organization of banks in places of three thousand inhabitants or less with a capital of $25,000 instead of $50,000, as formerly; and by allowing banks to issue circulation on the bonds deposited up to the par value of the bonds, instead of to ninety per cent. of their face value, as before.

This act was received with great satisfaction by the financial world, and was regarded generally as settling for some time to come the financial policy of the government. The Dingley tariff, however, was by no means satisfactory to the country at large, and the dissatisfaction which it occasioned deepened when it became evident that the Republican majorities in Congress had no intention of carrying out in good faith its reciprocity features. However vital and important the tariff policy of the government, in the campaign of 1900 it was side-tracked for other issues.

At one time it seemed that the questions growing out of the war with Spain would be the leading issues of the campaign: the Democratic national convention did, indeed, declare that it regarded imperialism as the "paramount issue," but it also adopted a silver plank and again nominated William J. Bryan as its candidate. Many of the thoughtful and conservative men of the country, who were opposed to the military and colonial policies of the Republican party, were even more strongly opposed to the silver tenets of Mr. Bryan. Instead of a clean-cut campaign on the single issue of imperialism, which was new and of transcendent importance, attention was diverted to a discussion of monetary standards, so that to the conservative men of the country it seemed a choice between free silver and imperialism.

Before the campaign opened it was evident that McKinley would be renominated by the Republican party, and it was almost equally certain that Bryan would be the Democratic candidate. For a time Admiral Dewey was a force to be reckoned with; but when he returned to this country in September, 1899, he said emphatically that he would not be a candidate for the presidency, and the American people took him at his word. Nevertheless, on April 4, 1900, he issued a statement, in which he said that he had "reached a different conclusion, inasmuch as so many assurances have come to me from my countrymen that I would be acceptable as a candidate for this great office." [1] He declined to state on what platform he would stand, but later let it be known that he regarded himself as a Democrat. But by this time the nomination of Bryan was practically a foregone conclusion, and Dewey's announcement was nowhere taken very seriously. Bryan's hold on the people was due to the widespread belief in his integrity of character and honesty of purpose. Although earnest, sincere, and patriotic, he selected issues without subjecting them to searching analysis, but when selected advocated them with a superb eloquence that would have adorned the highest statesmanship.

The campaign of 1900 is remarkable in the history of America for the number of parties in the field: at least twelve conventions met and adopted platforms, though not all of them nominated separate candidates. The People's party was the most significant of the third-party movements, but was soon found to be hopelessly divided into two wings. The Middle-of-the-Road, or Anti-fusion, Populists met at Cincinnati May 10, and nominated Wharton Barker, of Pennsylvania, for president, and Ignatius Donnelly, of Minnesota, for vice-president. The Fusion Populists, those who wished to act in co-operation with the Democrats, met the same day at Sioux Falls, South Dakota, and nominated Bryan

[1] *N. Y. World*, April 4, 1900.

for the presidency by acclamation, thus anticipating the action of the Democratic convention; Charles A. Towne, of Minnesota, for several years the recognized head of the Silver Republicans, was nominated for vice-president, though an effort had been made to keep this place open until the Democratic convention should meet. The most significant plank in the Populist platform, appearing in the platforms of both wings, was the government ownership of railroads as the remedy for trusts. The platform also denounced the gold-standard act, and declared against imperialism.[1]

In the national Republican convention, which met at Philadelphia, June 19, the proceedings were cut and dried. The Silver Republicans had left the party, the tariff question was in the background, and the only thing to be done seemed to be to indorse McKinley's administration. The platform was adopted on the second day with practically no opposition, and the following day McKinley was nominated by acclamation. Had Vice-President Hobart been alive it is probable that the convention would have nominated him and adjourned without incident. But who was to take Hobart's place? Some delegates favored John D. Long, secretary of the navy; Dolliver, of Iowa, had quite a following; Timothy L. Woodruff, of New York, and Elihu Root, secretary of war, were also mentioned; Root had positively declined to allow his name to be con-

[1] *World Almanac*, 1901, pp. 141, 143.

sidered. The most eligible candidate was Theodore Roosevelt, who in 1898 had been elected governor of New York; but in February he had issued a statement in which, with his usual emphasis, he said: "Under no circumstances could I, or would I, accept the nomination for the vice-presidency." It was generally expected that he would be renominated for governor of New York. He undoubtedly had presidential aspirations, and did not care to be side-tracked into the vice-presidency. But Roosevelt was acquiring great ascendency over the Republican party in New York, and was advocating reform measures which were opposed by the machine. Senator Platt, the Republican boss of New York, who was working in the interests of certain large corporations, came to the conclusion that it would be best to get Roosevelt out of New York politics, and that he would make a good candidate for vice-president. He therefore called in the help of Quay and the Pennsylvania machine, and started a boom for Roosevelt. This move met with a prompt response from the Far West, where Roosevelt's popularity was great. His speech seconding McKinley's nomination made a fine impression, and when, in spite of sincere protests, his name was placed in nomination by Lafayette Young, of Iowa, he received every vote in the convention except his own.[1]

The Republican platform contained little that was new or striking. It started out with an in-

[1] *Review of Reviews*, XXII., 7–9.

dorsement of President McKinley's administration, and the claim that the prosperity of the past four years was due to the Republican party. On the trust question the language was vague and general, recognizing "the necessity and propriety of the honest co-operation of capital to meet new business conditions, and especially to extend our rapidly increasing foreign trade." The party expressed a renewal of its faith in the policy of protection of American labor; favored legislative aid in building up the merchant marine; advocated the extension of trade with the Orient; commended the administration for its successful efforts to maintain the open door in China; approved the annexation of the Hawaiian Islands; commended the part taken by the United States in the peace conference at The Hague; asserted a steadfast adherence to the Monroe Doctrine; declared the acquisition of the Philippines and Porto Rico to have been a necessary result of our victories; and asserted that the pledge to Cuba had been performed to the letter.[1]

The Democratic party met in convention at Kansas City, July 4, 1900. As was expected, on the question of imperialism it declared: "We regard it as the paramount issue of the campaign." The main discussion took place with reference to what attitude the party should assume on silver. Mr. Bryan let it be known that if the demand for the immediate free coinage of silver were left out of

[1] *Republican Campaign Text-Book*, 1900, p. 421.

the platform he would refuse the nomination, and the convention was from the first completely under the influence of his friends, though it is probable that if the party had acted on its real sentiments it would have dropped the silver question.   There was a heated contest in the committee on resolutions, where there seemed to be a majority against the silver plank, and the decision depended on the New York delegation.   David B. Hill was opposed to the silver plank, but Richard Croker succeeded in keeping him off the committee, and threw the Tammany influence to Bryan.   Instead of putting the Republicans on the defensive by attacking imperialism, Bryan forced his party by the adoption of the silver plank to put itself in an apologetic attitude. A fact which now seriously embarrassed Bryan was that the Populists had nominated for vice-president Towne, whom personally he favored; but as it was evident that the Democrats could not afford to accept the entire Populist ticket, he did not insist on Towne's nomination.   Hill, representing the conservative element of the East, could have had the second place, but he positively declined to take it. Finally, Adlai E. Stevenson, who had served as vice-president during Cleveland's second term, was nominated for this place.   Bryan was thus associated with two candidates for the vice-presidency, and it became necessary for the Democrats and Populists in each state to agree on a common set of electors.

The Democratic platform was written in clear-cut, emphatic language. It began with the declaration that all governments derive their just powers from the consent of the governed, and continued: "We hold that the Constitution follows the flag and denounce the doctrine that an Executive or Congress, deriving their existence and their powers from the Constitution, can exercise lawful authority beyond it, or in violation of it." The platform denounced the Porto Rican tariff act, and demanded the fulfilment of our pledges to Cuba. It further denounced the whole Philippine policy of the Republican party, and declared: "We favor an immediate declaration of the nation's purpose to give to the Filipinos: first, a stable form of government; second, independence; and third, protection from outside interference such as has been given for nearly a century to the republics of Central and South America." On the trust question the Democratic platform was much more specific and emphatic than the Republican: it denounced the Dingley tariff law as "a trust-breeding measure"; favored publicity in the affairs of corporations engaged in interstate commerce; and advocated "such an enlargement of the scope of the Interstate Commerce law as will enable the commission to protect individuals and communities from discriminations and the people from unjust and unfair transportation rates." The financial plank denounced the recent gold-standard act and declared: "We reaffirm and indorse the principles of the

National Democratic platform adopted at Chicago
in 1896," and demand "the immediate restoration
of the free and unlimited coinage of silver and gold
at the present ratio of 16 to 1, without waiting for
the aid or consent of any other nation." Both
parties favored the irrigation of western lands,
and the granting of statehood to Arizona, New
Mexico, and Oklahoma.

Bryan was also indorsed by the Silver Republicans, who met in Kansas City the same week, and
by the Liberty Congress of the American League of
Anti-Imperialists, which met in Indianapolis August
16. A number of other parties put candidates in
the field, such as the Socialist Labor party, the
Social Democratic party, the Prohibition party, and
the United Christian party.

In the election in November thousands of Democrats voted for McKinley, some on account of their
opposition to the silver plank of the Democratic
platform, and some because they favored the new
colonial policy of the Republicans. Some Democrats, on the other hand, who had voted for McKinley in 1896, came back to the support of Bryan in
1900; and some prominent Republicans also supported the Democratic ticket, among them the
venerable George S. Boutwell, of Massachusetts,
and Senator Wellington, of Maryland. On the same
side were Carl Schurz, independent, and Edward
M. Shepard and Bourke Cockran, Gold Democrats.
Senator Hoar, who had been so vehement in his

opposition to the policies of the Republican administration, was greatly reproached by the Anti-Imperialists for voting for McKinley.

Senator Marcus A. Hanna, chairman of the Republican national committee, conducted a very clever campaign, making use of many devices, among them the "full dinner-pail" as an emblem of "McKinley prosperity." Posters were extensively used, and thousands of leaflets in foreign languages distributed in order to reach citizens of foreign speech. He succeeded in capturing a very large labor vote. President McKinley remained at home and took very little part in the canvass. Bryan pursued his characteristic method of travelling over the country and personally addressing hundreds of thousands of voters. But in this campaign his record as a speech-maker was rivalled by Theodore Roosevelt, who made a tour through the northern and western states, during which he attracted large crowds by his personality, and created enthusiasm by his aggressive manner of handling men and measures.

The campaign was much less exciting than that of 1896: the issues were confused, many Republicans being opposed to imperialism and lukewarm in their support of McKinley, and many Democrats refraining from voting on account of their objections to Bryan. On both sides thousands of voters, while sticking to their party, gave it only half-hearted support. Of 447 electoral votes, McKinley received 292, and Bryan 155. Of something less than 14,000,000 popular votes cast, McKinley received 7,206,677, and Bryan 6,374,397. As compared with the election of 1896, McKinley received about 100,000 more, and Bryan about 130,000 less, although the increase in population had added probably 1,000,000 to the electorate in the four years that had elapsed: many members of both parties plainly refrained from voting.[1]

President McKinley was inaugurated for his second term March 4, 1901, but his work was done. On September 6, while attending the Pan-American Exposition at Buffalo, he was shot by an anarchist, and died on the 14th of the same month, being the third president of the United States to fall by the hand of an assassin. His death was universally regretted: he had been singularly pure and blameless in his private life, honest in his public service, kindly and gentle in his contact with men, and skilful in handling them. He did much to close the last breach left by the Civil War.

His death placed in the presidential chair Theodore Roosevelt, of New York, one of the most active, aggressive, and picturesque characters that has appeared in American public life. In spite of his declaration on taking the oath of office that he would "continue absolutely unbroken the policy of President McKinley," there was little doubt in the public mind that he would make a record of his own.

---

[1] *World Almanac*, 1901, p. 119; Mosher, *Exec. Register of the U. S.*, 280.

CHAPTER VIII

THE STATUS OF DEPENDENCIES
(1898–1901)

THE annexations of 1898 raised questions new to the Constitution and to American experience. The McKinley administration took the view that the Constitution and laws of the United States did not apply to newly acquired territory until extended by Congress; while Congress later assumed that in legislating for the territories it was not necessarily bound by all the provisions of the Constitution. After two years of popular discussion as to whether "the Constitution followed the flag," the Supreme Court of the United States sustained the positions taken by the president and by Congress. It seems strange that, after a century of experience in annexing new territory, this question should still have been open to debate. There had never been a time when the territory of the United States consisted solely of states. When the Constitution was adopted, the bounds of the United States embraced an ·area organized into thirteen states and also a vast, undeveloped region west of the Alleghanies. A part of this national domain was subject to the Ordinance of 1787, which was older than the Constitution, and which contained certain articles of compact forever unalterable unless by the common consent of the original states and the people of the territory. The ordinance in terms provided that, after passing through a probationary period of national control, this territory was ultimately to be organized into states.

No express power was given by the Constitution to the federal government to acquire new territory, but the power has been held by the Supreme Court to be implied. As Chief-Justice Marshall put it: "The Constitution confers absolutely upon the government of the Union the powers of making war and of making treaties; consequently that government possesses the power of acquiring territory, either by conquest or by treaty." [1] This view is in thorough accord with the principles of our constitutional system, and does not require an argument, sometimes advanced, that territory may be acquired under an inherent power of sovereignty—an argument which ignores the fundamental principle of the Constitution that the federal government possesses only enumerated powers. [2]

As to the status of territory acquired by the United States, the Constitution is not specific, but there are two clauses bearing on the subject: (1) "The Congress shall have power to dispose of and

[1] Am. Insurance Co. *vs.* Canter, 7 Peters, 511.
[2] Willoughby, *Am. Constitutional System*, 146.

make all needful rules and regulations respecting the territory or other property belonging to the United States"; (2) "New States may be admitted by the Congress into this Union." These clauses have been upheld and expounded in numerous judicial decisions.

The first territory annexed by the new government was Louisiana, purchased from France in 1803. President Jefferson, as is well known, would have preferred a constitutional amendment authorizing the annexation, but his constitutional scruples were finally sacrificed to the demands of expediency. The question as to the political status of the inhabitants was, however, settled in the treaty: "The inhabitants of the ceded territory shall be incorporated in the Union of the United States, and admitted as soon as possible, according to the principles of the Federal Constitution, to the enjoyment of all the rights, advantages and immunities of citizens of the United States; and in the mean time they shall be maintained and protected in the free enjoyment of their liberty, property and the religion which they profess." [1]

The question as to the time when the Constitution and laws of the United States should be made to apply to the new territory was left to the discretion of Congress. By act of October 31, 1803, the government of the territory was temporarily vested

[1] *U. S. Treaties and Conventions*, 332; cf. Channing, *Jeffersonian System* (*Am. Nation*, XII.), chap. vi.

in the president in these words: "Until the expiration of the present session of Congress, unless provision for the temporary government of the said
territories be sooner made by Congress, all the military, civil, and judicial powers, exercised by the
officers of the existing government of the same,
shall be vested in such person and persons, and
shall be exercised in such manner, as the President
of the United States shall direct for maintaining and protecting the inhabitants of Louisiana in
the free enjoyment of their liberty, property and
religion." [1] President Jefferson interpreted this to
mean that the local laws of the province as they
then existed should continue in force until modified by Congress.   Accordingly, Albert Gallatin,
secretary of the treasury, wrote to the newly appointed governor of the territory the day the above
act was passed, saying: "It is understood that the
existing duties on imports and exports, which by
the Spanish laws are now levied within the province,
will continue until Congress shall have otherwise provided." [2] February 24, 1804, Congress passed an
act extending to Louisiana the laws of the United
States regulating duties on imports and tonnage;
and on March 26 another act was passed organizing a territorial government and extending to the
inhabitants specifically certain provisions of the

[1] *U. S. Statutes at Large* (Peters ed.), II., 245.
[2] Magoon, *Law of Civil Government under Military Occupation,*
159.

bill of rights, which act, by the well-known rules of
interpretation, withheld the provisions not specifically enumerated.[1] These facts seem to warrant
the statement that the view taken at this time was
that the Constitution did not extend *ex proprio vi-
gore* to newly annexed territory.

When Florida was annexed, Andrew Jackson as
governor, John Quincy Adams as secretary of state,
and James Monroe as president, as well as Congress,
all acted on the same principle—namely, that the
Constitution and laws of the United States did not
extend to newly acquired territory without express
action by Congress.[2]   Substantially the same course
of action was followed as to the Mexican cession of
1848,[3] the Gadsden Purchase of 1853, and the Alaska
purchase of 1867: in each of these cases the treaty
of cession provided specifically that the inhabitants
should at the proper time be admitted to the full
rights of citizens of the United States, so that the
withholding of portions of the Constitution and laws
of the United States was not intended to be of long
duration.

The treaty negotiated by President Harrison for
the annexation of the Hawaiian Islands in 1893,
later withdrawn from the Senate by President Cleve-

---

[1] *U. S. Statutes at Large* (Peters ed.), II., 283.

[2] For documents in the controversy between General Jackson
and Judge Fromentin, see Magoon, *Law of Civil Government
under Military Occupation*, 137.

[3] Cross *vs.* Harrison, 16 Howard, 164; cf. Garrison, *Westward
Extension* (*Am. Nation*, XVII.), chap. xix.

land,[1] likewise provided that these islands should become an integral part of the United States and that within one year Congress should extend to them the customs and navigation laws of the United States.[2]   In the mean time the existing commercial relations with the United States and with foreign countries were continued.

The annexations of 1898–1899, however, presented new problems, which called for new solutions.   Such was the case with the Hawaiian Islands, the annexation of which, while a natural consummation of American policy, was hastened by the war with Spain.   In June, 1897, President McKinley negotiated and submitted to the Senate a treaty providing for the annexation of this group of islands, under which they were to be "incorporated into the United States as an integral part thereof"; but, until legislation should be enacted extending the United States customs laws to the islands, the existing customs relations with the United States and other countries were to remain unchanged.[3]   This treaty was opposed in the Senate on grounds both of principle and of policy, so that in March, 1898, the advocates of annexation gave up all hope of securing a two-thirds majority for a treaty, and determined to gain their end by a joint resolution.   The new measure passed the

---

[1] Dewey, *National Problems* (*Am. Nation*, XXIV.), chap. xiii.
[2] Senate Com. on For. Rels., *Compilation of Reports*, VII., 281.
[3] *Ibid.*, 283.

House June 15, and the Senate July 6, during the
Spanish War, under pressure of Dewey's critical
position in Manila Bay following the victory of
May 1.

This resolution, signed by the president July 7,
1898, embodied almost the exact language of the
treaty: while it annexed the islands as "a part of
the territory of the United States," it left them
outside the customs limits, and contained a provision prohibiting Chinese from entering the United
States from Hawaii. It also provided that "the
municipal legislation of the Hawaiian Islands . . .
not inconsistent with this joint resolution nor contrary to the Constitution of the United States nor
to any existing treaty of the United States, shall
remain in full force until the Congress of the United
States shall otherwise determine." [1]   The islands
continued to occupy this status until the passage
of an organic act, April 30, 1900, which provided
for a territorial form of government on the usual
model, such as Arizona and New Mexico enjoy.
This act expressly extended the Constitution of
the United States to the territory of Hawaii, and
proclaimed all persons who were citizens of Hawaii
at the date of the transfer to be citizens of the
United States. [2]

The case of Porto Rico presents some radical
departures from earlier methods of procedure.   The

[1] *U. S. Statutes at Large*, XXX., 750.
[2] *Ibid.*, XXXI., 141.

treaty of cession of 1899 provided that "the civil rights and political status of the native inhabitants of the territory hereby ceded to the United States shall be determined by Congress." The military government established by the war department lasted for a little over eighteen months, when it was supplanted by an organic civil government, organized under the Foraker act of April 12, 1900.[1] Several features of this act made it plain that Congress had no immediate intention of incorporating the island fully within the territory of the United States, in the sense that the Constitution should extend over it or that its inhabitants should become entitled to the full privileges of citizens of the United States. Section 14 provided that the "statutory laws of the United States not locally inapplicable, except as hereinbefore or hereinafter otherwise provided, shall have the same force and effect in Porto Rico as in the United States." The inhabitants of the island continuing to reside there were to be considered "citizens of Porto Rico, and as such entitled to the protection of the United States."

Upon the question of including Porto Rico within the customs boundary of the United States, a decision was not so easily reached, although President McKinley had urged in his annual message of 1899 that the island be brought within the tariff limits at once. Against this proposition the beet-sugar and other protected interests were strongly arrayed,

[1] *U. S. Statutes at Large*, XXXI., 77.

and by the Foraker act a special tariff, amounting
to fifteen per cent. of the Dingley rates, was imposed
on all merchandise coming into the United States
from Porto Rico and coming into Porto Rico from
the United States; but, by a compromise extorted
by public opinion, this special tariff was not to
continue after March 1, 1902; and the duties collected under it were to be paid into the Porto-Rican
treasury. Congress thus held the view that Porto
Rico was not a part of the United States within
the meaning of the clause in the Constitution requiring that "all duties, imposts, and excises shall
be uniform throughout the United States." The
question unfortunately became entangled in discussions as to the constitutional status of the Philippines, and the discriminating measure passed the
House by a strict party vote, the fifteen per cent.
duties being imposed simply to show that Congress had the right. This feature of the act raised a
storm of protest throughout the country, and the
matter was soon taken into the courts.

The act also outlined a constitution for Porto
Rico essentially different from any form of territorial government previously adopted by Congress.
It provides for a governor, and an executive council
of eleven members, appointed by the president, with
the advice and consent of the Senate, for terms of
four years. The executive council consists of the
six heads of administrative departments—secretary,
attorney-general, treasurer, auditor, commissioner of

the interior, and commissioner of education — and
five other persons; at least five members of this
council to be native inhabitants of Porto Rico.
The heads of departments have an unusual degree
of authority, including the appointment of all sub-
ordinates in their respective departments.   This
practically takes the administration of affairs out
of the hands of the people of the island.[1]   The legislative power is vested in a legislative assembly consisting of the council just described and a house of
delegates composed of thirty-five members elected
biennially by the qualified voters of the island.   For
this purpose the island is divided into seven districts,
each of which sends five members voted for on a
general ticket.

The act makes provision for the usual United
States district court.   The system of insular courts
had been thoroughly overhauled by the military
government, and was not seriously modified by the
Foraker act.   The legislative assembly was given
full power to make any changes it saw fit, provided
that the justices of the supreme court be appointed
by the president with the advice and consent of the
Senate, and the justices of the district courts be
appointed by the governor with the advice and
consent of the executive council.   The legislative assembly has exercised its powers in this matter, and

[1] Willoughby, *Territories and Dependencies of the U. S.*, 85.
This book, by the treasurer of Porto Rico, is especially valuable
for the workings of the Foraker act.

the judiciary has been so completely reorganized that hardly a vestige of the old Spanish system remains. There is a supreme court, which has thus far been composed of three Porto-Ricans and two Americans. There are below this seven district courts, with one judge each, and twenty-four municipal courts. New civil and criminal codes have been adopted, and the judicial procedure altered in the direction of the American system. Trial by jury has been established in certain cases at the option of the accused.[1]

The most novel feature of the Porto-Rican government is the executive council, which not only sits for sixty days each year as an upper house, but is also required to act throughout the year as a general supervisory body. Its most important duties in the latter capacity are the granting of franchises and concessions of a public nature, and fixing the salaries of all officials not appointed by the president. Instead of a delegate to Congress, like the other territories, Porto Rico is allowed "a resident commissioner to the United States, who shall be entitled to official recognition as such by all the Departments." The people of Porto Rico have naturally desired to have greater governmental power in their hands; they have been especially dissatisfied with the organization of the council, and have wanted full territorial or statehood rights.[2]

Meanwhile the constitutionality of many measures

[1] Willoughby, *Territories and Dependencies of the U. S.*, 107.
[2] *Ibid.*, 117.

adopted by the president, as well as of these acts
of Congress, was being hotly contested in the courts.
Did the Constitution extend of its own force over
newly acquired territory, or was an act of Congress
necessary to extend it there? When Congress did
act for such territory, was it bound by the limitations imposed by the Constitution upon its powers,
or were these limitations confined to acts operative
within the territory of the states? Was an extension of the Constitution to new territory beyond the
repeal of later Congresses? The McKinley administration took the view that the Constitution and
laws of the United States did not apply to newly acquired territory unless extended there by Congress.
Consequently the collection of duties on goods imported from Porto Rico and the Philippines was continued. A number of cases involving these questions
in their various phases, and known as the "Insular
Cases," were carried to the Supreme Court of the
United States in the autumn of 1900, and decided
May 27, 1901.

The first case was that of De Lima *vs.* Bidwell,
to recover duties paid under protest on sugars imported from Porto Rico into the United States after
the ratification of the treaty but before the passage
of the Foraker act. The court held that the duties
were wrongfully exacted, on the ground that the
island of Porto Rico, after its cession to the United
States, though it had not formally been embraced
within the customs union of the States, was no

longer "foreign country" within the meaning of the Dingley law providing for duties upon articles "imported from foreign countries." The court affirmed the right of the United States to acquire territory by treaty, and declared that such territory was acquired as absolutely as if annexed by act of Congress; that a country could not be domestic for one purpose and foreign for another. The opinion of the court was delivered by Justice Brown, and concurred in by Chief-Justice Fuller and Justices Harlan, Brewer, and Peckham. From this opinion Justices Gray, McKenna, Shiras, and White dissented. Justice McKenna delivered a dissenting opinion of some length, holding that Porto Rico occupied a relation to the United States between that of foreign country and domestic territory; that the mere act of cession did not extend the Constitution and laws of the United States over the ceded territory, but that to accomplish this there must be an express provision in the treaty or a subsequent act of Congress; that the products of Porto Rico were, therefore, subject to the Dingley tariff duties.[1]

In the case of the "Fourteen Diamond Rings," decided December 2, 1901, the same questions were raised as to the status of the Philippine Islands, and the same conclusion reached—namely, that, as the Philippine Islands had ceased to be foreign territory, importations from the Philippines to the United States were not subject to the Dingley law.[2]

[1] 182 U. S., 1. [2] 183 U. S., 176.

The decision in the case of De Lima *vs.* Bidwell simply held that duties could not be collected under the Dingley act on goods imported from Porto Rico into the United States. It did not settle the question as to whether Congress had the constitutional right to impose duties on importations from Porto Rico. This issue was adjudicated upon, however, at the same term of the court in the case of Downes *vs.* Bidwell, decided May 27, 1901. In this case the court held that the island of Porto Rico, by the treaty of cession, became a territory appurtenant and belonging to the United States, but not a part of the United States within the revenue clauses of the Constitution, such as that requiring duties, imposts, and excises to be uniform throughout the United States; and, further, that the imposition of duties upon imports from Porto Rico by the act of Congress known as the Foraker act was a constitutional exercise of the power of Congress. Justice Brown delivered the decision in this case, and Justices White, Shiras, McKenna, and Gray concurred in the judgment; but not one of them agreed with Justice Brown in the process of reasoning by which he reached his conclusion.[1]

Justice Brown's argument was as follows: "The Constitution was created by the people of the *United States*, as a nation of *States*, to be governed solely by representatives of the *States;* and even the provision relied upon here, that all duties, imposts, and

[1] 182 U. S., 244.

excises shall be uniform 'throughout the United States,' is explained by subsequent provisions of the Constitution that 'no tax or duty shall be laid on articles exported from any *State*,' and 'no preference shall be given by any regulation of commerce or revenue to the ports of one *State* over those of another, nor shall vessels bound to or from one *State* be obliged to enter, clear, or pay duties in another.' In short, the Constitution deals with *States*, their people, and their representatives." The natural and logical conclusion from this argument would seem to be that the territories are entirely without the sphere of the Constitution, but Justice Brown did not go so far: he drew a distinction between certain rights peculiar to our system of jurisprudence guaranteed to citizens of the *states*, and certain natural rights the violation of which is prohibited in general terms in the Constitution. He disclaimed, therefore, "any intention to hold that the inhabitants of these territories are subject to an unrestrained power on the part of Congress to deal with them upon the theory that they have no rights which it is bound to protect."

Justice White reached the same conclusion, but based it on different grounds. In an assenting opinion, with which Justices Shiras and McKenna agreed, he laid down three propositions: that the United States has the right to acquire territory; that the Constitution confers upon Congress the right to govern such territory; and that in the

exercise of this right Congress is bound by the provisions of the Constitution so far as they are applicable.   "In the case of the territories, as in every
other instance, when a provision of the Constitution
is involved, the question which arises is, not whether
the Constitution is operative, for that is self-evident,
but whether the provision relied on is applicable."
He held, however, that Congress derives its authority
to levy local taxes within the territories, not from
the general grant of power to "lay and collect taxes,
duties, imposts, and excises," but from its right to
govern territories; therefore, in exercising the power
to tax in the territories, Congress is not bound by
the provision requiring uniformity.   To the view
here advanced by Justice White, the objection might
be raised that duties collected at the ports of the
United States are not local taxes.   But, he continues,
"the power just referred to, as well as the qualifica-
tion of uniformity, restrains Congress from imposing
an impost duty on goods coming into the United
States from a territory which has been incorporated
into and forms a part of the United States."   We
come back to the question, then, what was the
status of Porto Rico?   Justice White held that it
had not been fully incorporated, "that the treaty-
making power cannot incorporate territory into the
United States without the express or implied consent of Congress, that it may insert in a treaty express provisions against immediate incorporation,
and that on the other hand, when it has expressed

in the treaty the conditions favorable to incorporation, they will, if the treaty be not repudiated by
Congress, have the force of the law of the land, and
therefore by the fulfilment of such conditions cause
incorporation to result.   It must follow, therefore,
that where a treaty contains no conditions for incorporation, and, above all, where it not only has
no such conditions, but expressly provides to the
contrary, that incorporation does not arise until
in the wisdom of Congress it is deemed that the
acquired territory has reached that state where it is
proper that it should enter into and form a part of
the American family."   Justice Gray concurred in the
judgment and in substance agreed with the opinion
of Justice White, but prepared an opinion of his own.

Chief-Justice Fuller, with whom Justices Harlan,
Brewer, and Peckham concurred, prepared the dissenting opinion.   He denied that there was any
constitutional distinction between incorporated territories and territories unincorporated or merely appurtenant to the United States.   Justice Harlan added
some further remarks, in the course of which he said:
"I confess that I cannot grasp the thought that Congress, which lives and moves and has its being in
the Constitution, and is consequently the mere creat-
ure of that instrument, can, at its pleasure, legislate
or exclude its creator from territories which were
acquired only by authority of the Constitution."[1]

[1] See also *The Insular Cases*, comprising the records, briefs, and
arguments of counsel, *House Docs.*, 56 Cong., 2 Sess., No. 509.

In these cases four justices took the position that the Constitution extended of its own force to newly acquired territory, and four took the view that an act of Congress was necessary to extend it there; while Justice Brown based his conclusion in the Downes case on a principle that was repudiated by all eight of his colleagues. There was no constitutional doctrine, therefore, declared by a majority of the court.[1]

One other case of importance affecting the status of dependencies, or rather of their inhabitants, was decided by the Supreme Court. In the case of The Territory of Hawaii *vs.* Mankichi, decided June 1, 1903, the court held that prior to the organic act of April 30, 1900, the inhabitants of the Hawaiian Islands were not entitled to the privileges of the Fifth and Sixth Amendments to the Constitution, securing trial by jury. The annexing resolution had provided that "the municipal legislation of the Hawaiian Islands," not inconsistent with the joint resolution, nor contrary to the Constitution, nor to any existing treaty of the United States, should continue in force until Congress should otherwise determine. The defendant in error in this case was convicted of manslaughter without an indictment by a grand jury, and upon a verdict rendered by nine out of twelve jurors, in accordance with the local laws. Mankichi petitioned for a writ of *habeas corpus* on the ground that he was entitled to the

[1] On this point, see Willoughby, *Am. Constitutional System*, 238.

rights guaranteed by the Fifth and Sixth Amendments. On appeal to the Supreme Court, Justice Brown, who delivered the opinion, held that "most, if not all, the privileges and immunities contained in the Bill of Rights of the Constitution were intended to apply from the moment of annexation; but we place our decision of this case upon the ground that the two rights alleged to be violated in this case are not fundamental in their nature." This decision was rendered by five members of the court, but Justices McKenna and White expressed their concurrence in a separate opinion, holding that at the time the action was brought the islands had not been incorporated in the United States, and that the Fifth and Sixth Amendments were not applicable; in other words, that the case was controlled by the decision in Downes *vs*. Bidwell. From this decision four justices dissented (Fuller, Harlan, Brewer, and Peckham), holding that, waiving all discussion of the question whether the Constitution extended at once to the islands or not, by the annexing resolution Congress intended to invalidate so much of the existing Hawaiian legislation as was inconsistent with the Constitution.[1]

The status of the new annexations was practically settled, on commercial and political grounds, before the constitutional questions involved came up for adjudication. The dominant business interests of the country were opposed to the full

[1] 190 U. S., 197.

incorporation of the new possessions, and public opinion decided the question that way. When it came to the test the American nation, despite charges of inconsistency, applied to the situation the doctrine of inferior races and denied to the inhabitants of Porto Rico and the Philippines equal rights under the Constitution. The Supreme Court could not have reversed the decision of the American people, where such far-reaching acts of the president and of Congress were involved, without creating serious confusion. Consequently they bowed their heads before *un fait accompli*.

The decisions, confusing and unsatisfactory as they were from the stand-point of constitutional law, left Congress unhampered in the work of providing a government for the Philippine Islands. As in the case of Porto Rico, the type adopted was different from anything ever outlined by Congress before. It will be described at length in the next chapter.

CHAPTER IX

CIVIL GOVERNMENT IN THE PHILIPPINES
(1898–1907)

THE task of governing the Philippines began with the occupation of Manila by American troops August 13, 1898. The military rule thus established under the authority of the president, as commander-in-chief of the army, was continued without special authorization or interference on the part of Congress for more than two and a half years. The military governor was instructed from the first to act as far as possible through the ordinary agencies of the civil administration; and a commission was shortly sent out on the sole responsibility of the president to aid in the administration of civil affairs. While military and civil matters were thus gradually separated and placed in different hands, the government continued legally a military one and was administered through the secretary of war.

The problem of governing nearly eight million people, ranging from savagery to civilization, and divided into over eighty tribes representing a most complicated intermingling of races, customs, religions, and superstitions, presented so many new and

complex questions that Congress was in no hurry
to undertake the task of outlining a fundamental
law. Furthermore, the ultimate disposition of the
islands was still in the range of political controversy,
and it seemed best to await the verdict of the
American people in the next election. Although
this issue was confused with others in the election
of 1900, the victory of the Republican party was
accepted as a final decision in favor of retaining
the Philippines, and the Supreme Court soon made
decisions upholding substantially the policy the administration was pursuing.[1]

The treaty of peace was signed at Paris December 10, 1898, and on the 21st the president drew
up instructions for the secretary of war, directing
him to "extend the military government heretofore
maintained by the United States in the city, harbor,
and bay of Manila . . . with all possible dispatch
to the whole of the ceded territory." This order was
severely criticised at the time, because the treaty
was not ratified by the United States Senate until
February 6, 1899, and the ratifications were not
exchanged until April 11; but the situation was a
very precarious one, as the insurgents were preparing to occupy, and actually did occupy, places
evacuated by the Spanish troops; and it was fore-
seen that the latter would not be able to hold all
posts until the formal transfer to the United States
could be made.

[1] See chap. viii., above.

January 20, 1899, more than two weeks before
the ratification of the treaty, President McKinley
appointed a commission composed of Jacob Gould
Schurman, president of Cornell University, Rear-
Admiral George Dewey, Major-General Elwell S.
Otis, Charles Denby, and Dean C. Worcester, to
proceed to the Philippine Islands and try "to facili-
tate the most humane, pacific, and effective extension of authority throughout these islands, and to
secure, with the least possible delay, the benefits of
life and property to the inhabitants." When the
civilian members joined Dewey and Otis at Manila,
March 4, 1899, they found that conditions had
wholly changed since they left America, and that a
state of hostilities had existed for a month which
seriously interfered with the discharge of the duties intrusted to them. They issued a proclamation,
however, to the Philippine people, and held conferences with the agents of Aguinaldo, but without
practical results.[1] The commission then went to
work to investigate conditions in the islands, and
prepared an elaborate report on the people, resources, and climate, which was very helpful, inasmuch as the American people were for the most
part densely ignorant on all subjects relating to the
Philippines. Perhaps the most important conclusion of this commission related to the capacity of
the Filipinos for self-government: "Their lack of

[1] Schurman, *Philippine Affairs: A Retrospect and Outlook*,
8-13.

education and political experience, combined with
their racial and linguistic diversities, disqualify them,
in spite of their mental gifts and domestic virtues,
to undertake the task of governing the archipelago
at the present time." [1]

As a result of the report of the Schurman commission, President McKinley decided to appoint a
new commission, to be clothed with definite authority and to be made a permanent part of the
Philippine administration.   He selected William H.
Taft, of Ohio, as president, and Dean C. Worcester,
Luke E. Wright, Henry C. Ide, and Bernard Moses
as associate members.   The letter of instructions to
this commission, drawn up by Secretary Root, constitutes a most important and interesting document.
In it the commissioners were directed to proceed to
Manila and communicate with the military governor,
who was instructed to render them every assistance
within his power.   After becoming acquainted with
local conditions they were to proceed to organize
civil government from the bottom up, beginning
with the municipal governments in the cities and
in the rural communes.   Upon this foundation they
were to proceed later to organize governments in
the larger divisions or provinces.   Whenever the
commission should be of the opinion that the time
was ripe for the organization of a central government to take the place of the military government,

[1] Philippine [Schurman] Commission, *Report*, 1900, 4 vols.;
see also *Preliminary Report* of November 2, 1899.

they were directed to report that fact to the secretary of war with recommendations as to the form of central government to be established. In the distribution of powers among the governments organized by the commission, the smaller subdivisions were to be vested with all the powers they could properly exercise, so as to avoid centralization as much as possible.[1]

Beginning with September 1, 1900, the commission was to exercise, subject to the approval of the president through the secretary of war, the legislative authority theretofore exercised by the military governor. The latter was to remain the chief executive head of the government, and was to continue to exercise the executive authority then vested in him, subject, however, to the rules and orders enacted by the commission in accordance with the powers conferred upon it. When the commissioners entered upon their duties at Manila, September 1, General MacArthur was military governor, having succeeded General Otis on May 5. As both he and the commission acted under the secretary of war, there was little danger of serious conflict of authority. While this separation of powers gave the government in part a civil character, legally it was still a military government, for the president's authority was still merely that of commander-in-chief of the army of the United States.[2]

---

[1] Philippine Commission, *Reports*, 1900–1903 (collected), 5–11.
[2] *Ibid.*, 6.

The government of the Philippines was, however, put on a different footing by the "Spooner amendment" to the army appropriation act of March 2, 1901, under which "all military, civil, and judicial powers necessary to govern the Philippine Islands . . . shall, until otherwise provided by Congress, be vested in such person and persons and shall be exercised in such manner as the President of the United States shall direct, for the establishment of civil government and for maintaining and protecting the inhabitants of said islands in the free enjoyment of their liberty, property, and religion." [1] No president had ever before been clothed by Congress with such a degree of arbitrary power: the act of October 31, 1803, vesting the government of Louisiana in President Jefferson, the language of which was followed in part by the above act, did not confer upon him all powers necessary for governing Louisiana, but merely "the military, civil, and judicial powers exercised by the officers of the existing government." This was no arbitrary grant of power such as was conferred by the Spooner amendment.

The statute of March 2, 1901, enabled the president to make the separation of civil and military powers already undertaken by him more definite and complete. June 21 he issued an order through the secretary of war directing that, "on and after the fourth day of July, 1901, until it shall be otherwise ordered, the President of the Philippine Com-

[1] *U. S. Statutes at Large*, XXXI., 895.

mission will exercise the executive authority in all
civil affairs in the government of the Philippine
Islands heretofore exercised in such affairs by the
Military Governor of the Philippines, and to that
end the Hon. William H. Taft, President of the said
Commission, is hereby appointed Civil Governor of
the Philippine Islands." The order provided, further, that "The power to appoint civil officers, heretofore vested in the Philippine Commission, or in
the Military Governor, will be exercised by the Civil
Governor with the advice and consent of the Commission. The Military Governor of the Philippines
is hereby relieved from the performance, on and
after the said 4th day of July, of the civil duties
hereinbefore described, but his authority will continue to be exercised as heretofore, in those districts
in which insurrection against the authority of the
United States continues to exist, or in which public order is not sufficiently restored to enable provincial civil governments to be established under
the instructions to the Commission dated April 7,
1900." [1] Judge Taft was inaugurated as civil governor July 4, 1901.

By subsequent orders of the president, taking
effect September 1, 1901, two important steps were
taken. Three Filipinos—Dr. T. H. Pardo de Tavera,
Señor Benito Legarda, and Señor José Luzuriaga—
were added as members of the commission. By the
second order the executive government was organ-

[1] Sec. of War, *Annual Reports*, 1901, I., pt. x., 11.

ized in four departments under four members of the
original commission as heads: (1) department of the
interior under Commissioner Worcester; (2) department of commerce and police under Commissioner
Wright; (3) department of finance and justice under
Commissioner Ide; (4) department of public instruction under Commissioner Moses.[1]

When these changes were made the commission
was already in the midst of organizing the provinces.   About the middle of the preceding February
they decided to visit the capital of each province
for the purpose of creating, if the conditions seemed
favorable, civil provincial governments.   They first
passed through some of the provinces of central
Luzon, then proceeded south through the Visayas
as far as Mindanao, back to Manila by way of southern Luzon, and later covered the provinces in northern Luzon.   These visits occupied the greater part
of six months.   Thirty-three of the forty-nine Spanish provinces were visited, and in most of them provincial governments were established.   When the
commission reached the capital of a province they
usually conferred with the commanding officer concerning conditions, and later met in convention the
presidentes, the municipal councillors, and the principal men of each town, all of whom had been previously invited to meet the commission.   A discussion
followed, and a provincial act was then drawn up,

[1] Philippine Commission, *Reports*, 1900–1903 (collected), 140,
142.

with such modifications of the general plan as seemed to best meet local requirements. These visits of the commission were occasions of great festivities in which the natives displayed their wonted hospitality. In most cases the commissioners were accompanied by the ladies of their families. Several of the provinces thus transferred to the civil governor were later handed back to the military governor on account of insurrections.[1]

The work of organizing municipal and provincial governments was based on two acts of the commission: the municipal code of January 31, 1901, and the provincial government act of February 6, 1901.[2] The municipal code provided for the organization of "pueblos" as municipal corporations, with the old boundaries preserved and divided into "barrios." For administrative purposes the barrios were grouped in districts. The municipal district, like the old pueblo, embraced both urban and rural settlements. There were to be four classes of municipalities, divided according to population, the government of each vested in a president, a vice-president, and a municipal council, elected by the qualified voters for a term of two years. The suffrage was given to males twenty-three years of age who possessed any one of three qualifications: (1) who have held a municipal office; (2) own real property to the value

[1] Senate Docs., 57 Cong., 1 Sess., No. 331, pp. 4 et seq.; Sec. of War, Annual Reports, 1901, I., pt. x., 733.
[2] Philippine Commission, Acts, Nos. 82, 83.

of five hundred pesos, or pay thirty pesos taxes;
(3) speak, read, and write English or Spanish. The
municipal government thus constituted is charged
with the administration of local affairs. The code
provides in detail as to the levy and assessment of
taxes and the sources of revenue. This code does
not apply to the city of Manila, which has a special
form of government of its own, nor to the settlements of the non-Christian tribes, for which special
legislation was enacted later.

The provincial government act applies only to
the more civilized provinces. It provides that each
province shall be a body corporate, with power to
sue and be sued, to hold property, and make contracts. The principal officers of the province are
a governor, a secretary, a treasurer, a supervisor,
and a fiscal. No person is eligible for any of these
offices who is not either a citizen of the United
States, a native of the Philippines, or who has not
acquired the political rights of a native. With the
exception of the governor, all these officers are appointed by the commission and hold office at its
pleasure. The governor is elected by the councillors
of the organized municipalities within his province.
He is the chief executive officer of the province, but
has to report to the civil governor. The duties of
the secretary and treasurer are sufficiently indicated
by their titles. The supervisor has charge of all
public works. The fiscal is the attorney and legal
adviser of the provincial government. The real con-

trol of affairs is in the hands of the provincial board, consisting of the governor, the treasurer, and the supervisor. As two of these are appointed by the commission and serve during its pleasure, the control is practically reserved to the insular government. The provincial governments have charge of the construction of public works, the collection of revenues, the control over the constabulary, and a general supervision over municipal officers. The Neuva Vizcaya act, which was later followed in a number of other less civilized provinces, is modelled in the main after the general provincial act, but reserves a larger measure of control to the insular government.

As will be seen from this brief description, the provincial and municipal governments do not constitute local self-government in the American sense of the term at all. The Philippine people have practically no vestige of self-government: all that the provincial government act and the municipal code do is to decentralize to some extent the insular administration. The officers of the provincial government are appointed by the civil governor, may be removed or suspended by him at pleasure, and are at all times closely under his control.[1]

Within a year after the appointment of Judge Taft as civil governor, about thirty-five provinces were organized. With the exception of a few

[1] Cf. Willoughby, *Territories and Dependencies of the U. S.*, chaps. vii., viii.

sparsely settled districts these provinces included all
the Christian Filipinos, and thus left unorganized
and still under military rule only the country occupied by the Moros.[1]   The latter continued under
the Bates agreement,[2] which was never acted on by
Congress, until June 1, 1903, when the commission
passed an act providing for provincial and local
government in the Sulu Islands and in all territory
occupied by the Moro tribes.   The act created a
Moro province, divided into five districts, with a
governor, attorney, secretary, treasurer, superintendent of schools, and engineer, all appointed by
the civil governor with the advice and consent of
the commission.   Up to 1906 the military commander of the division, General Leonard Wood, held the
office of governor, the officers above mentioned constituting a legislative council with large powers.[3]
The commission has practically turned over the
whole region of the Moros to this council, retaining,
of course, general control.

The work of organizing local and provincial governments was undertaken and carried on without
any interference on the part of Congress.   The
president was given a free hand, and the executive
orders which he issued, first under the war power
and later under the Spooner amendment, were not
confined to the internal administration of the islands,

---

[1] Philippine Commission, *Reports*, 1900–1903 (collected), 293–
295.   [2] See p. 90 above.
[3] Philippine Commission, *Report*, 1906, pt. i., 340–358.

but embraced even tariffs within their scope. The McKinley administration took, of course, the same action as in the case of Porto Rico, and treated the Philippines as outside the customs limits of the United States; nor did the administration change its policy when the Supreme Court rendered its decision in the De Lima case, May 27, 1901.[1]

On goods imported into the Philippines duties were collected for a time under the Spanish laws. These were modified first by the orders of the military governor, and later by the commission. A tariff revision law of September 17, 1901,[2] was prepared by the commission, and then sent to Washington for approval. Governor Taft, in his testimony before the Senate committee, said: "We changed the principle of the (Spanish) tax, and attempted to make it quite low on all food-stuffs, on all necessities, and on agricultural implements, on machinery, and on everything that would tend to develop the country and improve the agricultural methods in the islands; and we attempted to put higher rates on luxuries." The duties were all specific, so as to avoid fraud and expense in assessment. In regard to the revision that was made in the war department, he says: "After consultations with merchants and persons interested in importing articles into the Philippines, it was sent to us in revised form, with a combination of specific duties and *ad valorem* limi-

[1] See p. 144 above.
[2] Philippine Commission, *Acts*, No. 230.

tations." [1]   The revision of this tariff in Washington
was simply an attempt, and a successful attempt,
to apply the principle of exploitation to the Philippines.[2]   It discriminated against the Philippines by
admitting American products into the islands at
duties ranging from fifteen to thirty per cent., while
Philippine products were still paying the Dingley
rates on coming into the United States.

The decision in the case of the "Fourteen Diamond Rings," rendered December 2, 1901, to the
effect that the Philippines were no longer foreign
territory within the meaning of the Dingley law,
and that therefore duties could not be collected
under that law on goods coming from these islands
into the United States, made it necessary for Congress to legislate on the subject.   After long discussions in committee, an act was passed March 8,
1902, approving and putting in force the tariff revision law passed by the commission September 17,
1901, and providing that articles imported into the
United States from the Philippines should pay the
regular duties, with the exception of Philippine products, which were to come in at a reduction of 25 per
cent. on the regular rate.[3]   The commission had
recommended in their report for 1901 a reduction
of 50 per cent., and Governor Taft urged in person

[1] *Senate Docs.*, 57 Cong., 1 Sess., No. 331, p. 151.
[2] R. F. Hoxie, "Am. Colonial Policy and the Tariff," in *Journal of Political Economy*, March, 1903, p. 213.
[3] *U. S. Statutes at Large*, XXXII., pt. i., 54.

before the Senate committee that a reduction of 75 per cent. would be much fairer. The duties collected under the act were to be paid into the Philippine treasury.[1]

The tariff act was soon followed by the Philippine government act of July 1, 1902, substituting congressional for presidential government, and setting up a more definite status.[2] This act contained organic or constitutional provisions as well as general legislation. In the first place it approved, ratified, and confirmed the action of the president in creating the Philippine commission and in conferring upon it the governmental powers set forth in his instructions of April 7, 1900; in creating the offices of civil governor and vice-governor with the powers set forth in the order of June 21, 1901; and in establishing the four executive departments of the government as set forth in the act of the commission of September 6, 1901. The government as thus organized was to be continued in all essential features until two years after the taking of a census provided for in the act. The only immediate change was that in future the appointment of civil governor, vice-governor, members of the commission, and heads of the executive departments was to be by the president with the advice and consent of the Senate. The act also declared the inhabitants of the islands to

[1] *Senate Docs.*, 57 Cong., 1 Sess., No. 331, p. 273; Philippine Commission, *Reports*, 1900–1903 (collected), 152.
[2] *U. S. Statutes at Large*, XXXII., pt. i., 691.

be "citizens of the Philippine Islands, and as such entitled to the protection of the United States." Practically all of the provisions of the Constitution of the United States guaranteeing the protection of life, liberty, and property were extended to the Filipinos by enumeration in this statute, except trial by jury, which could not well be grafted on to the civil law system.

The second feature of the act was the provision for the creation of a legislative assembly upon the fulfilment of certain conditions. As soon as the commission should certify to the president that the insurrection was at an end and general peace restored, he was to order a general census of the Philippine Islands to be taken, and it was made the duty of the president, two years after the completion and publication of the census, to direct the commission to hold a general election, except in the territory inhabited by the Moros and non-Christian tribes, for the choice of delegates to the Philippine assembly. After the convening of this assembly all legislative power is to be "vested in a legislature consisting of two houses—the Philippine Commission and the Philippine Assembly." The legislature is to hold stated annual sessions of ninety days, beginning on the first Monday in February. The act also dealt with the question of public lands, franchises, coinage, bond issues, and a number of other questions. The last section provided that the division of insular affairs of the war department, organized by the orders of the secretary of war of December 13, 1898, and December 10, 1900, be continued, and be known thereafter as the bureau of insular affairs.

One remarkable omission from this act was all reference to the salaries and expenses of the commission. The Schurman commission had been paid by the department of state. When the Taft commission was appointed the sum of fifty thousand dollars was advanced from the funds of the United States, and this amount was subsequently reimbursed from funds derived from the Philippine treasury.[1] No reference to the salaries paid the commissioners out of the Philippine treasury is to be found in any of the reports of the commission or of the secretary of war. Even the Senate committee on the Philippines had great difficulty in extracting this information from Governor Taft when he gave his testimony before them. It appears, however, that when the commission first went to the Philippines the president was paid $17,500 annually, and the other members $15,000 each. When Mr. Taft was appointed civil governor, his salary was raised to $20,000, and he was given in addition the palace formerly occupied by the Spanish governor-general as his official residence. The amount of these salaries was fixed by the president and secretary of war.[2]

---

[1] Statement of Secretary Root, *Senate Docs.*, 57 Cong., 1 Sess., No. 416.

[2] Taft's testimony before the Senate Committee, *Senate Docs.*, 57 Cong., 1 Sess., No. 331, pp. 257–262.

American government has proved very expensive to the Filipinos, and there has been much complaint of the burden of taxation: they would prefer a less efficient government with lower taxes. From the American point of view the experiment in colonial government has not been a financial success. The total cost of the Philippines to the United States, from 1898 to 1902, was officially stated by Secretary Root at $169,853,512.82 in actual expenditures, exclusive of the purchase money.[1] Edward Atkinson estimated the cost of the war with Spain, including the direct and indirect expenses of our colonial policy, from 1898 to 1904, at $1,000,000,000.[2]

. American control of the Philippines has not, up to 1907, demonstrated its success. The islands have not yet recovered from the disastrous effects of the insurrection, during which large districts were deserted, homes devastated, trade interrupted, and agriculture suspended. Then a disease, probably rinderpest, attacked the cattle, carrying off in two years, according to Governor Taft's testimony before the Senate committee in 1902, three-fourths of all in the archipelago. Most of these were carabao, the chief reliance for industry, especially for the cultivation of rice. Their loss caused a further suspension of agriculture and consequent famine.[3] The United States has been too eager to American-

[1] *Senate Docs.*, 57 Cong., 1 Sess., No. 416.
[2] Atkinson, *Cost of War and Warfare.*
[3] *Senate Docs.*, 57 Cong., 1 Sess., No. 331., p. 28.

ize the Filipinos through political and legal reforms, and it will doubtless be many years before their needs and capacities will be sufficiently understood to legislate wisely in their behalf.

One of the greatest difficulties has been the adjustment of the church question, especially the titles of the lands held by the friars.   This question is on the surface ecclesiastical, but in reality political and economic.   Of the three orders holding agricultural lands at the time of the American occupation, the Dominicans had 161,953 acres; the Augustinians, 151,742; and the Recolletos, 93,035; making a total of over 400,000 acres, including the best land in most of the provinces.[1]   These lands were rented to the natives on shares in small holdings, and tenancy usually continued for years in the same family. When the friars were driven out by the insurgents,[2] they transferred their agricultural lands, to be held in trust, to corporations; in the case of the Dominicans, to an individual; but the tenants refused in most cases to pay rent, and naturally opposed the return of the friars.[3]   The Philippine commission early proposed the purchase of these lands by the American government, and was given the necessary authority in the civil government act of July 1, 1902; but the friars demanded exorbitant prices, and long negotiations followed, necessitating direct relations

[1] Philippine Commission, *Reports*, 1900–1903 (collected), 44.
[2] See p. 83 above.
[3] Philippine Commission, *Reports*, 1900–1903 (collected), 46.

with the papacy, Governor Taft visiting Rome for
that purpose.[1]   The price finally agreed on in 1903
for 410,000 acres, was $7,239,000.[2]   This purchase
by no means solved the problem, for the plan of the
commission was to sell to the tenants; but many
of them, claiming that they had just as good titles
as the friars, and that the rents they formerly paid
had been extorted through political influence, refused to buy back what they regarded as their own.[3]

The American authorities have from the first real-
ized the importance of conciliating the Roman Catholic church and securing its co-operation in the work
of pacifying the islands.   To this end they sought
to encourage the introduction of American priests
to take the place of the friars, but very few Americans were available for the work.[4]   The whole church
question has been further complicated by the Agli-
payan movement, which resulted in the formation
of an Independent Filipino Catholic church.   Grego-
rio Aglipay was a native priest of the Roman Church
before the insurrection.   He identified himself with
Aguinaldo's government and became one of the leaders of the insurrection in northern Luzon.   After his
surrender to the American forces he became quite
active in the propaganda among the native priests
to prevent the return of the friars.   The refusal of

---

[1] Philippine Commission, *Reports*, 1900–1903 (collected), 304.
[2] *Ibid.*, p. 501.
[3] Willis, *Our Philippine Problem*, chap. ix.
[4] Philippine Commission, *Reports*, 1900–1903 (collected), 503.

the pope to withdraw the Spanish friars from the
islands was made the occasion for the formation of
the Independent Filipino church, which grew with
astonishing rapidity in 1902 and 1903, and became
a prime factor in local politics.[1] The seizure of
church property by Aglipayans gave rise to riots
and bloodshed, and the American authorities had to
interfere for the protection of life and property.
The commission finally passed an act, July 24, 1905,
giving the supreme court original jurisdiction in all
controversies relating to the possession of church
property, and a number of actions were begun, but
at the date of the report of 1906 none of them had
been brought to a conclusion.[2]

The census of the Philippine Islands having been
completed and published March 27, 1905, and a condition of general peace having continued for two
years thereafter,[3] President Roosevelt issued an executive order March 28, 1907, directing the commission to call a general election for the choice of
delegates to the Philippine assembly. An election
law was shortly afterwards promulgated by the
commission,[4] and an election held July 30, 1907, in
which, though the vote was small, the Nationalists
won by a large majority. The assembly, which will
consist of eighty-one members, is expected to con-

[1] Philippine Commission, *Reports*, 1900–1903 (collected), 319.
[2] *Ibid.*, 1906, pt. i., 58.   [3] See p. 168 above.
[4] See the election law of January 9, 1907, Philippine Commission. *Acts*, No. 1582.

vene in the early part of October.   The organization
and workings of this body will be watched with close
interest, especially since the party which favors national independence will be in the majority; for if
the Filipinos develop a fair degree of governmental
efficiency, the United States may be glad of the opportunity of giving up the internal government of
the islands, retaining simply a protectorate.

CHAPTER X

THE REPUBLIC OF CUBA
(1899–1907)

WHEN the Congress of the United States decided to demand the withdrawal of Spain from Cuba, its action was accompanied by the so-called Teller resolution: "That the United States hereby disclaims any disposition or intention to exercise sovereignty, jurisdiction or control over said island except for the pacification thereof, and asserts its determination, when that is accomplished, to leave the government and control of the island with its people." [1] Never has a resolution made by a nation under such circumstances been more faithfully carried out. In the treaty of peace of 1899 the United States expressly agreed that, so long as its military occupation of Cuba should last, it would assume and discharge the obligations that might under international law result from the fact of such occupation for the protection of life and property.

The Spanish troops and officials evacuated Havana January 1, 1899, and transferred the government of the island to a military governor representing the

[1] See p. 27 above.

president of the United States. The cities and towns were crowded with refugees and reconcentrados, and a large Spanish population remained, between whom and the Cubans a bitter feeling of hostility existed. The occupation of the island by the United States having been accomplished without disorder, the task that presented itself to the Americans was the creation of "a stable government administered by the Cuban people, republican in form, and competent to discharge the obligations of the international relationship and be entitled to a place in the family of nations."

The first step was to take a census of the several provinces, in order to acquire the necessary data for fixing the representation and the qualifications for suffrage. The treaty of peace provided that Spanish residents might retain their Spanish citizenship by filing a declaration of their intention to do so prior to April 11, 1900, so that no civil government based on popular election could be inaugurated before that time. It was found by the census that two-thirds of the inhabitants could not read and write. After conference with the leading Cubans as to the proper basis of suffrage, it was agreed "that every native male Cuban or Spaniard who had elected to take Cuban citizenship, of full age, might vote if he could read and write, or owned real or personal property to the value of $250, or had served in and been honorably discharged from the Cuban army." [1]

---

[1] *Senate Docs.*, 58 Cong., 2 Sess., No. 312, p. 7.

The first municipal elections were held June 16,
1900, under an election law promulgated by the
military governor. The boards of registration and
election were composed of Cubans, and no United
States soldier or officer was present at any polling-
place. On September 15 the first general election
was held, under the orders of the military governor, for the purpose of choosing delegates to a convention "to frame and adopt a constitution for the
people of Cuba, and, as a part thereof, to provide for
and agree with the government of the United States
upon the relations to exist between that government and the government of Cuba." [1] The constitutional convention, assembled as a result of this
election and composed of thirty-one members, was
called to order by General Leonard Wood, the military governor, in the city of Havana, November 5,
1900.

The convention finally agreed upon a constitution
for the republic of Cuba, which was adopted. February 21, 1901. The legislative power was vested
in a congress of two houses—a Senate and a House
of Representatives; the executive power was vested
in a president; and the judicial power in a supreme
court of justice and in such other courts as might
be established by law. The Senate was composed of
four senators from each of the six provinces, chosen
by an electoral board for a period of eight years.
The House of Representatives was composed of one

[1] *Foreign Relations*, 1902, p. 358.

member for every twenty-five thousand inhabitants, elected for four years by direct vote, one-half to be elected every two years. The president was elected by presidential electors for four years, not to serve for three consecutive terms. The constitution provided for the recognition of the public debts legitimately contracted by the insurgent government, but was silent on the subject of future relations with the United States.[1]

This subject had been brought to the attention of the convention early in February by General Wood, who, acting under instructions from Washington, required that there should be incorporated in the constitution provisions to the effect (1) that the government of Cuba would never make any treaty impairing the independence of the island, (2) that it would never contract any public debt in excess of its capacity to meet by the ordinary revenues, (3) that the United States should have the right to intervene for the protection of Cuban independence, (4) that the acts of the military government during the period of American occupation should be recognized as legal, (5) that the United States should be granted naval stations in Cuba.[2] The convention was willing to accept the first and fourth proposals, but not the others, on the ground that they impaired the independence and sovereignty of the island, and that it was their duty to make Cuba "independent

---

[1] Sec. of War, *Annual Reports*, 1902, I., pt. i., 84.
[2] *Ibid.*, 1901, I., pt. i., 46.

of every other nation, the great and noble American nation included." [1]

The United States was, however, master of the situation, and had no intention of withdrawing from the island until this matter was satisfactorily adjusted. A provision, known as the Platt amendment, was therefore inserted in the army appropriation bill of March 2, 1901, directing the president to leave the control of the island to its people so soon as a government should be established under a constitution which defined the future relations with the United States substantially as follows:

" I. That the government of Cuba shall never enter into any treaty or other compact with any foreign power or powers which will impair or tend to impair the independence of Cuba, nor in any manner authorize or permit any foreign power or powers to obtain by colonization or for military or naval purposes or otherwise, lodgment in or control over any portion of said island.

" II. That the said government shall not assume or contract any public debt, to pay the interest upon which, and to make reasonable sinking fund provision for the ultimate discharge of which, the ordinary revenues of the island, after defraying the current expenses of the government shall be inadequate.

" III. That the government of Cuba consents that the United States may exercise the right to intervene for the preservation of Cuban independence, the

[1] *Foreign Relations*, 1902, p. 362.

maintenance of a government adequate for the protection of life, property, and individual liberty, and for discharging the obligations with respect to Cuba imposed by the treaty of Paris on the United States, now to be assumed and undertaken by the government of Cuba.

"IV. That all acts of the United States in Cuba during its military occupancy thereof are ratified and validated, and all lawful rights acquired thereunder shall be maintained and protected.

"V. That the government of Cuba will execute, and as far as necessary extend, the plans already devised or other plans to be mutually agreed upon, for the sanitation of the cities of the island. . . .

"VI. That the Isle of Pines shall be omitted from the proposed constitutional boundaries of Cuba, the title thereof being left to future adjustment by treaty.

"VII. That to enable the United States to maintain the independence of Cuba, and to protect the people thereof, as well as for its own defense, the government of Cuba will sell or lease to the United States lands necessary for coaling or naval stations at certain specified points, to be agreed upon with the President of the United States.

"VIII. That by way of further assurance the government of Cuba will embody the foregoing provisions in a permanent treaty with the United States." [1]

In order to allay the doubts raised by certain

[1] *U. S. Statutes at Large*, XXXI., 897, 898.

members of the convention in regard to the third clause, Secretary Root authorized General Wood to state officially that the intervention described in this clause did not mean intermeddling in the affairs of the Cuban government, but formal action on the part of the United States, based upon just and substantial grounds.[1] With this assurance the convention adopted the Platt amendment, June 12, 1901, and added it as an appendix to the constitution.

The last act of the convention was the adoption of an election law providing for a general election to be held December 31, 1901. On this date governors of provinces, provincial councillors, members of the House of Representatives, and presidential and senatorial electors were chosen. The electors met February 24, 1902, and chose Tomas Estrada Palma as president, and Luis Esteves Romero as vice-president. A month later General Wood was instructed to provide for the inauguration of the new government, for the withdrawal of American troops, and for the transference of authority to President Palma. On May 20, 1902, the new government entered on its independent career, with the cordial good-will of the United States.[2]

The work done by General Wood and his associates in the civil administration of Cuba during the period of military occupation was remarkable both

---

[1] *Senate Docs.*, 58 Cong., 2 Sess., No. 312, p. 12.

[2] *Documentary History of the Inauguration of the Cuban Government*, in Sec. of War, *Annual Reports*, 1902, App. A.

for its scope and thoroughness. The only governmental machinery in existence when they took
charge was that of the municipalities, and they had
to organize a complete system of insular government
in all departments. They established order, relieved
distress, organized hospitals and charitable institutions, undertook extensive public works, achieved
notable success in the reorganization of the system
of public schools, and put Havana, Santiago, and
the other principal cities in first-class sanitary condition.[1] Streets were cleaned, sewers opened, cess-
pools and sinks emptied, and water supplies improved. The sanitation of Havana was the marvel
of the age. No such popular demonstration of the
truth of modern scientific theories of health and
sanitation has elsewhere been given to the world.
In the course of bacteriological experiments conducted at Quemados in the summer of 1900, Major
Walter Reed, a surgeon in the United States army,
established the fact that yellow-fever is transmitted
by the bite of a mosquito. This discovery is justly
regarded as one of the great achievements of modern
medical science. Sanitary measures based on the
work of Major Reed were subsequently adopted and
put into effect by the health officers of Havana, with
the result that the city was rendered free from yellow-fever for the first time in one hundred and forty
years.[2] The total amount expended for sanitation

[1] Military governor of Cuba, *Report*, 8 vols., 1901.
[2] Sec. of War, *Annual Reports*, 1901, I., pt. i., 39, 40.

in the entire island under American occupation was nearly ten million dollars. The customs service, which furnished the principal part of the public revenues, was administered by General Tasker H. Bliss. The total receipts for the entire period were $57,197,140.80, and the expenditures $55,405,031.28, leaving a surplus of $1,792,109.52 in the treasury.[1]

While there had been a definite understanding before the withdrawal of the American troops as to the political relations that were to exist in future between the island and the United States, there had been no agreement on the subject of commercial relations, and Congress had failed to make any concessions to Cuban products. The principal agricultural product of the island is sugar. This industry was almost entirely destroyed by the insurrection, and its restoration was hindered not only by the fact that the plantations were heavily mortgaged and their machinery destroyed, but also because the uncertainty regarding the future government of the island and its trade relations with the United States made it difficult for the planters to raise the capital to restore their machinery. This doubt as to the future market for the sugar output was the main hinderance to industrial development. Entirely new methods of production on a large scale were necessary to enable Cuban sugar to compete with the bounty-fed beet-sugar of Europe, and with the sugars of

[1] *Senate Docs.*, 58 Cong., 2 Sess., No. 312, p. 31; Sec. of War, *Annual Reports*, 1902, App. B.

Porto Rico and Hawaii, which were now admitted
to the American market free of duty.   As the United
States was the great market for Cuban sugar, it was
evident that the future of the sugar industry depended upon the willingness of the United States to
arrange for a reduction of its tariff in favor of the
Cuban product.

The president had hoped to settle this question
with Cuba on a basis of reciprocity before the withdrawal of American troops, and in his annual message of December 3, 1901, urged that considerations
of honor as well as of expediency made it incumbent
upon Congress to provide for a substantial reduction
in the tariff duties on Cuban imports into the United
States; but a powerful opposition at once made itself
felt, and succeeded in thwarting for two years the
efforts of the administration to do justice to Cuba.
The opposition was organized by the American beet-
sugar interests of the North and West, which were
combined in a sort of trust comprising all the factories in the country and known as the American Beet
Sugar Association.   With them were allied the cane-
sugar planters of Louisiana, and they succeeded in
gaining the active support of various farmers' associations, on the ground that they were fighting for
American agricultural interests, whereas as a matter
of fact the farmers had much to gain from reciprocity.   They appealed also successfully to the high
tariffites, urging that a concession to Cuba would
strike a blow at the principle of protection; that the

Dingley tariff had been a pledge to the beet-sugar pro-
ducers, and that millions of dollars had been invested
in that industry, all of which would be lost if Cuban
sugar should be admitted at the proposed rates.[1]

The American Sugar Refining Company, generally
known as the "Sugar Trust," which controlled the
refining and marketing of cane-sugar, wanted all the
raw sugar it could get, and was therefore in favor of
the administration's policy. The beet-sugar contin-
gent made the plausible claim that a reduction in the
tariff would not benefit the Cuban planter, for whom
it was intended, but would simply lower the price, to
the sole benefit of the trust. Rarely has a lobby
displayed greater determination to defeat a wise
measure of policy or drawn to itself stronger support
by fallacious arguments. Even if the entire sugar
crop of Cuba had been admitted free of duty, like
that of Porto Rico and Hawaii, the beet-sugar pro-
ducers would still have enjoyed a high rate of protection, for the reason that there would have remained a large unsatisfied demand in the United States to
be supplied from Europe. As long as this was the
case the price of sugar could not materially decline.[2]

In January, 1902, the beet-sugar lobby and the
Cuban sugar planters, the largest of whom were
Americans, arrived at a compromise, whereby the
high rates were to continue to be collected so as not
to lower the price, and a rebate was to be paid the

[1] Laughlin and Willis, *Reciprocity*, chap. xi.
[2] *Review of Reviews*, XXV., 392-394.

Cuban planter; but the rebate plan did not appeal
to the ways and means committee, which had the
matter in charge, and the scheme came to naught.
At first it was thought that a 50-per-cent. reduction
would be necessary to revive the sugar industry of
Cuba, but so great was the opposition that the committee finally agreed that 20 per cent. was as much
as there was any prospect of getting through Congress, and reported a bill to that effect in April, 1902,
which passed the House.   The opposition in the
Senate, led by Senator Burrows, of Michigan, was so
strong, and the outlook for the bill so discouraging,
that President Roosevelt sent a special message to
Congress June 13, urging favorable action.[1]   About
this time the beet-sugar lobby discovered that F. B.
Thurber, of New York, who as president of the
United States Export Association had been distributing reciprocity literature throughout the country, was in the employ of President Havemeyer, of
the Sugar Trust, and also of General Leonard Wood,
military governor of Cuba.   The House called on the
secretary of war for the facts, and he submitted a
statement from General Wood, July 1, 1902, in
which the latter admitted that he had expended
$15,526.82, most of which had passed through Thur-
ber's hands, in distributing newspapers and circulars
on reciprocity and in sending delegations of Cubans
to Washington.   He said that the disbursements had
been made by him as governor of Cuba, and that it

[1] *Senate Docs.*, 57 Cong., 1 Sess., No. 405.

was "an expenditure of Cuban funds for the purpose of promoting Cuban interests." [1] This exposure, though of little real significance, killed any chances that the bill had for passing the Senate at this session.

After the withdrawal of the United States from Cuba, the question of reciprocity was taken up in the ordinary diplomatic way and a convention signed December 11, 1902, under which Cuban products were to be admitted to the United States at a reduction of 20 per cent., while certain classes of American goods were to be admitted to Cuba at reductions of 25, 30, and 40 per cent. The convention further stipulated that so long as it was in force no sugar should be admitted to the United States from any other foreign country, by treaty or convention, at a lower rate of duty than that provided by the Dingley tariff. [2] This was the death-blow to the general principle of reciprocity, since sugar was the basis of reciprocity with most countries.

The Senate failed to act on this treaty at the second session of the Fifty-seventh Congress, but a special session of the Senate was convened by the president on March 5, 1903 partly to consider the Cuban treaty and partly to discuss the canal treaty with Colombia. Two weeks later the Cuban treaty was ratified, with amendments, and with the very unusual provision that it should not go into effect until approved by Congress. As the House was not in

[1] *House Docs.*, 57 Cong., 1 Sess., No. 679.
[2] *Foreign Relations*, 1903, p. 375.

session, this meant that the treaty had to go over until the fall.

Meanwhile the Cuban situation was represented as being very bad, and in order to relieve it the president convened the Fifty-eighth Congress in extraordinary session on November 9, 1903, in order that it might give its approval to the treaty. In his message next day he urged the enactment of the necessary legislation mainly on the ground that the Platt amendment had brought the island within our system of international policy, and that it necessarily followed that it must also to a certain degree come within the lines of our economic system. The Republican party was divided on the issue: the friends of the administration urged the passage of the bill approving the treaty, on the ground of plain duty to Cuba; while other Republicans, in their zeal to foster the domestic sugar interests, refused to support the president's policy. Of the Democrats, some favored reciprocity, while others preferred letting the Republicans fight the matter out among themselves. John Sharp Williams, the new Democratic floor leader, regarding reciprocity as a step towards tariff revision, took the position that the Democrats should support the bill, although he would have preferred some amendments. The Louisiana Democrats remained firm in their opposition. The bill passed the House November 19 by the overwhelming vote of 335 to 21.

The bill then went to the Senate, and although

that body had ratified the treaty, its opponents debated at length the measure which was to give it effect. The result was that the extra session expired without conclusive action. The expiration of the extra session and the beginning of the regular session occurred at the same moment, twelve o'clock, December 7, 1903. The president took the view that there was a "constructive recess," or recess in contemplation of law, and renewed the appointment of General Wood as a major-general, much to the chagrin of the Senate, which had made a determined fight against him. Taking advantage of the president's "constructive recess," the members of Congress in turn voted to themselves the mileage which would have accrued if there had been an interval between the sessions. The Cuban treaty bill was made the special order each day in the Senate until December 16, when the final vote was taken and it passed.

In accordance with the terms of the Platt amendment, the Cuban government had already leased to the United States as naval stations Guantanamo, on the southeastern coast of the island, and Bahia Honda, on the northwestern coast.[1] The treaty embodying the provisions of the Platt amendment was concluded May 22, 1903, and ratifications exchanged July 1, 1904.[2]

Under the reciprocity treaty trade relations with Cuba steadily increased. Exports from the United States to the island rose from $26,000,000, in 1902,

---

[1] *Foreign Relations*, 1903, p. 350.   [2] *Ibid.*, 1904, p. 243.

to $38,000,000, in 1905; and during the same period imports into the United States from Cuba gained from $34,000,000 to $86,000,000.

The Cuban Republic seemed fairly established on solid foundations, and the United States felt a reasonable pride in its work; but it soon developed that the Cubans had not learned the primary lesson of democracy—submission to the will of the majority.   Towards the latter part of August, 1906, following the re-election of President Palma, an insurrectionary movement began which had for its object the overthrow of his government.   About the middle of September, President Roosevelt decided to send Secretary Taft and Assistant Secretary of State Bacon to Havana for the purpose of reconciling the contending factions; and at the same time he addressed a letter to Mr. Quesada, Cuban minister to the United States, in which he said: "Our intervention in Cuban affairs will only come if Cuba herself shows that she has fallen into the insurrectionary habit, that she lacks the self-restraint necessary to secure peaceful self-government, and that her contending factions have plunged the country into anarchy."   Secretary Taft's efforts proving unavailing, President Palma resigned.

When the time for the assembling of the Cuban congress, which had been convened, arrived, it was found to be impossible to command a quorum. President Palma having refused to withdraw his resignation, and there being no congress to adopt other measures for continuing the government, Secretary Taft assumed control September 29, and proclaimed a provisional government for the restoration of order and the protection of life and property. This action was taken under authority of President Roosevelt, in accordance with the provisions of the Platt amendment.[1] Secretary Taft stated in his proclamation that "the provisional government hereby established will be maintained only long enough to restore order, peace, and public confidence, by direction of and in the name of the President of the United States, and then to hold such elections as may be necessary to determine on those persons upon whom the permanent government of the republic should devolve." A body of United States troops was sent to Cuba under command of Brigadier-General Franklin Bell. October 3, 1906, Secretary Taft was relieved of the duties of provisional governor in order that he might resume his labors in Washington, and Charles E. Magoon was appointed to take his place at Havana. In his message to Congress, December 3, 1906, the president made it perfectly clear that while the United States had no desire to annex Cuba, it was "absolutely out of the question that the island should continue independent" if the "insurrectionary habit" should become "confirmed."[2]

[1] See p. 179 above.
[2] Secretary Taft's report on the Cuban situation was sent to Congress December 17, 1906.

CHAPTER XI

THE ALASKAN BOUNDARY

(1898–1903)

THE settlement of the Alaskan boundary dispute in October, 1903, removed the last cause of friction likely to arise from a question of that kind with England. When Alaska was acquired from Russia by purchase in 1867,[1] the boundary-line separating that territory from the British possessions had never been marked or even accurately surveyed, though the treaty between Great Britain and Russia, on which the controversy turned, had been made as far back as 1825.[2] The language of this treaty seemed to exclude Great Britain altogether from the coast north of 54 degrees and 40 minutes. The importance of marking the boundary before the country became more thickly settled was urged by President Grant in his annual message of December 2, 1872, and was discussed by succeeding presidents and secretaries of state; but owing mainly to the expenses of a survey in that deserted region the matter was indefinitely deferred by both govern-

---

[1] Dunning, *Reconstruction* (*Am. Nation*, XXII.), chap. x.
[2] Turner, *New West* (*Am. Nation*, XIV.), chap. xii.

ments. There had never been any difference of opinion expressed as to the general interpretation to be
given to the treaty, and the question of marking the
boundary was regarded merely as a surveying problem to be settled by commissioners appointed in the
usual way and with the usual powers.

The discovery of gold in the Klondike district,
on the upper tributaries of the Yukon, in Canadian
territory, in 1897, put a very different aspect on the
matter. The shortest and quickest route to the
gold-bearing region was by the trails leading up
from Dyea and Skagway on the headwaters of Lynn
Canal—Skagway being about 1115 miles from Seattle and less than 600 miles from Dawson. The
Yukon, or all-water route, was much easier but
slower—the distance from Seattle to St. Michael by
ocean steamer being 2700 miles, and from that point
to Dawson by river steamer 1300 miles.[1] Dyea and
Skagway soon became important places, and the
population rapidly increased. The Canadians now
laid claim to these ports on Lynn Canal, and pushed
their outposts down in that direction. Serious difficulties threatened from the conflict of authority over
the collection of customs. The general question of
the boundary was, therefore, referred to the Anglo-
American joint high commission, which met at
Quebec in the summer of 1898 for the purpose of
adjusting matters relating to commercial reciproc-

[1] U. S. Geological Survey, *Map of Alaska with Descriptive
Text*, 11.

ity and fisheries. The commission not only failed
to reach an agreement on this question, but it developed here for the first time that the Canadians
had set up an entirely new theory as to the interpretation to be given to the treaty of 1825, so as
greatly to narrow the American coast strip and
throw the boundary-line across the heads of inlets
and channels in such a way as to give the Canadians
access to several deep-water harbors.[1] It seems to
have been the aim of the Canadian commissioners,
without regard to any consistent interpretation of
the treaty, to lump the boundary question with
other matters, and in the course of negotiations to
effect a compromise that would give them at least
one harbor on Lynn Canal. The United States commissioners naturally did not feel authorized to trade
off American territory in this way.

When this interpretation was set up, it became at
once evident that the permanent adjustment of the
boundary was a matter that would require long
diplomatic negotiation. Meanwhile there was a
steady movement of men and supplies to the Klondike by way of Dyea and Skagway; and the situation on the headwaters of Lynn Canal, where both
United States and Canadian officials claimed jurisdiction, was growing serious. Under these circum-

[1] *Maps and Charts Accompanying the Case and Counter Case
of the U. S. before the Alaskan Boundary Tribunal*, No. 27; John
W. Foster, "Alaskan Boundary," in *National Geog. Magazine*,
November, 1899, p. 453.

stances the United States agreed upon a *modus vivendi* with Great Britain, fixing a provisional line at certain points, and accordingly notes were exchanged October 20, 1899: the line thus established gave the Canadians temporary possession of several points which had always been regarded as within American jurisdiction. The main question was left for future adjustment, it being specifically provided that this provisional line was fixed " without prejudice to the claims of either party in the permanent adjustment of the international boundary."[1] This temporary concession on the part of the American government was severely criticised in the United States, on the ground that it tended to discredit claims which were too well established to admit of any doubt. It undoubtedly did encourage the Canadians to hope for ultimate success in their efforts, and it gave the British government some ground for adopting the Canadian view of the case.[2]

Finally, on January 24, 1903, Mr. Hay signed a convention with Sir Michael Herbert, agreeing to submit the question to a limited sort of arbitration; the tribunal was to consist of three Americans and three British members. It had been proposed at first to constitute it in the usual way of a mixed commission with an umpire from outside to determine all points of difference, but to this arrangement President Roosevelt would not agree, as we

[1] *Foreign Relations*, 1899, p. 330.
[2] *Review of Reviews*, XXVIII., 527.

could not possibly gain by such an arrangement and
Canada had nothing to lose. As the tribunal was
finally constituted, no decision could be reached unless at least one commissioner failed to sustain the
contention of his own government and upheld that
of the other. The American members were Elihu
Root, at that time secretary of war; Senator Henry
Cabot Lodge, of Massachusetts; and ex - Senator
George Turner, of Washington. The British members were Lord Alverstone, chief-justice of England;
Sir Louis Amable Jetté, lieutenant-governor of the
province of Quebec; and Allen B. Aylesworth, of
Toronto.

As it was not likely that any evidence would be
submitted in so clear a case which would cause the
American members to change their minds, and as
it was well known that the two Canadian members
were thoroughly committed to the Canadian view,
it was evident from the first that the trial was really
before Lord Alverstone, the chief-justice of England;
in case he sustained the American contention, there
would be an end of the controversy; in case he sustained the Canadian view, there would be an even
division, and matters would stand as they stood before the trial began, except that a great deal more
feeling would have been engendered, and the United
States might have had to make good its claims by
force. But with Lord Alverstone as judge the American government was willing to take the risk, rather
than to allow the controversy to drag on indefinitely.

After a good deal of diplomatic sparring over points
connected with the presentation of the cases, the
members of the tribunal met in London September
3, 1903.[1] The main question to be decided was the
interpretation to be given the articles defining the
boundary in the Anglo-Russian treaty of 1825, the
text of which is as follows:

"ARTICLE III.

"The line of demarcation between the possessions
of the High Contracting Parties upon the coast of
the continent and the islands of America to the
northwest, shall be drawn in the following manner:

"Commencing from the southernmost point of
the island called Prince of Wales Island, which point
lies in the parallel of 54 degrees 40 minutes north
latitude, and between the 131st and the 133d degree of west longitude, the said line shall ascend
to the north along the channel called Portland
Channel, as far as the point of the continent where
it strikes the 56th degree of north latitude; from
this last-mentioned point, the line of demarcation
shall follow the summit of the mountains situated
parallel to the coast, as far as the point of intersection of the 141st degree of west longitude; and
finally, from the said point of intersection, the said
meridian line of the 141st degree, in its prolongation
as far as the Frozen Ocean, shall form the limit be-

[1] *Foreign Relations*, 1903, pp. 493–543.

tween the Russian and the British Possessions on
the continent of America to the northwest.   ·

"ARTICLE IV.

"With reference to the line ·of demarcation laid
down in the preceding Article, it is understood:

"First. That the island called Prince of Wales
Island shall belong wholly to Russia.

"Second. That wherever the summit of the mountains which extend in a direction parallel to the
coast from the 56th degree of north latitude to the
point of intersection of the 141st degree of west
longitude shall prove to be at the distance of more
than ten marine leagues from the ocean, the limit
between the British Possessions and the line of the
coast (*la lisière de côte*) which is to belong to Russia,
as above mentioned, shall be formed by a line parallel to the windings (*sinuosités*) of the coast, and
which shall never exceed the distance of ten marine
leagues therefrom." [1]

This language was indefinite in several particu-
lars. In the first part of the boundary described—
that is, from the southernmost point of Prince of
Wales Island along Portland Channel to the 56th
degree, there was room for doubt as to the side of
the line on which the islands at the mouth of Portland Channel should fall; and there was the further
difficulty that Portland Channel does not extend as

---

[1] Moore, *Digest of Int. Law*, I., 466; cf. *U. S. Treaties and Conventions*, 939.

far north as the 56th degree. In the second part of the line described—that is, from the 56th degree of north latitude to the 141st degree of west longitude (Mount St. Elias approximately)—there is no dominant range of mountains parallel to the coast corresponding to the language of the treaty, though such a range was prominently marked on the maps of Vancouver of 1798,[1] and on the maps of other cartographers prior to 1825. In 1893 a joint international survey of the coast between Portland Channel and Lynn Channel was undertaken by the United States and Great Britain, and in their report the American commissioners testified "that throughout the *lisière* the mountains are composed of numerous isolated peaks and short ridges running in different directions, and that within ten marine leagues of tide-water there is no defined and continuous range such as appears upon the early maps and charts following the sinuosities of the coast."[2] As to the third section of the line—that is, from Mount St. Elias to the Arctic Ocean—there has never been any dispute.

A number of specific questions were submitted to the tribunal for decision. The most important of these was number five: "Was it the intention and meaning of said convention of 1825 that there should remain in the exclusive possession of Russia a con-

---

[1] *Maps and Charts Accompanying the Case and Counter Case of the United States before the Alaskan Boundary Tribunal*, Nos. 4 and 5.   [2] *Case of the United States*, 85, and App. 529–538.

tinuous fringe or strip of coast on the mainland, not exceeding ten marine leagues in. width, separating the British possessions from the bays, ports, inlets, havens, and waters of the ocean?" If this question should be answered in the negative, the tribunal was to tell how the *lisière* was to be measured, whether from the line of the general direction of the mainland coast, or from the line separating the territorial waters from the waters of the ocean, or from the heads of inlets and bays.[1]

The English contention was that the line should follow certain peaks along the coast, and run parallel with the general direction of the mainland coast, cutting through inlets, bays, and headlands.[2] This interpretation ignored the meaning of the word *sinuosités*, and failed to construe the plain intent of the negotiators.

The United States claimed: (1) that the treaty of 1825 confirmed in full sovereignty to Russia a strip of territory along the continental shore from the head of Portland Canal to Mount St. Elias, ten marine leagues in width measured from the heads of all gulfs, bays, inlets, and arms of the sea— that is, from tide-water—unless within that distance from tide-water there was a range of mountains lying parallel to the sinuosities of the coast, in which case the summit of such range was to form the boundary; (2) that the acts of Great Britain subsequent

---

[1] *Foreign Relations*, 1903, p. 488.
[2] Alaskan Boundary Tribunal, *Proceedings*, III., 73–78.

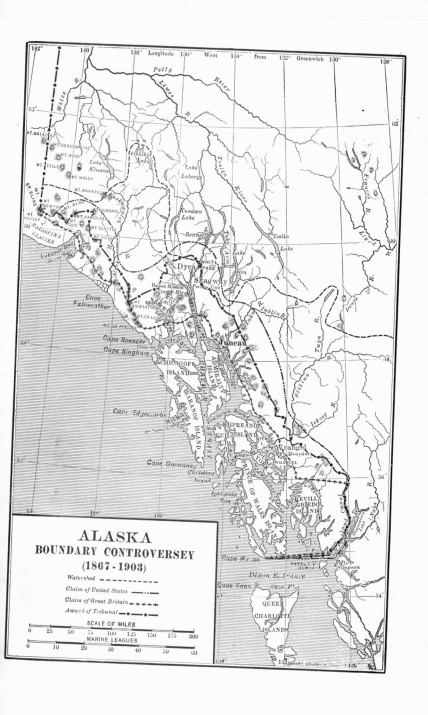

ALASKA
BOUNDARY CONTROVERSEY
(1867 - 1903)

Watershed − − − − − −
Claim of United States − · − · −
Claim of Great Britain + + + +
Award of Tribunal − · − · −

SCALE OF MILES
0   25   50   75   100   125   150   175   200
MARINE LEAGUES
0   10   20   30   40   50   60

to this treaty, and the universal interpretation given it by governments, geographers, cartographers, and historians, agreed with and confirmed the intention and meaning as above stated; (3) that the United States purchased Alaska, entered into possession of and occupied the *lisière* above described, and exercised sovereign rights therein, and remained in possession for thirty years without any notice from Great Britain that she claimed any portion of the territory ceded by Russia; (4) that there being no continuous range of mountains between Portland Channel and Mount St. Elias parallel with the sinuosities of the coast, the width of the *lisière* above described was limited by the agreed distance of ten marine leagues from tide-water.[1]

In support of its claims the United States showed from the records of the negotiations leading up to the treaty of 1825 that Sir Charles Bagot, the English negotiator, made effort after effort to secure an outlet to deep water through the *lisière*, and was finally forced to yield the point. The most interesting feature of the case was the overwhelming array of maps presented by the United States, including British and Canadian, showing the boundary-line claimed by Russia and the United States.[2] It was also shown that both the Canadian and British

---

[1] Alaskan Boundary Tribunal, *Proceedings*, I., pt. ii., pp. 1–106.
[2] See especially the series of eight maps from British sources, *U. S. Atlas*, No. 28, showing the progressive advance of the British frontier between 1884 and 1898.

authorities had, by repeated acts, recognized our title
to the strip in dispute.

The decision of the tribunal was rendered October
20, 1903. On all the important points the vote
stood four to two, Lord Alverstone, Root, Lodge,
and Turner concurring in the decision; and the two
Canadian members dissenting. The decision sustained in the main the American claim, holding that
it was the intention of the treaty of 1825 to shut
England out from access to tide-water through the
lisière. Wales and Pearse islands, at the entrance
of Portland Channel, were awarded to England, and
the line from the head of Portland Channel to Mount
St. Elias was slightly drawn in, though it ran well
around the heads of all inlets. The tribunal desig-
nated certain mountain peaks as the mountains
referred to as parallel to the coast, except between
the Stikine and Taku rivers. For the greater part
of the distance between these rivers the tribunal
declared that " in the absence of further survey the
evidence is not sufficient to enable the Tribunal to
say which are the mountains parallel to the coast
within the meaning of the treaty." [1] The commissioners appointed later to complete this part of the
boundary agreed on what is practically a straight
line, and this was accepted by both governments as
final. [2] The decision was, of course, a disappoint-

---

[1] Alaskan Boundary Tribunal, *Proceedings*, I., 29–32; *Foreign
Relations*, 1903, p. 543.

[2] *Foreign Relations*, 1904, p. 324.

ment to the Canadians, but it did not justify the
charge that Lord Alverstone had sacrificed their
interests in order to further the British policy of
friendly relations with the United States.

CHAPTER XII

THE PANAMA CANAL

(1898–1907)

IN the construction of an interoceanic canal, as in many other things, the Spanish War was a turning-point. The voyage of the *Oregon* around the Horn, which held for weeks the attention of the American people, impressed upon them as nothing else could do the importance of a canal from a naval point of view. The question is now so closely connected with the policies of commercial and colonial expansion upon which the nation has entered as to make a canal a generally recognized necessity. Although the piercing of the isthmus has always been considered a perfectly feasible undertaking, on approaching it the difficulties have been found to be very great. Even the preliminary question as to the choice of routes has delayed and defeated more than one plan for the execution of the project.

The diplomatic problems involved in the control of an interoceanic canal have been as great a hinderance to its construction as the engineering difficulties. The insignificance of the Spanish-American republics, whose territories embrace the available

routes, and their recognized inability either to construct or protect such a gigantic work, have rendered
the co-operation of foreign capital and foreign states
necessary. For the organization and control of a
canal three plans have been proposed: (1) a canal
constructed by a private corporation under international control; (2) a canal constructed by a private
corporation under the exclusive control of the United
States; (3) a canal constructed, owned, operated,
and controlled by the United States as a government
enterprise.

The Clayton-Bulwer convention of 1850[1] provided
for a canal of the first type, constructed by private
capital under the political control of Great Britain
and the United States, and such other powers as
might unite with them in guaranteeing its complete
neutralization, a plan similar in most respects to
the one adopted by the Constantinople convention
of 1888 for the regulation of the Suez Canal. The
organization of a French company by De Lesseps,
and the prospect of the speedy construction of a
canal at Panama under French auspices, led to the
change of policy announced by President Hayes,
when he declared in 1880 that any canal that might
be constructed between the Atlantic and Pacific
oceans should be under American control; and that
the line of such canal should be considered "a part
of the coast line of the United States." [2] The

[1] Smith, *Parties and Slavery* (*Am. Nation*, XVIII.), chap. vi.
[2] Richardson, *Messages and Papers*, VII., 585.

lengthy discussions with England that followed this change of policy and the efforts of Blaine and Frelinghuysen to secure modifications of the Clayton-Bulwer treaty have been discussed in an earlier volume of this series.[1] Their arguments to show that the United States had outgrown the treaty and that it was really voidable at pleasure made little impression on the British government, which simply adhered to its rights under that instrument.[2] President Cleveland reverted in 1885 to the policy of a neutralized canal under international guarantee;[3] and Secretary Olney declared, in 1896, that the only way to modify the stipulations of 1850 was through a direct appeal to Great Britain for a reconsideration of the whole matter.[4]

Precisely in this spirit Secretary Hay undertook, in 1899, to negotiate a new treaty with England. The original draught of the Hay-Pauncefote treaty,[5] signed February 5, 1900, authorized the United States to construct and assume the management of a canal either directly or through a company, but retained the principle of neutralization and adopted a set of rules which were substantially the same as those of the Constantinople convention above re-

[1] Sparks, *National Development* (*Am. Nation*, XXIII.), chap. xiii.

[2] Sec. of State, *Corresp. in Relation to the Proposed Interoceanic Canal, the Clayton-Bulwer Treaty, and the Monroe Doctrine*, 322-367.

[3] Dewey, *National Problems* (*Am. Nation*, XXIV.), chaps. vii., xix.   [4] Moore, *Digest of Int. Law*, III., 209.

[5] *Senate Docs.*, 56 Cong., 1 Sess., No. 160.

ferred to. The Senate, however, amended the treaty: (1) by declaring that the Clayton-Bulwer treaty was thereby superseded; (2) by providing that the regulations governing the use of the canal should not apply to measures which the United States might adopt for its own defence and the maintenance of public order along the canal; (3) by cutting out entirely the article providing for the adherence of other powers. The British government refused to accept the amendments.[1]

After the lapse of a year a new agreement, which was a compromise between the first draught and the Senate amendments, was submitted to the Senate, and ratified December 16, 1901. The new treaty abrogated in express terms the Clayton-Bulwer convention, and provided that the United States might construct a canal under its direct auspices, to be under its exclusive management. The principle of neutralization was nominally retained, but under the sole guarantee of the United States, with power to police the canal; and the clause of the first draught forbidding fortifications was omitted.[2] A unilateral guarantee amounts to nothing: the effect of the Hay-Pauncefote treaty, therefore, is to place the canal politically as well as commercially under the absolute control of the United States.[3]

[1] Moore, *Digest of Int. Law*, III., 211.
[2] *Foreign Relations*, 1901, p. 245.
[3] Latané, "Neutralization Features of the Hay - Pauncefote Treaty," in Am. Hist. Assoc., *Annual Report*, 1902, pp. 289–303.

For several years the United States had been investigating the cost of constructing a canal through Nicaragua, and two commissions—one in 1895 and another in 1897—had reported favorably on the practicability of that route. A third commission, with Admiral John G. Walker as chairman, was appointed under act of March 3, 1899, which authorized an expenditure of $1,000,000 for the purpose of making a thorough investigation of all the facts bearing on the choice of routes. But this question had now become a political rather than an engineering problem.

While there were many disinterested men in and out of Congress who were striving to arrive at a conclusion based on the merits of the case, the activity of others derived its chief stimulus from financial considerations. The New Panama Canal Company had secured, at the time of the reorganization, an extension of its concession to October, 1904, and subsequently another extension to October, 1910; but the validity of the latter arrangement, which did not receive the approval of the Colombian Congress, was doubtful. The company, which could not raise the necessary funds to continue the work, was therefore threatened with the forfeiture of its franchise and property. This danger, combined with the strong opposition in the United States to a canal under foreign management, and the serious consideration Congress was giving to the Nicaragua project, led the French company to conclude that its only hope lay in transferring its concession and property to the American government. To this end an active lobby was maintained at Washington, and powerful agencies employed to influence public opinion in favor of the Panama route.

But the rivalry of Nicaragua was not easily overcome. The Maritime Canal Company, which under a charter from the Congress of the United States and a concession from Nicaragua had begun work at Greytown in 1890, and been forced for lack of funds to stop work in 1893, was also urging Congress to make its enterprise a national one. It found an indomitable champion in Senator Morgan, of Alabama, who, during the ten years' fight for Nicaragua, never wavered in his convictions as to the superiority of that route. In 1900 Nicaragua declared the concession of this company null and void, and granted a new concession to the Grace-Eyre-Cragin Syndicate, a body of prominent New York capitalists; but the Maritime Canal Company refused to abandon its claims, and the contest between the two concerns was carried to the lobbies of Congress. The opposition of the transcontinental railroads to a canal at either point brought into play another set of powerful interests, usually arrayed against the plan which appeared for the time being most likely to succeed.[1]

Meanwhile the Walker commission had been carrying on investigations in Nicaragua, at Panama,

[1] Johnson, *Four Centuries of the Panama Canal*, chap. viii.

and at Paris, since the status of the French company
and its willingness and ability to sell were important
elements in the recommendation of a route. The
report, dated November 16, 1901, placed the estimated cost of construction of the Nicaragua Canal
at $189,864,062, and the cost of completing the
Panama Canal at $144,233,358. To this latter sum
had to be added the cost of acquiring the rights and
property of the French company, offered to the
United States at $109,141,500, making the total cost
of the Panama Canal $253,374,858. The commis-
sion also expressed the opinion that the United
States should not pay over $40,000,000 for the in-
terests of the New Panama Canal Company. In
conclusion, the report stated: "After considering
all the facts developed by the investigations made
by the Commission and the actual situation as it
now stands, and having in view the terms offered
by the New Panama Canal Company, this Commission is of the opinion that the most practicable and
feasible route for an isthmian canal, to be under
the control, management, and ownership of the
United States, is that known as the Nicaragua
route." [1]

This report created a crisis in the affairs of the
French company, which protested that the commission had tried to force its hand by misrepresenting
its statement of values and reporting it as the price

[1] Isthmian Canal Commission, 1899–1901, *Report* (*Senate Docs.*,
57 Cong., 1 Sess., No. 54,) p. 263.

the company had fixed for the transfer of its interests. The president and most of the directors resigned, but at a general meeting of the stockholders
it was decided to negotiate for a sale to the United
States on the ʰest terms that could be secured, and
on January 4, 1902, a definite offer to sell at $40,-
000,000 was made to the commission by cable.[1]
That body promptly took the matter under consideration again, and in a supplementary report of
January 18 recommended to the president the adoption of the Panama route instead of the Nicaragua.

In December Mr. Hepburn had introduced into
the House a bill providing for the construction of a
canal through Nicaragua, and January 9, 1902, more
than a week before the commission made its supplementary report, this bill passed the House by
the almost unanimous vote of 308 to 2.[2] When the
question came up in the Senate, Senator Morgan
continued to fight for Nicaragua as the traditional
American route, declaring that the Panama Company
could not give a valid transfer of its property and
interests. But this objection was cleverly met by
Senator Spooner, who offered an amendment, which
was virtually a substitute, authorizing the president
to acquire the rights and property of the Panama
Canal Company at a cost not exceeding $40,000,000;
to acquire from the republic of Colombia, upon such
terms as he might deem reasonable, perpetual con-

[1] Johnson, *Four Centuries of the Panama Canal*, 124.
[2] *Cong. Record*, 57 Cong., 1 Sess., 481, 513, 540, 557, 558.

trol of a strip of land, not less than six miles in width, extending from the Caribbean Sea to the Pacific Ocean, with jurisdiction over said strip; to proceed, as soon as these rights were acquired, to construct a canal through the Isthmian Canal Commission created by this act; but should he be unable to obtain a satisfactory title to the property of the French company, and the control of the necessary territory of the republic of Colombia within "a reasonable time and upon reasonable terms," then the president was instructed to secure control of the necessary strip through Nicaragua and proceed to construct a canal there.

Senator Hanna made a strong speech in favor of Panama, basing his opposition to the Nicaragua route on its liability to volcanic disturbances. Taking advantage of the popular excitement over Mont Pelée and La Soufrière, still in active eruption, he illustrated his points with an array of maps and charts spread before him in the Senate chamber that carried conviction and changed a number of votes. The bill as amended passed the Senate June 19, 1902, by a vote of 67 to 6.[1] The House at first refused to concur in the Senate amendments; but after a conference the Spooner measure was adopted by a vote of 260 to 8,[2] and the act was signed by the president June 28.[3]

After a thorough investigation of the affairs of

---

[1] *Cong. Record*, 57 Cong., 1 Sess., 7059.   [2] *Ibid.*, 7416, 7441.
[3] *U. S. Statutes at Large*, XXXII., pt. i., 481.

the Panama Company, Attorney-General Knox reported that it could give a clear title.   Negotiations between Secretary Hay and Mr. Herran, the Colombian *chargé d'affaires*, resulted, after considerable delay, in the signature, January 22, 1903, of the Hay-Herran convention, by the terms of which the United States agreed to pay Colombia $10,000,000 cash and an annuity of $250,000 for the lease of a strip of land six miles wide across the isthmus.   Although objection was raised against this treaty because it failed to secure for the United States full governmental authority over the zone, it was nevertheless ratified by the Senate March 17, 1903.

The Colombian Congress met in extra session June 20, mainly for the purpose of considering this treaty. When the vote was finally taken August 12, the treaty was rejected by the unanimous vote of all the senators present.[1]   President Roosevelt later declared that this action was due to the "anti-social spirit" of Colombia and to the cupidity of the government leaders, who proposed to wait until they could confiscate the $40,000,000 worth of property belonging to the French company and then sell it to the United States.[2]   This view is not borne out by the despatches of Mr. Beaupré, the American minister, who repeatedly warned Secretary Hay that there was a "tremendous tide of public opinion

[1] *Senate Docs.*, 58 Cong., 2 Sess., No. 51, p. 56.
[2] Message of January 4, 1904, *Senate Docs.*, 58 Cong., 2 Sess., No. 53, pp. 5, 26.

against the canal treaty," which even the Colombian government could not ignore.[1]   The people of
Colombia felt that Panama was their greatest asset.
They knew perfectly well that, in spite of threats
to the contrary, President Roosevelt was determined
not to adopt the alternative of the Spooner amendment and go to Nicaragua; consequently they opposed the treaty with the expectation that they
could get better terms, and particularly that they
might reserve a fuller measure of sovereignty over
the isthmus.   The charge of bad faith against Colombia does not come in good grace from a country
whose Constitution also requires the ratification of
treaties by the Senate.

With the failure of the Hay-Herran convention
the advocates of the Nicaragua route began to take
courage and to demand that as the "reasonable
time" allowed in the Spooner act for the president
to acquire a right of way through Panama had expired, it was now his duty to turn to Nicaragua.
The directors of the Panama Company, on the other
hand, were in a state of consternation.   If they
could not sell to the United States, they would have
to sacrifice their property entirely, or sell to some
other purchaser at a lower figure.   It was persist-
ently rumored that Germany was disposed to buy
their interests, but it is not probable that such a
step was seriously contemplated by the German
government.   Offers of a tentative nature were

---

[1] *Senate Docs.*, 58 Cong., 2 Sess., No. 51, pp. 5, 7, 16.

made, however, from some quarter, and so complete was the demoralization of the directors that William Nelson Cromwell, the American attorney for the company, hastened to Paris to dissuade them from taking any rash step.

The inhabitants of the isthmus were also greatly excited at what they considered a sacrifice of their interests, and two of the foremost citizens — José Agustin Arango and Dr. Manuel Amador Guerrero— conferred with Captain J. R. Beers, the freight agent of the Panama Railroad Company, as to the advisability of organizing a revolution. As a result, Dr. Amador visited the United States, and had conferences with William Nelson Cromwell and with Secretary Hay. The latter was of course guarded in his replies, but outlined what he considered the rights and duties of the United States under the treaty of 1846.[1] Amador was greatly encouraged at this time by the sudden arrival in New York of Philippe Bunau-Varilla, the former chief-engineer of the French company, who entered with enthusiasm into the revolutionary project.[2]

When Amador returned to Panama his friends were at first inclined to doubt the intentions of the United States, but these apprehensions were removed when the United States gun-boat *Nashville* arrived off Colon November 2. The *Boston*, *Dixie*, and *Atlanta* had also received orders to proceed

---

[1] See p. 219 below.
[2] Johnson, *Four Centuries of the Panama Canal*, 162–171.

within easy reach of the isthmus. The Colombian
Congress adjourned October 31 without reconsideration of the treaty, and two days later orders were
cabled to the American naval commanders to keep
the transit open and to "prevent the landing of
any armed force with hostile intent, either Government or insurgent, at any point within 50 miles of
Panama." [1]   It can hardly be denied that this was
creating a situation very favorable to revolution.

But the revolutionists were slow in taking advantage of their opportunities, and the government
at Washington was growing impatient. At 3.40
P.M., November 3, the following despatch was sent
to the American consuls at Panama and Colon:
"Uprising on Isthmus reported. Keep Department
promptly and fully informed. Loomis, Acting."
At 8.15 a reply was received from Consul Ehrman,
at Panama: "No uprising yet. Reported will be in
the night. Situation is critical." At 9.50 P.M. a
second despatch was received from the same source:
"Uprising occurred to-night, 6; no bloodshed. Army
and Navy officials taken prisoners. Government will
be organized to-night." [2]

Before the *Nashville* received the order to prevent
the landing of armed forces, four hundred and fifty
Colombian troops arrived at Colon. The principal
officers hurried across the isthmus in a special train
to Panama, expecting their troops to follow, and were

---

[1] *Senate Docs.*, 58 Cong., 2 Sess., No. 53, p. 13.
[2] *House Docs.*, 58 Cong., 1 Sess., No. 8, p. 2.

there seized by the revolutionary leaders and locked up for safe keeping. The next day Commander Hubbard landed fifty marines from the *Nashville* at Colon, and a day later the officer in charge of the Colombian forces was persuaded by a generous bribe to reimbark his troops and leave.[1] Events continued to follow one another with startling rapidity. On the 6th Secretary Hay instructed the American consul to recognize the *de facto* government. On the same day Bunau-Varilla was appointed envoy extraordinary and minister plenipotentiary of the Panama republic at Washington, and a week later he was formally received by President Roosevelt.

Such hasty recognition of a new government was, of course, without precedent in the annals of American diplomacy,[2] and it naturally confirmed the rumors that the whole affair had been prearranged. In the *Review of Reviews* for November, 1903, Dr. Albert Shaw, a close personal friend of President Roosevelt, had discussed the question, "What if Panama should revolt?" and outlined with remarkable prophetic insight the future course of events. It turned out some months later, however, that his editorial had been inspired by the following letter which he had received from the president, dated October 10: "My dear Dr. Shaw: I enclose you, purely for your own information, a copy of a letter of September 5 from our Minister to Colombia. I

[1] Johnson, *Four Centuries of the Panama Canal*, 173–180.
[2] Paxson, *Independence of the South American Republics*.

think it might interest you to see that there was absolutely not the slightest chance of securing by treaty any more than we endeavored to secure. The alternatives were to go to Nicaragua, against the advice of the great majority of competent engineers—some of the most competent saying that we had better have no canal at this time than go there —or else to take the territory by force without any attempt at getting a treaty. I cast aside the proposition at this time to foment the secession of Panama. Whatever other governments can do, the United States can not go into the securing, by such underhand means, the cession. Privately, I freely say to you that I should be delighted if Panama were an independent state, or if it made itself so at this moment; but for me to say so publicly would amount to an instigation of a revolt, and therefore I cannot say it.

"With great regard, sincerely yours, Theodore Roosevelt."[1]

In his annual message of December 7, 1903, the president undertook to justify the course of the administration by showing the ingratitude of Colombia for the work of the United States in maintaining order on the isthmus for over fifty years under the treaty of 1846, and her utter inability to control the situation and prevent riot and revolution. This message by no means allayed the criticism of the president's course; and on January 4, 1904, he sent

[1] *Literary Digest*, October 29, 1904.

a special message to Congress in defence of his
action. He held that Colombia was not entitled
"to bar the transit of the world's traffic across the
isthmus," and that the intervention of the United
States was justified—(1) by our treaty rights, (2) by
our national interests, (3) by the interests of collective civilization.

In answer to the president's arguments, it may
be said in regard to the first point that the treaty
obligations were obligations to Colombia: the United
States agreed in the convention of 1846 that in
return for the right of way across the isthmus it
would keep it open and guarantee Colombia's sovereignty over the same. It is difficult to adopt the
president's view that this was an obligation to the
world at large. Nor, in the second place, could it
be rightly claimed that the safety of the United
States was directly involved, when it is remembered
that a majority of Congress were in favor of the
Nicaragua route and had voted for the Spooner act
on the contingency that a right of way through
Panama might not be secured, and that the president would then go to Nicaragua. The third point
involved the recognition of the president as the
agent of collective civilization, clothed with the
power to exercise an international right of eminent
domain.

Admitting the force of the president's views as
to the advantages of the Panama route over that
through Nicaragua, the question arises, was he jus-

tified in adopting measures amounting in themselves to open acts of war in order to secure that route? The act of Congress could not possibly be so construed; hence the emphasis on the interests of collective civilization. The president knew that when Congress convened in December, the situation remaining unchanged, he would be compelled to go to the Nicaragua route. His object, therefore, was to make the choice of the Panama route an accomplished fact before Congress should meet. This was the attitude distinctly assumed in the message of January 4, 1904, in the course of which he said: "The only question now before us is that of the ratification of the treaty. For it is to be remembered that a failure to ratify the treaty will not undo what has been done, will not restore Panama to Colombia, and will not alter our obligation to keep the transit open across the Isthmus, and to prevent any outside power from menacing this transit." [1]

The treaty referred to was the convention with Panama which had been signed November 18, 1903, and which was ratified by the Senate February 23, 1904, by a vote of 66 to 14. By the terms of this agreement the United States guaranteed the independence of the Panama republic; and in return Panama granted to the United States in perpetuity the use, occupation, and control of a zone of land ten miles wide for the construction of a canal, the United States receiving as full power and author-

[1] *Senate Docs.*, 58 Cong., 2 Sess., No. 53, p. 28.

ity over this strip and the waters adjacent as if it were the sovereign of the said territory. The United States further agreed to pay the republic of Panama the sum of $10,000,000 upon the exchange of ratifications, and the sum of $250,000 a year beginning nine years thereafter.[1]

An act approved April 28, 1904, appropriated $10,000,000 to pay the sum stipulated, and vested the powers of temporary government of the zone in the president.[2] By executive order of May 9, 1904, the president placed the government of the territory as well as the construction of the canal in the hands of the Isthmian Canal Commission, with Rear-Admiral John G. Walker as chairman, Major-General George W. Davis as governor of the zone, and John F. Wallace as chief-engineer. In less than a year the commission was reorganized by the appointment of Theodore P. Shonts as chairman, Charles E. Magoon as governor, John F. Wallace as chief-engineer, and four associate members, at salaries ranging from $30,000 to $7500. Wallace resigned June 29, 1905, to accept a more lucrative position in the United States, and John F. Stevens was appointed chief-engineer in his place.

In November, 1905, a board of European and American engineers, appointed by the president to recommend the type of canal to be adopted, reported in favor of a sea-level canal, by a vote of

---

[1] *Foreign Relations*, 1904, p. 543.
[2] *U. S. Statutes at Large*, XXXIII., pt. i., 429.

8 to 5; but the majority of the commission, including Chief-Engineer Stevens, were in favor of a lock
canal, and this type was finally adopted by Congress. The cost of a sea-level canal, estimated at
$300,000,000, and the time required for construction,
at least fifteen years, were serious objections to the
adoption of that type; but the plan for a high-level
lock canal, in addition to being cheaper, has certain
positive advantages: it contemplates a lake formed
by the locks at Gatun, which will take care of the
flood-waters of the Chagres—a very difficult problem; this lake, moreover, will be 30 miles long and
have a channel ranging from 1000 feet to 8 miles in
width, whereas a sea-level canal would have a channel varying from 150 to 200 feet. It is claimed that
steamships, in traversing the lake, will gain much
more time than they will lose in going through
the locks, and the entire transit will occupy less
time than would the passage through a sea-level
canal.

Many difficulties yet remain unsolved, labor conditions, owing to the deadly climate, being especially
hard to contend with. West-Indians having proven
inefficient, and American labor, except for the higher
skilled occupations, being out of the question, it was
proposed at one time to try Chinese coolies, but
against this proposition the American labor unions
were solidly arrayed. Similarly the proposition advanced by Secretary Taft to purchase supplies in
the cheapest markets of the world encountered vio-

lent opposition from the protected interests in the United States and had to be abandoned.

Early in 1907 it was announced that the president had decided to carry on the work through private contractors, and bids were invited. As a result of this decision Chairman Shonts resigned; and late in February Chief-Engineer Stevens, after some disagreement with the president, tendered his resignation also. Greatly to the surprise of the public, it was announced a few days later that all bids, including that of the Oliver Company, which was much lower than the others, had been rejected and that President Roosevelt had decided to commit the great undertaking to army engineers. Lieutenant-Colonel George W. Goethals was made chief-engineer, and Majors David Du B. Gaillard and William L. Sibert assistant engineers. While, owing to the repeated change of engineers, no great progress has been made up to 1907, the way has been prepared by the sanitation of the isthmus and the assemblage of material.[1]

[1] *Review of Reviews*, **XXXV.**, **269, 397.**

CHAPTER XIII

THE ELECTION OF 1904

(1901–1904)

THOSE who expected of Theodore Roosevelt, when he succeeded to the presidency in the autumn of 1901, a special moderation and reserve, were soon filled with astonishment. The three years that followed broke many of the precedents of our political history. Other vice - presidents who had succeeded to the office of president had failed to hold their own party together: neither Tyler nor Fillmore nor Johnson nor Arthur had been able to build up a party of his own; and all were succeeded by presidents of an opposite party. But Theodore Roosevelt was made of different stuff: his attitude from the first was that of aggressive leadership. It was soon apparent that he regarded himself as possessed of all the attributes of an elected president; and, what was more to the point, he made others so regard him. His foreign policy was in part, owing to the retention of John Hay as secretary of state, a continuation of that of President McKinley's administration; in part it was characteristically aggressive. He adhered to the policy of the "open

door" in the East, though with only partial success.
He gave a new interpretation to the Monroe Doc-
trine, virtually constituting the United States the
regulator of the financial relations of the Latin-
American republics. In his hasty recognition of
Panama he departed from all precedents.

His activity in national affairs was equally striking and unusual. He astonished the country by his
interference in the anthracite coal strike and the
consequent adjustment of a dispute which seriously
threatened industrial peace and the welfare of thousands of individuals. In his first message to Congress he began an attack on trusts and large aggre-
gations of capital, and put his principles to the test
in the successful prosecution of the Northern Securities Company. In many things he utterly disre-
garded the wishes and prejudices of whole sections
and classes: by inviting Booker Washington, a leader of the negroes, to his table at the White House,
and by the appointment of negroes to office in the
South, he antagonized that section. The advance-
ment of General Wood, formerly colonel of the
Rough Riders, to a high position in the army raised
a storm of opposition, but the president did not
flinch from his purpose. He interfered openly in
the politics of several states, notably in Maryland,
New York, and Ohio. The death of Senator Hanna,
February 15, 1904, removed the last centre of opposition, leaving Roosevelt in control in Ohio and
without a formidable rival for the next nomination.

Serious concern was caused to the administration by the discovery in 1903 of extensive public land and postal frauds. For three or four years intimations had been whispered in Washington that the administration of the post - office department was thoroughly corrupt. The higher officials of the department tried repeatedly and with remarkable success to discredit these rumors. Finally, in January, 1903, the president instituted an investigation, which resulted in a number of indictments and in several convictions. These cases revealed a large number of fraudulent contracts by which the government had been robbed of thousands of dollars. No such wholesale "graft" had been exposed since the star-route frauds of thirty years before. The exposure of corruption in the administration of the public lands was equally sensational, involving, as it did, the criminal conviction of two United States senators. While the Republican leaders had endeavored to hush these cases up and to conceal the extent of the "graft," the president finally took the matter up in spite of them and had it investigated. So far from injuring him, these investigations greatly enhanced the high regard which the masses had for his integrity and honesty of purpose.

Roosevelt's popularity was the despair and confusion of the Republican machine and of the Democrats alike. Probably no man in American public life has ever been so constantly before the people, either in cartoon and caricature, or in photographs and sketches in the papers and magazines. He was shown in the costume of a rough-rider and a ranch-man, sitting on his porch at Sagamore Hill, hunting the grizzly in the Far West, or taking a fence on a fine mount. The "strenuous life"—the title of one of his essays—became a by-word and a fad, and all the while his popularity increased. A man with so many human interests combined with many human failings, outspoken and blunt, moved alternately by anger, by enthusiasm, and by noble purpose, ap-pealed to the people in a peculiar way. John Hay, with his discriminating pen, has described him as "Of gentle birth and breeding, yet a man of the people in the best sense; with the training of a scholar and the breezy accessibility of a ranchman; a man of the library and a man of the world; an athlete and a thinker; a soldier and a statesman; a reader, a writer, and a maker of history; with the sensibility of a poet and the steel nerve of a rough rider; one who never did, and never could, turn his back on a friend or on an enemy." [1]

Such was the man whom the Democrats had to face in the campaign of 1904. It was evident from the first that it was to be a contest not of platforms, but of men. Policies counted for little: the per-sonal element had come to the front once more; people had lost faith in the efficacy of measures; they were looking for men, tried men; honesty and

[1] Speech at Jackson, Michigan, July 6, 1904, *Addresses of John Hay*, 298.

efficiency were the standards of comparison. The Democrats unfortunately were without a leader, and their eventual candidate, Judge Parker, was put forward in order to prevent the nomination of Hearst.

So complete was the ascendency of Roosevelt in his party that no candidate was suggested against him, and the Republican national convention, which met at Chicago June 21, 1904, was a decidedly humdrum affair. Elihu Root, of New York, as temporary chairman, delivered a notable speech in which he set forth the achievements of the party and particularly of President Roosevelt's administration. He challenged "judgment upon this record of effective performance," and called upon the people to indorse it and to continue to intrust the government of the country to the Republican party. This speech was the keynote of the campaign. The proceedings of the convention were marked by even greater unanimity than those of the Philadelphia convention four years before. The only incidents to mar the harmony of the preliminary proceedings were fights between state factions in Illinois and Wisconsin. The Wisconsin contest reflected the growing popularity of Governor La Follette, who was trying to organize the state against Senator Spooner. The national committee decided against La Follette, who later got control of the legislature and was sent to the United States Senate.

The entire programme was carefully prearranged, and the convention was swayed by the administration forces. "Uncle Joe" Cannon, who had become widely popular on account of the imperturbable humor with which as speaker he dominated the Fifty-eighth Congress, was made permanent chairman. The platform was presented June 22 by Senator Lodge, who had prepared it in advance of the convention; and the next day Roosevelt was unanimously nominated. For vice - president Congressman Hitt, of Illinois, had been a leading candidate; but before the convention met it was apparent that Senator Fairbanks, of Indiana, was in the lead. At the instance of President Roosevelt, Cortelyou, secretary of commerce and labor, was made chairman of the national committee—a decided innovation, inasmuch as he was not a politician in the ordinary sense of the term.

The Republican platform was brief and devoid of startling or sensational features. The significant thing about it was not so much what it contained as what it did not contain: tariff revision and reciprocity had been dropped, and it was evident that the party had determined, in the political slang of the day, to "stand pat" and boldly challenge a vote of confidence from the people.[1]

The Democratic national convention was held at St. Louis July 6–10. The fight for control had been waged for months, for the Democratic party, which first split on the money issue in 1894, was still divided into two camps, the conservatives, or fol-

[1] *Republican Campaign Text-Book*, 1904, p. 485.

lowers of ex-President Cleveland, and the radicals, led by William R. Hearst, formerly of California, but since 1895 proprietor of the *New York Journal*, a radical and socialistic newspaper, which claimed to have brought on the Spanish War. Senator Arthur P. Gorman, the Democratic boss of Maryland, who had long aspired to the presidency, made a last effort to secure a following, particularly in the southern states, which still felt a certain degree of gratitude to him for the part he had played in the defeat of the "Force Bill" of 1890; but the party was not looking for a smooth and elusive politician of his type. Bryan held aloof and remained non - committal as to Hearst, but actively opposed the campaign conducted by David B. Hill in favor of Judge Parker, of the New York bench, and a return to "safe and sane Democracy." The early successes of the Hearst boom forced the conservatives to rally round Judge Parker, though he had been out of active politics for twenty years. When the convention met, Bryan favored ex-Governor Pattison, of Pennsylvania, or Senator Cockrell, of Missouri. Had he made a fight for either one of these earlier in the canvass, he might have defeated the nomination of Parker, as the rule of the Democratic conventions requires a two-thirds vote to nominate.

The St. Louis convention was one of the most exciting and sensational in the history of the Democratic party. It was called to order Wednesday, July 6, by John Sharp Williams, the minority leader in the House of Representatives, who delivered a long speech, clever, sarcastic, ironical, but lacking in the element of constructive leadership. At the afternoon session next day Bryan appeared on the platform for the purpose of reading a minority report in favor of seating the Hearst delegates in the Illinois contest. This was the signal for one of those tremendous demonstrations for which this convention will ever be memorable; it lasted for over half an hour, producing a bewildering and deafening uproar and creating disorder which continued during the remainder of the session. When Bryan's speech was over the vote was 647 to 299 against him and in favor of the majority report, the first test of Judge Parker's strength.

By Thursday night the sub-committee on resolutions had agreed upon a platform and was ready to report it to the full committee. The text of this proposed platform was given to the Associated Press and published throughout the country, and its adoption was confidently expected; but the unexpected happened. The full committee refused to accept the work of its sub-committee, and proceeded to overhaul its platform. Instead of a short session, there was sixteen hours of hot and at times angry debate in the committee, and when the convention met next morning it was necessary to adjourn till that night.

The main fight before the committee was on the financial plank. John Sharp Williams framed the basis of the sub-committee's proposition as follows:

"The discoveries of gold within the last few years, and the greatly increased production thereof, adding $2,000,000,000 to the world's supply, of which $700,-000,000 falls to the, share of the United States, have contributed to the maintenance of a money standard of values no longer open to question, removing that issue from the field of political contention." The adverse vote encountered by Bryan in the convention was taken as an indication that he was not to be allowed to dictate as he had to the Kansas City convention four years before; and the financial plank adopted by the sub-committee greatly pleased the eastern Democrats. The country was, therefore, amazed to learn that Bryan had appeared before the full committee and made a determined fight against the financial plank, and after a memorable all-night session carried his point by the sheer force of his remarkable personality. The platform as finally adopted contained no reference whatever to the questions of money and banking: Williams introduced an income-tax amendment, but withdrew it at the urgent appeal of Hill; Bryan, however, insisted on its retention, and the final result was the dropping of both planks. The committee agreed to this compromise by a vote of 35 to 15, and the platform was presented to the convention Friday night, and adopted, in great confusion, without further discussion.[1]

[1] *Review of Reviews*, XXX., 132–146; *Baltimore Sun*, July 6–11, 1904.

The nomination of candidates was next in order, and most of the night was consumed in nominating speeches. Finally, at five o'clock Saturday morning the first ballot was taken: Parker received 658 votes; Hearst, 200; Cockrell, 42; Olney, 38; and a few scattering. As Judge Parker lacked only a few votes of the necessary two-thirds, several of the smaller delegations changed their votes to him, and a motion to make his nomination unanimous was carried. The convention then took a recess until the afternoon, when Henry G. Davis, of West Virginia, was nominated as candidate for vice-president.

At this final session came the most sensational incident of a sensational convention in the following telegram addressed to William F. Sheehan, of the New York delegation:

"I regard the gold standard as firmly and irrevocably established, and shall act accordingly if the act of the convention to-day shall be ratified by the people. As the platform is silent on the subject, my view should be known to the convention; and if it is proved to be unsatisfactory to the majority, I request you to decline the nomination for me, so that another may be nominated before adjournment. —Alton B. Parker." [1]

The reading of this telegram caused for the time being intense excitement. There was talk of revising the platform, and also of nominating another

[1] *Democratic Campaign Text-Book*, 1904, p. 23.

man; but finally, at the urgent insistence of Till-
man, of South Carolina, and others, it was decided
to let the platform and candidate remain the same,
and to send in reply the following telegram: "The
platform adopted by this convention is silent on the
question of the monetary standard because it is not
regarded by us as a possible issue in this campaign,
and only campaign issues were mentioned in the
platform." [1]

Judge Parker's telegram was the subject of much
discussion in the papers for days after the adjournment of the convention. Some looked upon it as
an act of the greatest courage, others as a clever bit
of strategy; while Bryan asserted in an interview
that if the telegram had been received before the
nomination some one else would have been selected.
The plain fact is that Bryan's unexpected domina-
tion of the convention in its last hours created an
unfavorable impression upon the conservative element of the East, and caused Parker to define his
position beyond dispute.

Judge Parker was recognized by all parties as a
thoroughly upright judge and a man of the highest
integrity; he was popular in his own state, but not
well known outside its limits, and without experience
in national politics. His telegram made a very favorable impression, and led the public to suppose that
he would rise to the occasion and make an active
and aggressive campaign. But in this they were

[1] *Democratic Campaign Text-Book*, 1904, p. 23.

mistaken. His conduct of his campaign was without striking incident; he proved to be a man of good sense, but thoroughly conservative and without initiative, when aggressive leadership was needed. The campaign that followed was decidedly commonplace. The usual number of small parties was in the field, but they did not affect the issue.

The Democrats had to some extent healed the breach in their party: the eastern gold men came back into the fold, and the silver wing gave the ticket a nominal, though not a very enthusiastic, support. The issues were not clearly drawn: both parties repudiated all connection with the trusts; the Republican platform advocated protection, which was a reason why the trusts should support the Republican ticket; Roosevelt, on the other hand, had begun attacks on the trusts, and his record was pointed to for the satisfaction of the anti-trust vote.

On the question of the Philippines, the two parties were not as far apart as they had been in 1900: the Republicans had come around to the promise of self-government; the Democratic platform advocated for the Philippines the same treatment that had been accorded to Cuba. Root, the most competent person in the country to speak on the Philippine situation, declared in his Chicago speech that it was only a question of time when such treatment would be accorded them.[1] In Judge Parker's speech of acceptance he advocated for the Filipinos "the

[1] *Republican Campaign Text-Book*, 1904, p. 473.

right of self-government," explaining later that he
used the term as equivalent to "independence."
Whatever the mistakes of the Republican party in
its dealings with the Philippines, and they were
many, it is difficult to see what changes in policy
could have been brought about if a Democratic
administration had come into power at that late
day.   Later on in the campaign Judge Parker made
charges against the administration in the Philippines,
relating to actual conditions as they then existed.
These charges were of a wholesale and most extrava-
gant nature, and when denied in emphatic terms by
Governor Wright in a cablegram, Judge Parker was
unable to substantiate them.

As the campaign developed, the trust question
became the most important issue, and was handled
with unusual bitterness on both sides.   The Republican managers paraded Roosevelt as a "trust-
buster," and undertook to show that the Wall
Street interests were all arrayed against his nomination and working for Judge Parker.   The Democrats charged, on the other hand, that the trusts
and great corporations were contributing heavily to
the Republican campaign fund.   Finally Parker,
who had remained at his home at Esopus, on the
Hudson, during the greater part of the campaign,
made several speeches in New York, in which he
called attention to the fact that Cortelyou had resigned the position of secretary of commerce and
labor, a position in which he had been charged with

the investigation of the affairs of the great corporations engaged in interstate business, in order to become chairman of the Republican campaign committee; and charged that he was using information
he had acquired as a member of the cabinet for the
purpose of collecting contributions from corporations. For some days the public expected a reply
from Cortelyou, but none was forthcoming. November 5, however, three days before the election,
there appeared in all the papers a signed statement
from the president discussing the charges at length,
and concluding with the assertion that "the statements made by Mr. Parker are unqualifiedly and
atrociously false." This was the closing incident of
the campaign.[1]

Subsequent revelations as to the amounts contributed by the insurance companies to the Republican campaign fund showed that the president's
strong language was hardly warranted by the facts.
Judge Parker's statement as to the reasons for Cortelyou's appointment was merely an inference, it is
true, but the fact remains that Cortelyou received
and used the contributions; and that President
Roosevelt was in a peculiar sense responsible, having dictated the appointment of Cortelyou and kept
in close touch with him all through the campaign.

Additional light was thrown on the subject of
Judge Parker's charges early in April, 1907, when
there appeared surreptitiously in the public press a

---

[1] *Review of Reviews*, XXX., 644.

letter written more than a year before by E. H. Harriman, the railroad king, to Sidney Webster, in which the writer stated that President Roosevelt had summoned him to Washington in the autumn of 1904, about a week before the election, and asked him to help in raising the necessary funds to carry New York; that the president promised to appoint Senator Depew ambassador to Paris; that upon Harriman's return to New York he raised, with the help of Depew's friends, the sum of $200,000, of which he himself subscribed $50,000, and turned the amount over to Treasurer Bliss.   In explanation of the appearance of the letter at the time that the Interstate Commerce Commission was investigating some of Harriman's railroad transactions, the latter said that it had been sold to the New York *World* by a discharged stenographer and that he had made every effort to stop its publication.   The president published in reply a letter in which he said: "Any such statement is a deliberate and wilful untruth—by rights it should be characterized by an even shorter and more ugly word. . . . I never requested Mr. Harriman to raise a dollar for the Presidential campaign of 1904."   This was drawing a rather nice distinction between the national and the state campaign.   Other letters made public by the president showed that he had been on cordial terms with Harriman and had invited him to the White House shortly before the election.[1]

[1] *Literary Digest*, April 13, 1907.

The total number of votes cast in the election of 1904 was smaller than in the election of 1900— 13,528,979, as against 13,961,566. Of these Roosevelt received 7,624,489, and Parker 5,082,754,[1] and the electoral vote was 336 to 140. Roosevelt's popular vote and popular majority were the largest ever recorded for any president. He carried even Missouri, thus breaking the solid South, while Parker did not carry a single state outside the South.

A remarkable feature of this election was the success of five Democratic governors in states that gave Roosevelt large majorities: Douglas in Massachusetts, Johnson in Minnesota, Toole in Montana, Adams in Colorado, and Folk in Missouri. This result showed that the individual man was no longer dominated to the same extent as formerly by party organizations. The election of Folk, a young man of thirty - five, who had shown marked ability and courage in prosecuting numerous bribery cases in St. Louis, was one of the many signs of a great civic awakening that was sweeping over the entire country. This movement, though already under way as the result of conditions that were no longer tolerable, undoubtedly received a great impetus from the action and utterances of President Roosevelt. It was particularly strong in the larger cities, resulting in the overthrow of bosses and political machines, and marking the beginning of a veritable municipal re-

[1] *World Almanac*, 1905, p. 445.

naissance.   In many cities the reform movement
was identified with the advocacy of municipal ownership, an avowed remedy for the abuses of municipal franchises by public-service corporations.   In
Chicago, Edward F. Dunne was elected mayor on
such a platform in 1905.   The same year witnessed
a temporary municipal revolution in Philadelphia
under Mayor Weaver, and the re-election of Je-
rome, as an independent candidate, to the office
of district attorney in New York City, an event of
great significance as showing the extent to which
the public conscience had been freed from political
control.

As the result of charges made during the campaign
against the great corporations in New York, a joint
committee of the senate and assembly of that state
was appointed to investigate the management of
life-insurance companies.   This committee, of which
William W. Armstrong was chairman and Charles
E. Hughes counsel, began its sittings September
6, 1905, and soon uncovered an almost incredible
state of corruption in the Wall Street circles of high
finance.   The report of this committee, dated February 22, 1906, not only led to a thorough-going
reorganization of the insurance companies, but gave
the impulse and afforded the justification for a
searching investigation, by national and state governments, into the affairs of great corporations generally, the end of which is not yet in sight, but which
is undoubtedly destined to lead to fundamental

changes in the existing system. The temper of the New York public was shown by the election of Hughes in the fall of 1906 to the office of governor on the Republican ticket, without reference to the wishes of the machine.

CHAPTER XIV

INTERNATIONAL ARBITRATION

(1899–1907)

IN spite of recent wars there has developed among the peoples of the earth a strong undercurrent of sentiment in favor of peace, and the principle of international arbitration has received wide recognition. From pulpit and press, from philanthropic associations, from chambers of commerce, from conferences of lawyers, national and international, the demand has come for the peaceful adjustment of international disputes; and this demand has been met by the negotiation of arbitration treaties, a score or more of which have already been entered into by the leading powers of the world. This subject is of special interest to Americans for the reason that the nations on this continent have so frequently resorted to arbitration, and no country has done more to encourage this method of procedure than the United States.

It is difficult to determine the exact number of cases that have gone before specially constituted international courts or mixed commissions during the past hundred years, but the number has increased with each decade. Great Britain and the United States have led the way, each having been a party to about sixty arbitrations.[1] The organization of temporary tribunals under special treaties involves unnecessary expense and delay, and it has long been held by the advocates of arbitration that the ever increasing number of cases submitted to this method of settlement justified some more permanent arrangement. It was with this view that an arbitration treaty between England and the United States was negotiated by secretary Olney and Lord Pauncefote and submitted by President Cleveland to the Senate in January, 1897. That body unfortunately rejected the treaty, though it lacked only two votes of the necessary two-thirds.[2]

A year later the czar of Russia invited the powers to a peace conference, which met at The Hague during the summer of 1899. Twenty-six states were represented, and the total number of delegates was one hundred, all of whom were present at the opening session. Invitations were extended only to powers maintaining diplomatic representatives at the Russian court; this limitation excluded the Central and South American republics; so that the United States and Mexico were the only American states who sent delegates. President McKinley appointed to represent the United States Andrew D. White, am-

[1] Moore, *Am. Diplomacy*, 215, 216.
[2] Moore, *Int. Arbitrations*, I., 962–989; Senate Com. on For. Rels., *Compilation of Reports*, VIII., 389–425.

bassador to Germany; Seth Low; Stanford Newel;
Captain A. T. Mahan; Captain William Crozier; and
Frederick William Holls, as secretary and counsel.
The other governments sent men of equal standing
—statesmen, diplomats, jurists, and soldiers.

In calling the conference the czar referred to the
overwhelming economic burden imposed upon the
people by the "armed peace" of Europe, and proposed as one of the principal topics for discussion
the possible means of "placing a limit upon the
progressive increase of land and naval armaments."[1]
The press of Europe at once characterized the proposed gathering of diplomats as the "Disarmament
Conference," and when it became evident, in the
early sessions, that this subject could not be safely
discussed, the majority of the newspaper correspondents declared the movement a failure. But such
was far from being the case. Besides discussing a
number of important international questions, and
draughting new conventions for the regulation of
warfare on land and sea, the conference made a great
stride forward in the adoption of "A Convention
for the Peaceful Adjustment of International Differences." This document, which was ratified by all
the powers represented at the conference except
Turkey,[2] and later indorsed by the Pan-American
Conference of 1901, offers three methods of settling
disputes without an appeal to arms: (1) through
good offices and mediation; (2) through interna-

---

[1] *Foreign Relations*, 1898, pp. 541, 551.   [2] *Ibid.*, p. 691.

tional commissions of inquiry; (3) by submission
to the permanent court of arbitration provided for
in the convention.[1]

The tender of good offices is nothing new in international relations, but under the provisions of this
treaty the signatory powers have the right to make
an appeal, such as President Roosevelt made to
Russia and Japan in 1905, without incurring resentment.[2]   International commissions of inquiry constitute a novel method of procedure in "differences
of an international nature involving neither honor
nor vital interests, and arising from a difference of
opinion on points of fact."   The practical value of
this provision was tested during the Russo-Japanese
war of 1904, when England and Russia appointed
an international commission of inquiry to investigate an attack by the Russian Baltic Squadron upon
a fleet of English fishing-vessels off Dogger Bank.
By the time the facts were ascertained popular excitement had subsided, and Russia quietly agreed to
pay an indemnity.[3]   In such times of great national
excitement the value of a moment gained is incal-
culable.

By far the most important work of the peace
conference of 1899, however, was the creation of a
permanent court of arbitration.   To this step Ger-

[1] On the proceedings of the conference, see Holls, *Peace Conference at The Hague;* White, *Autobiography,* II., chaps. xlv.–xlix.
[2] See p. 118 above.
[3] Hershey, *Int. Law and Diplomacy of the Russo-Japanese War,*
chap. viii.

many, which at that time had never submitted any
dispute to arbitration, was stoutly opposed, and her
delegates had inflexible instructions to vote against
any such proposal; but this opposition, which threatened to defeat the whole plan, was finally overcome
by Andrew D. White, who made a skilful and con-
vincing appeal to the emperor.   The Hague court,
as finally constituted, was to consist of a large body
of judges, each of the signatory powers being allowed to appoint as many as four, for terms of six
years.   The judges so appointed were to constitute
a permanent court, but they were not to sit as a
collective body, or to receive pay unless called upon
to serve.   When two or more nations should have
a dispute to be adjudicated, the convention provided
that they should select any desired number of arbitrators for the special tribunal from the general list
or panel of the court, and sign "a special act (compromis), in which the subject of the difference shall
be precisely defined, as well as the extent of the
powers of the arbitrators.   This act implies an agreement by each party to submit in good faith to the
award."

The court held its first session September 15, 1902,
to hear the case of the United States vs. Mexico
in the matter of the Pious Fund of the Californias.
The tribunal was composed of five judges.   The
trust fund under dispute was started by Jesuits in
the seventeenth century for the conversion of the
California Indians; and after the expulsion of the

order from Mexico the fund was administered first by the king of Spain and later by the independent government of Mexico. After the purchase of upper California by the United States in 1848, Mexico refused to pay any part of the income to the Catholic bishops of that state, who brought their case in 1868 before a mixed claims commission, which decided in their favor. Mexico paid the accrued interest, but failed to keep it up. In 1891 the state department took up the claim, and Mexico finally agreed to submit the question to the Hague court. That tribunal decided that under the principle of *res judicata* Mexico was bound by the decision of the commission of 1868 to pay to the United States, for the benefit of the archbishop of San Francisco and the bishop of Monterey, the interest that had accrued since that date, and for the future an annuity of $43,050.99.[1]

The second case to be referred to the Hague court grew out of the intervention of Germany, Great Britain, and Italy in Venezuela in 1902, and involved the question as to whether these powers had acquired by the use of force any rights which other creditor nations did not possess.[2] A third case arose out of a dispute between Japan on the one side and Great Britain, Germany, and France on the other, as to the right of Japan to tax buildings erected on land held by foreigners under perpetual leases. The United States and several other powers were also

---

[1] *Foreign Relations*, 1902, App. II.
[2] See chap. xvi., below.

interested in the matter, but on the promise of Japan
to accord them like treatment with the litigant powers they refrained from entering as parties to the
suit.   The court held, in a decision rendered May
22, 1905, that the incorporation of the foreign settlements with the Japanese communes, following
the admission of Japan to full international standing
and the surrender by foreigners of exterritorial rights,
did not interfere with the permanent leases or render
the buildings erected on them subject to taxation.[1]
A fourth case, also decided in 1905, was a dispute
between Great Britain and France as to the meaning
of certain provisions of the treaty of 1862, by which
they agreed reciprocally to respect the independence
of the sultans of Muscat and Zanzibar.   The decision,
though somewhat in the nature of a compromise, was
in the main favorable to England.[2]

The Hague convention did not bind any power
to submit any dispute to arbitration: resort to the
court was purely optional.   But during the years
1903, 1904, and 1905 thirty-three separate treaties
were concluded between different European powers,
binding the contracting parties to submit to the
Hague court differences which were of a legal nature
or which related to the interpretation of treaties, provided they did not affect " the vital interests, the in-

[1] *Revue Générale de Droit Int. Pub.*, XII., 492–516; *Foreign
Relations*, 1905, p. 692.
[2] *Archives Diplomatiques*, 1905, p. 554; *Revue Générale de Droit
Int. Pub.*, XIII., 145.

dependence, or the honor of the two contracting states." [1] The value of these treaties, most of which were modelled after the Anglo-French treaty of October 14, 1903, is somewhat uncertain; many people think them not worth the paper they are written on. While, of course, the reservation of questions affecting honor or vital interests is comprehensive enough to cover almost any question that a state chooses to include, nevertheless such a treaty enables a weaker state to make a dignified demand for arbitration and puts the burden of a refusal on the stronger state. Then, too, once the habit of arbitrating minor differences is formed, it is only a step to the settlement of more important matters by the same means.

November 1, 1904, Secretary Hay and the French ambassador signed a limited compulsory arbitration treaty similar to the ones above referred to, and treaties of like tenor were later signed with Germany, Switzerland, Portugal, and Great Britain; while assurances were received from Italy, Russia, Mexico, and other powers that they were ready to conclude similar agreements. [2] The first batch of treaties was submitted to the Senate in December, 1904, but they were amended in such a way as to render them unacceptable to the president. The first protest against them in the original form came from certain southern senators, who feared that under their terms the foreign holders of the repu-

[1] *Am. Journal of Int. Law*, I., 681.
[2] *Foreign Relations*, 1904, p. 9.

diated bonds of some of the southern states might
bring their claims before the Hague court; and
Senator Bacon proposed an amendment excluding
from arbitration under these treaties claims against
any state of the Union.

But opposition of a wholly different character
soon developed. The interpretation put by the
executive upon one clause of the treaties seemed
to strike a blow at the constitutional prerogatives
of the Senate. The difficulty arose as to the meaning of the word "agreement" in the second article,
which read as follows: "In each individual case
the high contracting parties, before appealing to the
Permanent Court of Arbitration, shall conclude a
special agreement defining clearly the matter in dispute." The question was raised as to whether the
term "agreement" meant the same as treaty and
required the concurrence of the Senate, or whether
the president could make such an agreement without the consent of the Senate. When it was found
that the president and Secretary Hay took the latter view, an amendment was proposed substituting
the word "treaty" for "agreement" in the article
above quoted. This amendment not only met the
objection raised by the southern senators, but it
further safeguarded the constitutional prerogatives
of the Senate.

During the previous thirty years no less than
fifteen arbitration agreements had been entered
into by the president without the concurrence of the

Senate and without general treaties;[1] and President Roosevelt showed no small degree of impatience and even of irritation at the proposed amendment. In a letter to Senator Cullom, chairman of the committee on foreign relations, February 10, 1905, he stated his views at length, and declared that if the proposed amendment should be adopted he would not refer the treaties back to the other powers for ratification, for in the amended form "they probably represent not a step forward, but a slight step backward as regards the question of international arbitration."

This protest was of no avail. The next day the Senate ratified the treaties in the amended form, the amendment being adopted by a vote of 50 to 9; the nine votes sustaining the president were cast by the committee on foreign relations. Even stanch supporters of the president, like Senator Lodge, opposed his views in this matter. The Senate was undoubtedly greatly influenced by the fact, which had just come to their knowledge, that the president had committed the government to a radically new policy in regard to Santo Domingo affairs without consulting them. It was felt that he was too impatient of restraint on his power to manage international questions, and that he apparently did not fully appreciate the constitutional limitations imposed upon the executive.

The view taken by the Senate, that under our

[1] *Senate Docs.*, 58 Cong., 3 Sess., No. 158, pp. 8, 9.

constitutional system each agreement defining the
questions at issue and the extent of the powers of
the arbitrators should be submitted to it for ratification, did not nullify the compulsory features of the
treaties, for the Senate as a co-ordinate branch of
the government is just as much bound as the president to carry out in good faith obligations to foreign
powers.   All it demanded was the right to pass upon
such agreements, and to decide whether they came
within the scope of the general treaties.   The question of the repudiated bonds of certain states is a
case in point.   A president might decide that they
were in the class of questions covered by the general
arbitration treaties, while the Senate might take a
different view.   That the action of the Senate was
not a blow at the principle of arbitration was pointed
out at the time by reference to the past record of
that body.   It appeared that of the forty-four arbitration treaties that had been submitted to the
Senate prior to those under discussion, forty-three
had been ratified and one rejected; of the forty-
three ratified, six had been ratified with amendments
and thirty-seven without.[1]   Wisely or unwisely, the
Constitution does impose restraints upon the executive in matters of foreign policy.   At any rate, the
Senate acted clearly within its rights, and it was
unfortunate that the president should have repudiated the treaties because the Senate undertook
to safeguard its constitutional prerogatives by strik-

[1] *Senate Docs.*, 58 Cong., 3 Sess., No. 158, p. 8.

ing out an ambiguous word and substituting one about which there could be no misunderstanding.

While the Hague court has not measured up to the hopes of its friends in all respects, it has far surpassed the expectations of its enemies. A great discouragement to many of its friends was the fact that some of the powers which had participated in the conference of 1899 were soon engaged in wars, but it should be remembered that the questions involved in the Boer War of 1899–1902, and in the Russo-Japanese War of 1904–1905, were not of such a character as to admit of judicial determination, and were quite beyond the scope and intent of the convention which created the court. The first conference left many questions unsettled and expressed the hope that future gatherings would continue the work. In October, 1904, President Roosevelt proposed a second conference,[1] and while favorable replies were received from most of the powers, Russia declined to take part during the continuance of the war with Japan. After the close of that war, the Russian government took the matter up and issued invitations for a meeting during the summer of 1906, which at the suggestion of the United States was postponed so as not to interfere with the meeting of the Pan - American Conference at Rio Janeiro, already arranged. June 15, 1907, was finally set for the meeting of the second conference at The Hague, and the South American republics were in-

[1] *Foreign Relations*, 1904, p. 10.

vited, so that it might be in the fullest sense a
world conference.[1] Although this body did not decree disarmament, or even place a limit on military
and naval expenditures, nevertheless it reaffirmed
the principle of international arbitration, took steps
looking to the establishment of an international
prize court, defined more clearly the rights and
duties of neutrals, and adopted new rules relating to
warfare on land and sea.   Disarmament is an ideal
to be dreamed of; arbitration is a practical method
of avoiding war, capable of indefinite extension.
Apart from other considerations, international congresses have a most beneficial influence in making
the leading men of the world acquainted with one
another, and thereby removing national prejudice
and establishing lines of pacification.

[1] *Am. Journal of Int. Law*, I., 431-440.

CHAPTER XV

THE MONROE DOCTRINE AND WORLD POLITICS
(1895–1902)

SOME one has remarked that there is a latent tendency in the human mind to define a thing in order to avoid the necessity of understanding it. This is strikingly illustrated in the case of the Monroe Doctrine. Certain writers have undertaken to determine precisely what President Monroe and John Quincy Adams had in mind when the message of 1823 was being prepared, and to apply this standard to all subsequent appeals to the principle.[1] Such a method would relegate the Monroe Doctrine to the realm of past issues, possessing merely an historical interest; for the international situation of 1823 can never be reproduced, and hence the demand for the application of President Monroe's celebrated declaration, with the precise meaning he gave it, can never again arise. But the public policy of a state develops just as the law of a state develops; and with the lapse of years the Monroe Doctrine has been modified to meet changing conditions, and has become

[1] On the original Monroe Doctrine, see Turner, *New West* (*Am. Nation*, XIV.), chap. xii.

more widely extended in its application than its authors ever contemplated. President Roosevelt expressed this idea very aptly when he said in 1905: " If we had refused to apply the Doctrine to changing conditions it would now be completely outworn, it would not meet any of the needs of the present day, and indeed would probably by this time have sunk into complete oblivion.   It is useful at home, and is meeting with recognition abroad because we have adapted our application of it to meet the growing and changing needs of the Hemisphere.   When we announce a policy, such as the Monroe Doctrine, we thereby commit ourselves to the consequences of the policy, and those consequences from time to time alter." [1]

Of the various appeals that have been made to the Monroe Doctrine since its first enunciation, some may be regarded as unwarranted extensions and others as natural developments of the original declaration.   Owing to wide divergences of opinion as to whether this principle was really involved in certain specific cases, and the tendency that politicians have shown at times to juggle with it, critics have called it the " will-o'-the-wisp of American politics," and have applied the term Pseudo-Monroeism to some of its later applications; but in spite of all such attacks, it stands to-day as " the cardinal principle of American foreign policy."

The various phases of development through which

[1] *Foreign Relations*, 1905, p. xxxiii.

the Monroe Doctrine has passed need not here be discussed. Understanding by it the broad principle that American interests are unalterably opposed to the establishment of new European colonies in America, or the interference of European powers in the political concerns of the independent states of this continent, it is safe to assert that it has received the almost unanimous sanction of American statesmen of all shades of political belief since its enunciation. The nearest approach to its abandonment was in President Grant's administration, when Secretary Hamilton Fish made an unsuccessful attempt to get the powers of Europe to co-operate with the United States, or at least to acquiesce, in a settlement of the Cuban question.[1]

The failure of Secretaries Blaine and Frelinghuysen, a few years later, to oust England from the joint control of the isthmian canal, which had been conceded to her by the Clayton-Bulwer treaty, on the ground that the expanded interests of the United States had operated to annul that agreement,[2] tended to bring the Monroe Doctrine into further disrepute, but it was suddenly revived and rehabilitated in a most striking and sensational way by President Cleveland in the Venezuelan affair.

The most striking feature of this case was that

[1] Latané, *Dipl. Relations of the U. S. and Spanish America*, 163-173.
[2] Sparks, *National Development* (*Am. Nation*, XXIII.), chap. xiii.

Mr. Olney, in a despatch of July 20, 1895, appealed to the Monroe Doctrine by name and claimed that it was a principle of international law, not because of its assertion by President Monroe and succeeding presidents, but as an American statement of a well recognized principle — namely, the right of a state to intervene in a controversy between other states when it deems its own interests involved.   President Cleveland, who made this despatch his own, found an aggressive policy a complete success: Congress promptly made the necessary appropriation for the expenses of the boundary commission which he proposed to appoint; and thus, for the first time since its enunciation over seventy years before, the Monroe Doctrine received something approaching legislative sanction.[1]   No sooner was the commission appointed than the British government, which had taken issue quite hotly with Mr. Olney's arguments, changed front completely and assumed a most friendly tone, placing at the disposal of the commission all the information in its archives.[2]

Strange to say the Venezuelan incident was the beginning of a warm friendship between the United States and England, which soon showed itself in the cordial diplomatic support given by England during and after the war with Spain, and in the relinquish-

[1] Foster, *Century of Am. Diplomacy*, 477.
[2] Latané, *Dipl. Relations of the U. S. and Spanish America*, 273–284; cf. Dewey, *National Problems* (*Am. Nation*, XXIV.), chap. xix.

ment of the principle of joint control in the canal.
The Hay-Pauncefote treaty of 1901 frankly recognized the paramount interest of the United States
in this enterprise, and left it free to proceed with it
in its own way.[1] Great Britain's surrender of her
interests in the American canal was the natural and
logical outcome of the interest she had acquired in
the Suez Canal by the purchase of the French holdings in 1875 and the occupation of Egypt in 1881;
"for it was unreasonable that any nation should
control one of the two great artificial arteries of
world commerce, and at the same time retain at
least a half interest in the other." [2]

In most of the discussions of the question prior
to the war with Spain, the Monroe Doctrine found
its sanction in the doctrine of the political separation of the two hemispheres. The use of the term
"hemisphere" proved unfortunate and misleading;
for, no sooner had the United States decided to retain the Philippine Islands than the cry arose that it
had abrogated the Monroe Doctrine; that having in-
vaded the eastern hemisphere, it could not consistently continue to keep the powers of Europe out of
the western hemisphere. Although this line of argument carried great weight both in this country and
in Europe, it was nevertheless based on a logical

---

[1] See p. 207 above.
[2] Hart, *Monroe Doctrine in its Territorial Extent and Application* (U. S. Naval Institute, *Proceedings*, XXXII., No. 3, pp. 785,
789).

fallacy. It is manifest to one who reads the official papers relating to this question. that, in using the terms "eastern hemisphere" and "western hemisphere," the authors from President Monroe to President Roosevelt had reference to the spheres of European and American interests respectively. While the term "western hemisphere" is fairly descriptive of the sphere of American interests and is frequently employed, the term "eastern hemisphere" is rarely ever used in this connection, for the simple reason that it is not regarded as synonymous with the sphere of European interests. The coast of Asia never came within the scope of these discussions, for the reason that it constitutes a third sphere with a set of primary interests of its own.

When the United States acquired the Philippines its main object was to use them as a base for the protection of its commercial interests in China, then on the point, apparently, of being partitioned out among the powers.[1] At that time American trade with China was second only to that of England, and the United States had as much right there as any other power; but the seizure of a portion of Chinese territory, being contrary to the cherished American principle of non-interference in the internal affairs of an independent nation, was out of the question. It seemed wise, therefore, to the administration to hold the Philippine Islands, which the fortune of war had brought within its grasp. The permanent

[1] See p. 72 above.

occupation of these islands has undoubtedly brought the country more fully into the current of world politics; but the proposition that it will lead to interference in the internal politics of any European state or give any European state a pretext for interfering in the domestic concerns of any state on this continent cannot logically be maintained. There is no necessary reason why the events of 1898 should in any way disturb the existing principle that governs the political relations of Europe and America in their domestic spheres. The Monroe Doctrine has always been regarded as a sort of *quid pro quo;* as Jefferson said in his letter of advice to Monroe: "Our first and fundamental maxim should be, never to entangle ourselves in the broils of Europe. Our second, never to suffer Europe to meddle with cisatlantic affairs"; and as Mr. Olney, in the course of the Venezuelan affair, expressed it: "American non-intervention in Europe implied European non-intervention in America." As long as this principle is maintained there can be no fair charge of inconsistency.

While the United States has always been a world power in the sense that its influence has been exerted, and for the most part effectively, in the interests of peace, humanity, and neutral rights, the war with Spain brought new prestige to the republic and gave it added weight in the councils of the nations. The enlarged activity of the United States in international affairs is, it is true, attended with new dangers and new responsibilities; but it is no longer a weak and struggling nation, whose main desire is to be let alone.   There is no longer any need for the isolation of the early days.   For the benefit of those who deplore the growing activity of the nation in the field of world politics as an unwise departure from the teachings of the fathers, it may be well to recall the ground on which Washington based the policy of isolation which he bequeathed as a legacy to his countrymen.   "With me," he said, "a predominant motive has been to endeavor to gain time to our country to settle and mature its yet recent institutions, and to progress without interruption to that degree of strength and consistency which is necessary to give it, humanly speaking, the command of its own fortunes."[1]   That time has long since elapsed; and the United States has now command not only of its own fortunes but of the fortunes of others, and cannot shirk the responsibilities that such a position brings with it.

One of the first acts in the "new rôle of a world power" was the despatch of troops to China in 1900 to co-operate with the European powers in the relief of the legations at Peking.[2]   American participation in this expedition was not due to a desire to intervene in the affairs of the Chinese empire; next to the rescue of the minister, the object was to see that the powers of Europe did not go too far in their

---

[1] Richardson, *Messages and Papers*, I., 224.
[2] See p. 107 above.

interference.   The United States more than any other power was anxious at this juncture to preserve
the integrity of the Chinese empire and the independence of the Chinese government.   Japan was
in thorough sympathy with that purpose, though
the present tendency of her policy seems to be
towards the assertion of the paramount interest of
Japan in the affairs of eastern Asia, and the development of a sort of Monroe Doctrine of her own for the
protection of China against the exploitation of foreign powers, including the United States.   The part
played by the United States in the formation of the
new Japanese doctrine is almost exactly analogous
to the part played by England in the formation of
the Monroe Doctrine.   In each case the new doctrine
was soon turned against the nation that assisted in
its formation.

Those who thought that the war with Spain had
brought about the abrogation of the Monroe Doctrine were soon disabused.   It would have been
strange indeed if the United States, after maintaining in weakness and with great effort the Monroe
Doctrine, had surrendered it in the time of strength.
American participation with the powers of Europe
in the peace conference at The Hague in 1899 was
taken by many Americans to mark the end of the
old order and the beginning of a new era in American
diplomacy; but, contrary to their expectations, this
meeting was made the occasion for the most emphatic and effective declaration of adherence to the

Monroe Doctrine that has ever been made to the nations of Europe. The treaty was signed by the American delegation under the express reservation of a declaration previously read in open session that "Nothing contained in this convention shall be so construed as to require the United States of America to depart from its traditional policy of not intruding upon, interfering with, or entangling itself in the political questions or policy or internal administration of any foreign state; nor shall anything contained in the said convention be construed to imply a relinquishment by the United States of America of its traditional attitude toward purely American questions." [1]

The Hague conference was concerned with questions of general international interest, and had no bearing upon the internal affairs of any state, European or American; but such was not the character of the conference which convened at Algeciras, Spain, December 15, 1905, for the purpose of instituting certain administrative reforms in Morocco. The United States decided, in view of its rights in Morocco under a treaty of 1880, to take part in the conference. Having no political interests at stake, its delegates were able to offer impartial advice; and they were instrumental in composing many of the differences that arose during the proceedings, especially those between Germany and France. The treaty was signed by the American representatives under a

---

[1] *Foreign Relations*, 1899, p. xxxvi.

reservation somewhat similar to that read at the
Hague conference, to the effect that the United
States acquiesced in the regulations and declarations
of the conference and accepted their application to
American citizens and interests in Morocco "without assuming obligation or responsibility for the
enforcement thereof." [1] Not satisfied with this declaration, the Senate attached to its resolution of
ratification a further disclaimer to the effect that
the participation of the United States in the conference was solely for the protection of its commerce
and the life, liberty, and property of its citizens in
Morocco, and was "without purpose to depart from
the traditional American foreign policy which for-
bids participation by the United States in the settlement of political questions which are entirely European in their scope." [2]

This determination not to interfere in the internal
politics of European states has not prevented diplomatic protests in the name of humanity against
the harsh treatment accorded the Jews in Roumania.
The United States had more than a philanthropic
interest in this matter, however, as was shown by
Secretary Hay in his note of July 17, 1902, when he
stated that the enforced emigration of the Jews from
Roumania in a condition of utter destitution was
"the mere transplantation of an artificially produced

[1] *Foreign Relations*, 1905, p. 678.
[2] Resolution of December 12, 1906, in *Am. Pol. Science Review*,
I., 330.

diseased growth to a new place"; and that, as the
United States was practically their only place of
refuge, we had a clearly established right of remon-
strance.[1] As regards the treatment of Jews in Russia, information has repeatedly been sought through
diplomatic channels as to the extent of destitution
among them, and permission has been requested for
the distribution of relief funds raised in the United
States. Such inquiries have been so framed as to
amount to diplomatic protests. In his annual message of 1904 President Roosevelt went further and
openly expressed the horror of the nation at the
massacre of the Jews at Kishenef.[2] These protests
were, however, purely diplomatic in character; there
was not the slightest hint at intervention.

So far from abandoning the Monroe Doctrine,
President Roosevelt has given it greater prominence
than any other president. His messages to Congress
as well as his public addresses throughout the country are filled with discussions of this principle of
policy and of the rights and duties in connection
with it. The fullest recognition of the Monroe Doctrine on the part of a European power came from
Germany in 1901, when, on December 11, the German ambassador, in informing the state department
of the intention of his government to use forcible
measures in the collection of claims of its citizens
against Venezuela, declared that the German government had "no purpose or intention to make even

[1] *Foreign Relations*, 1902, p. 910.   [2] *Ibid.*, 1904, p. xliii.

the smallest acquisition of territory on the South American continent or the islands adjacent." [1]   This action was taken in order to prevent a subsequent appeal to the Monroe Doctrine, and was regarded as an open acknowledgment of that principle.

The president, of course, received earlier intimations of Germany's intentions, and had already defined his views in his message of December 3 as follows: "This doctrine has nothing to do with the commercial relations of any American power, save that it in truth allows each of them to form such as it desires.   In other words, it is really a guarantee of the commercial independence of the Americas. We do not ask under this doctrine for any exclusive commercial dealings with any other American state. We do not guarantee any state against punishment if it misconducts itself, provided that punishment does not take the form of the acquisition of territory by any non-American power." [2]

The intervention of the powers in Venezuela in 1902 gave rise to many complicated questions, and led President Roosevelt later on to a different solution of this question.   With reference to Santo Domingo he took the position that, as the forcible collection of public debts from an American by a European power would practically lead to a weakening or violation of the Monroe Doctrine, the only way out of the difficulty in such cases was for the United States to exercise " an international police

---

[1] *Foreign Relations*, 1901, p. 195.   [2] *Ibid.*, p. xxxvi.

power"[1] and act as the agent in such collection.
This conclusion has been called the Roosevelt corol-
lary of the Monroe Doctrine.   The problem here presented is the most difficult that has ever arisen in
connection with the Monroe Doctrine, and one of
the most perplexing in the whole range of modern
diplomacy; further consideration of it will be reserved for the next chapter.

[1] See p. 278 below.

CHAPTER XVI

THE FORCIBLE COLLECTION OF PUBLIC DEBTS
(1901–1907)

CLAIMS of citizens of one country against the government of another may arise in several ways. They may be based, in the first place, on injury to person, such as cruel or inhuman treatment, false imprisonment, or mob violence. Where such injuries are real (whether committed directly, by the officers or authorized agents of the government, or indirectly, by the failure of the government to afford protection), and where legal remedy is denied, it is the right and duty of the state whose citizens have suffered to come to their assistance and to demand redress.

A second class of claims arises from the destruction or confiscation of the property of resident aliens. The property may be taken for military purposes as a matter of necessity; it may be destroyed in the ordinary course of military operations; it may be taken by forced loans; or it may be pillaged by soldiers or by mobs. The general rule of international law applying to such cases is that resident aliens are entitled to no greater exemption or protection than citizens.

There is a third and distinct class of claims, however, in regard to which the practice of states is not so well settled: they are claims for breach of contract, usually called "pecuniary claims"; and the contracts on which they are based may be government bonds, charters, franchises, or concessions, the guarantee of dividends on investments, or contracts for furnishing military supplies or for constructing public works. This class of claims has received little attention from writers on international law, for the reason that states have in the past usually drawn a sharp distinction between contractual and other claims, largely disregarding the former.

In 1848 Lord Palmerston stated in a circular despatch, which has been much quoted, that the government of Great Britain had usually considered it undesirable that its subjects should invest their capital in loans to foreign governments, instead of employing it in profitable undertakings at home; and that with a view to discouraging hazardous loans to foreign governments the British government had hitherto thought it best to abstain from taking up as international questions complaints made by British subjects against foreign states. This policy was reaffirmed by Lord Salisbury in 1880.[1]

The policy of the United States, which is substantially in accord with the above, is well summarized

[1] Hall, *Int. Law* (5th ed.), 281 *n.*

in a despatch of Secretary Bayard, dated June 24, 1885:

"1. All that our Government undertakes, when the claim is merely contractual, is to interpose its good offices; in other words, to ask the attention of the foreign sovereign to the claim; and this is only done when the claim is one susceptible of strong and clear proof.

"2. If the sovereign appealed to denies the validity of the claim or refuses its payment, the matter drops, since it is not consistent with the dignity of the United States to press, after such a refusal or denial, a contractual claim for the repudiation of which, by the law of nations, there is no redress." [1]

The intervention of Germany, Great Britain, and Italy in Venezuela in 1902, for the purpose of collecting debts alleged to be due their subjects, raised issues which greatly embarrassed the United States, and which had not come up in such an acute form since the somewhat similar action of France, England, and Spain in Mexico nearly half a century before.[2] The German claims may be taken as typical: the principal one was for seven-per-cent. dividends guaranteed by the Venezuelan government on the capital stock of a railroad built by German subjects at a cost of nearly $20,000,000, and for the recovery

---

[1] Moore, *Digest of Int. Law*, VI., 716.
[2] Dunning, *Reconstruction* (*Am. Nation*, XXII.), chap. x; see also Latané, *Dipl. Relations of the U. S. and Spanish America*, chap. v.

of interest seven years in arrears on five-per-cent. public bonds issued to cover the above; another claim amounting to about $400,000 was for the recovery of forced loans and military requisitions made during the civil wars of 1898–1900.[1]   The British demands included claims for destruction of property during the civil wars and for the recovery of interest on the public debt of 1881.[2]

The German claims were brought to the attention of the United States government by the German ambassador December 11, 1901.[3] Their dubious character, regarded from the stand-point of international law, led Germany to make a frank avowal of her intentions to the United States,[4] and to secure for her action the acquiescence of that government. After disavowing any intention of violating the Monroe Doctrine, the German ambassador stated that his government had decided to "ask the Venezuelan government to make a declaration immediately, that it recognizes in principle the correctness of these demands, and is willing to accept the decision of a mixed commission, with the object of having them determined and assured in all their details." To this note Secretary Hay replied December 16, 1901, thanking the German government for its voluntary and frank declaration, and stating that he did not consider it necessary to discuss the claims in ques-

---

[1] *Foreign Relations*, 1901, p. 193; 1903, p. 429.
[2] *Senate Docs.*, 58 Cong., 2 Sess., No. 316, pp. 292 et seq.
[3] *Foreign Relations*, 1901, p. 192.   [4] See p. 266 above.

tion; but he called attention to President Roosevelt's reference to the Monroe Doctrine in his annual message of December 3, 1901.[1]

After a year of fruitless negotiations it was announced that, "owing to the evasive attitude" of President Castro, the German government proposed, in conjunction with Great Britain, to establish a pacific blockade of Venezuelan harbors.[2] Secretary Hay at once directed Ambassador Tower to say to the German government that the United States adhered to the position taken by it in relation to the Cretan blockade of 1897,[3] and did "not acquiesce in any extension of the doctrine of pacific blockade which may adversely affect the rights of states not parties to the controversy, or discriminate against the commerce of neutral nations," and that the United States reserved all its rights in the premises.[4] The powers then proposed to establish a "warlike blockade," but "without any declaration of war."[5] This device was resorted to at the suggestion of the German government, in order to avoid a formal declaration of war, which could not be made without the consent of the Bundesrath. Meanwhile Venezuela's gun-boats had been seized and her ports blockaded, acts which Mr. Balfour admitted on the floor of the House of Commons constituted a state of

[1] See p. 267 above.
[2] *Foreign Relations*, 1903, p. 419.   [3] *Ibid.*, 1897, p. 255.
[4] *Ibid.*, 1903, p. 420; Moore, *Digest of Int. Law*, VII., p. 140.
[5] *Foreign Relations*, 1903, p. 454.

war; and on December 20 a formal blockade was announced in accordance with the law of nations, which created a status of belligerency.[1]

The hostilities thus commenced were brought to a close in February, 1903, by the diplomatic intervention of the United States.   As the result of negotiations with the powers, conducted on behalf of Venezuela by Herbert W. Bowen, the American minister, an agreement was reached in which Venezuela recognized the justice of a part of the claims and promised to set aside thirty per cent. of her customs receipts for their payment.   The powers, on the other hand, agreed to submit their claims to the arbitration of mixed commissions.   The situation was further complicated by the demands of the blockading powers that the sums ascertained by the mixed commissions to be due them should be paid in full before anything was paid on the claims of the peace powers.   Venezuela insisted that all her creditors be treated alike, and at the suggestion of President Roosevelt, who declined an invitation to act as arbitrator, it was finally agreed, May 7, 1903, that the demand for preferential treatment should be submitted to the Hague court.[2]

During the summer of 1903 ten mixed commissions sat at Caracas to adjudicate upon the claims of as many states against Venezuela.   The awards of these commissions are highly instructive, as they show the injustice of resorting to measures of coer-

[1] Moore, *Digest of Int. Law*, VII., 141.   [2] *Ibid.*, VI., 590, 591.

cion for the collection of pecuniary claims which have
not been submitted to arbitration; it appears that
there is a need for international justice and morality
on the part of the creditor powers as well as on the
part of the debtor nations. In the following table
the claims and awards are both expressed in *bolivars*,
worth about twenty cents in gold:

	Amt. of claims [1]	Amt. of awards [2]
Great Britain.	14,743,572	9,401,267
Germany	7,376,685	2,091,908
France	17,888,512	2,667,079
Spain..............	5,307,626	1,974,818
Belgium	14,921,805	10,898,643
Sweden and Norway..	1,047,701	174,359
The Netherlands.....	5,242,519	544,301
The United States ...	81,410,952	2,313,711
Mexico	2,893,040	2,577,328
Italy	39,844,258	5,785,962
	190,676,670	38,429,376

Before the Hague tribunal, Germany, Great Britain, and Italy claimed that they had acquired by
the use of force rights which the other creditor nations did not possess; while Belgium, France, Holland,
Mexico, Norway and Sweden, Spain, and the United
States demanded that all the creditors of Venezuela
should be treated alike. In the award, rendered
February 22, 1904, the tribunal decided that the
three allied powers were entitled to preferential pay-

[1] *Venezuelan Arbitrations of 1903 (Senate Docs.,* 58 Cong., 2
Sess., No. 316).
[2] *Foreign Relations,* 1904, p. 871.

ment; that Venezuela had recognized in principle
the justice of their claims in the protocols of February 13 and May 7, 1903, while she had not recognized
the claims of the neutral powers; that the latter
had profited to some extent by the operations of the
allies; and that their rights remained for the future
absolutely intact.[1]

Against President Roosevelt's position that the
coercion of an American state was not contrary to
the Monroe Doctrine, provided that it did "not take
the form of the acquisition of territory by any non-
American power," [2] Señor Drago, Argentine minister
of foreign affairs, vigorously protested in a note dated
December 29, 1902, containing a statement of the
"Calvo Doctrine," which takes its name from a celebrated Argentine publicist.   In his well-known work
on international law, Calvo contends that a state has
no right to take up, even as a matter of diplomatic
action, the pecuniary claims of its citizens against
another state.   This doctrine, which has received the
indorsement of most of the Latin-American states,
was so ably expounded in the note of the Argentine
minister that it is now usually known as the "Drago
Doctrine," though as stated by Drago it is less comprehensive and more specific than as enunciated by
Calvo.   One of Drago's contentions was that "the
collection of loans by military means implies terri-

---

[1] *Foreign Relations*, 1904, p. 506.   For a full report of the case,
see *Senate Docs.*, 58 Cong., 3 Sess., No. 119.
[2] See p. 267 above.

torial occupation to make them effective, and territorial occupation signifies the suppression or sub-
ordination of the governments of the countries on
which it is imposed."[1]

Should forcible collection of international claims
of a purely pecuniary origin be adopted as a general
practice by the great powers, the means of coercion
would have to be clearly defined, as well as the rights
of third parties.   Under present conditions, however,
the forcible collection of such claims raises several
questions of a very perplexing character.

The first consideration is one of equity between
the repudiating and the coercing state.   Intervention, such as that of England and Germany in Venezuela, coming in the midst of civil insurrection, en-
dangers the very existence of the state; and the
right to a continued existence is the most sacred of
all sovereign rights.   It is not always possible for a
state to pay its debts, and of that fact the state
itself is the sole judge; for if this question is to be
settled by foreign states, the very existence of that
state is at the mercy of its creditors.   The most that
a foreigner has the right to expect is that his claims
shall receive the same consideration as those of subjects.

The second consideration in intervention of this
kind involves the claims of third parties.   Intervening states are not the only ones holding claims
against the debtor state, yet when a settlement is

_____
[1] *Foreign Relations*, 1903, p. 1.

forced the coercing states usually demand preferential treatment, and in the Venezuelan case the Hague court sustained this claim.

A third and still more difficult problem is how far measures of coercion should be allowed to interfere with the commerce of the non-coercing states. This consideration raises the question as to the means to be employed in the act of coercion. The most effective measure falling short of war is " pacific blockade," but the United States does not recognize such a blockade as binding on third parties.

The only other effective measure of coercion seems to be the seizure of custom-houses and the collection of dues; but such a step frequently, though not necessarily, leads to the permanent occupation of territory, which in the case of American states is in direct conflict with the Monroe Doctrine. President Roosevelt's solution of this latter phase of the question is stated in his message of December 6, 1904: " Any country whose people conduct themselves well can count upon our hearty friendship. If a nation shows that it knows how to act with reasonable efficiency and decency in social and political matters, if it keeps order and pays its obligations, it need fear no interference from the United States. Chronic wrong-doing, or an impotence which results in a general loosening of the ties of civilized society, may in America, as elsewhere, ultimately require intervention by some civilized nation, and, in the western hemisphere, the adherence of the United States to the Monroe Doctrine may force the United States, however reluctantly, in flagrant cases of such wrong-doing or impotence, to the exercise of an international police power."[1]

The last clause of this message contains the principle upon which the president's Santo-Dominican policy has been based. The debt of Santo Domingo, as reported to the state department by Minister Dawson September 12, 1904, was $32,280,000; the estimated revenues under Dominican management of custom-houses were $1,850,000, and the proposed budget for current expenses was $1,300,000, leaving only $550,000 with which to meet the payments of interest, amounting during the ensuing year to $1,700,000, which, together with arrearages of $900,-000, made a total of $2,600,000.[2] About $22,000,000 of this debt was due to European creditors, and over $18,000,000 had been more or less formally recognized. Most of this indebtedness had been incurred by revolutionary or military chieftains who had at various times taken forcible possession of the government and hastened to raise all the money they could by the sale of bonds, leaving the responsibility with their successors. In view of the practical bankruptcy of the Dominican government, certain European powers intimated towards the close of 1904 that unless the United States would take charge of the Dominican customs and guarantee an equitable distribution of the revenue, they would be compelled in

[1] *Foreign Relations*, 1904, p. xli.   [2] *Ibid.*, 1905, p. 302.

the interests of their citizens to resort to measures of coercion.

December 30, 1904, Minister Dawson was directed by Secretary Hay to suggest to the Dominican government that it request the United States to take charge of its customs.[1]   In pursuance of this suggestion a protocol was concluded between Santo Domingo and the United States February 4, 1905, providing that the United States should guarantee the territorial integrity of the Dominican republic, take charge of its custom-houses, administer its finances, and settle its obligations, foreign as well as domestic.[2] In short, the Dominican republic was to be treated as a bankrupt corporation, and the United States was to act as receiver.   The Senate failed to ratify this treaty; but under a *modus vivendi* the president of Santo Domingo appointed a receiver of customs, named unofficially by President Roosevelt, who proceeded to administer the affairs of the republic, under the protection of the United States navy, in accordance with the original programme.[3]

The president's course met with determined opposition, both in and out of Congress, but as he was determined to have his way and continued to carry out his policy without the sanction of the Senate, that body finally decided that it would be best to

---

[1] *Foreign Relations*, 1905, p. 298.

[2] *Executive Docs.*, V., 58 Cong., 3 Sess.; Moore, *Digest of Int. Law*, VI., 518–529; *Foreign Relations*, 1905, pp. 298–391.

[3] *Ibid.*, pp. 365–370.

recognize the *modus vivendi* and give the arrangement a definite legal status.   February 25, 1907, the Senate signed a revised treaty with Santo Domingo, which omitted the territorial-guarantee clause, but provided that the president of the United States should appoint a general receiver of Dominican customs and such assistants as he might deem necessary; that the government of the United States should afford them such protection as might be necessary for the performance of their duties; and that until the bonded debt should be paid in full the Dominican republic should not increase its debt except with the consent of the United States.[1]   In the mean time, under the *interim* arrangement, conditions in Santo Domingo had greatly improved, the customs receipts had nearly doubled, and the creditors had agreed to compromise their claims, so that the total debt at the time the above treaty was ratified amounted to not more than $17,000,000.[2]

President Roosevelt's policy undoubtedly warded off serious difficulty in the case of Santo Domingo, but the ultimate effects of that policy are not yet evident; for, if it be taken as a precedent that the United States will in every case assume responsibility for the payment of the debts of American states, the bankers of Europe will find it profitable to buy

---

[1] *Am. Journal of Int. Law*, I., Official Documents, 231.
[2] Hollander, "Convention of 1907 between the U. S. and the Dominican Republic," in *Am. Journal of Int. Law*, I., 287.

up all doubtful claims against American states and urge their governments to press for payment. Our navy would thus be converted into a debt-collecting agency for the powers of Europe, and the only escape from such a predicament would be the establishment of a protectorate over the weaker Latin-American states, and the imposition upon them of a provision like the "Platt Amendment," [1] by which Cuba has bound herself not to contract any foreign debt without the consent of the United States "the payment of which cannot be provided for by the ordinary revenues of the island."

There is one other solution of the question: at the Second International American Conference, held in the city of Mexico in 1901, a treaty was drawn up containing the following clause: "The high contracting parties agree to submit to arbitration all claims for pecuniary loss or damage which may be presented by their respective citizens, and which can not be amicably adjusted through diplomatic channels, and when said claims are of sufficient importance to warrant the expenses of arbitration." [2] It provided, further, that all controversies of this character should be submitted to the Hague court for arbitration, unless both parties should prefer that a special tribunal be organized. This treaty was signed by the representatives of seventeen powers, but it was

[1] See p. 179 above.
[2] *Senate Docs.*, 57 Cong., 1 Sess., No. 330; *Foreign Relations*, 1905, p. 650.

ratified only by Guatemala, Salvador, Peru, Honduras, the United States, and Mexico.[1]

The question of the forcible collection of pecuniary claims was also given a place on the programme of the Third International Conference of American States, which met at Rio Janeiro in July, 1906; but as the majority of the states represented were debtor states, it was not deemed advisable for the conference to indorse the "Drago Doctrine," as some of its members urged. The question was simply referred back to the governments represented, with the recommendation that they consider the advisability of inviting the second peace conference at The Hague, in 1907, to "consider the question of the forcible collection of public debts and the best means tending to diminish conflicts which have their origin in pecuniary claims." [2]

The Hague conference, after an animated discussion, finally adopted the proposals of General Horace Porter, of the American delegation, in the following terms:

"The contracting powers agree not to have recourse to armed force for the recovery of contract debts claimed from the government of one country by the government of another country as being due to its citizens.

---

[1] Moore, *Digest of Int. Law*, VII., 95; *Foreign Relations*, 1905, p. 653.

[2] Reinsch, "Third International Conference of American States," in *Am. Pol. Sci. Review*, I., 189.

"This undertaking is, however, not applicable when the debtor state refuses or neglects to reply to an offer of arbitration, or, after accepting the offer, prevents any *compromis* from being agreed on, or, after the arbitration, fails to submit to the award." The adoption of this agreement by the vote of thirty-nine of the forty-four states represented in the conference marks a great gain for the cause of arbitration.[1]

[1] For a fuller discussion of certain phases of this question, see Latané, " Forcible Collection of International Debts," in *Atlantic Monthly*, October, 1906.

CHAPTER XVII

IMMIGRATION

(1880–1907)

THE year 1905 broke all previous records in the history of immigration to the United States, the number of immigrants recorded for the twelve months ending June 30 being 1,026,499. But the numerical strength of the movement was not its most serious aspect: the character of immigration has undergone radical changes in the past few years.[1] Prior to 1880 three-fourths of all persons who migrated to America came from the Celtic and Teutonic countries of northern and western Europe, mostly from the United Kingdom and Germany, while less than one per cent. came from Italy, Austria-Hungary, Russia, and Poland. About 1880 the numbers from the latter countries began to increase, and assumed larger and larger proportions, until in 1905 the Slavic and Iberian countries of eastern and southern Europe furnished nearly three-fourths of

[1] See Sparks, *National Development* (*Am. Nation*, XXIII.), chap. i.

the total.[1] The following table shows the racial elements for 1905: [2]

Italians (South)	186,390
Hebrews	129,910
Poles	102,137
Germans	82,360
Scandinavians	62,284
Irish	54,266
Slovaks	52,368
English	50,865
Magyars	46,030
Italians (North)	39,930
Croatians and Slovenians	35,104
Lithuanians	18,604
Finnish	17,012
Scotch	16,144
Ruthenians	14,473
Greeks	12,144
Bohemians and Moravians	11,757
French	11,347
Japanese	11,021
All others	72,353
Total	1,026,499

The very high rate of illiteracy among immigrants from southeastern Europe, together with racial, social, religious, and political distinctions of a fundamental character, renders them less assimilable, and therefore less desirable, than immigrants from northern Europe.

The stream of immigration always flows towards the relatively prosperous country, and its volume is a fair gauge of economic and industrial conditions.

[1] Commissioner-General of Immigration, *Report*, 1905, p. 110.
[2] *Ibid.*, p. 11.

The number of immigrants to the United States did
not reach the 100,000 mark in any one year until
1842, when 104,565 landed on our shores. By 1854
the number had risen to 427,833; and in that year
an anti-foreign agitation became a factor in American politics. The sudden increase was coincident
with hard times in Ireland, revolution in Germany,
and the development of the western country. The
financial depression of 1857 and the outbreak of the
Civil War reduced the number by 1862 to 72,183.
The year 1873 broke the record again, showing the
entry of 459,803 immigrants. The panic of that
year and the financial depression that followed reduced the number by 1878 to 138,469. There was
a sudden rise in 1880, and in 1882 the number reached
788,992, a figure not equalled again for twenty-one
years. The financial crisis of 1893 and the succeeding years of depression caused a drop to 229,299 by
1898. Since that time there has been a rapid increase, until now over 1,000,000 aliens come annually
to our shores.[1] President Roosevelt has called attention to the startling fact that the number of
immigrants in the single year 1905 exceeded the
entire number of colonists that came to America
during the one hundred and sixty-nine years which
elapsed between the first landing at Jamestown and
the Declaration of Independence.[2] As compared
with the total population of the country, however,

[1] Commissioner-General of Immigration, *Report*, 1905, pp. 42,
43.   [2] *Foreign Relations*, 1905, p. xlvi.

the percentage is lower than during the periods 1849–1854 and 1881–1882;[1] and there is, furthermore, a large emigration from this country of which no official record is kept, but it is considerably in excess of 200,000 a year.[2]

The general prosperity of America is undoubtedly the most important cause of immigration, for most of the immigrants come at the inducement of friends and relatives who have preceded them. Steamship agents testified in 1901 that from 40 to 55 per cent. of those who come to our shores have their passage prepaid by friends in this country; if to this be added those to whom money is sent from this side for the purchase of tickets abroad, the proportion taking passage at the expense of their friends would amount to about two-thirds of the whole.[3] The facility of transportation and the activity of steamship agents are powerful aids to emigration, but they do not, in the long-run, determine its direction.

Religious persecution, or rather anti-Semitism, which is a compound of religious persecution and race antagonism, is still an active cause of emigration from Russia, Austria-Hungary, and Roumania. These persecutions began in Russia about 1880 and continued for two or three years, when they ceased to some extent, but were renewed in 1891 and have

[1] Industrial Commission, *Report*, XIX., 958.
[2] Commissioner-General of Immigration, *Report*, 1906, p. 56.
[3] Industrial Commission, *Report*, XV., 95, 115, 118.

continued off and on until 1907. In three months of 1900 more than 20,000 Jews left Roumania, in a most helpless and pitiable condition; and many of them had to be assisted to emigrate by the agents of the Baron Hirsch Fund. There are still over 8,000,000 Jews in Europe, mostly in Russia, Austria, the Balkan States, and Germany, subject to more or less unfavorable discrimination and liable at any time to come in larger numbers to the United States. Some of the Jewish leaders are trying to check this movement for fear of arousing an anti-Semitic agitation here.[1]

It is frequently charged that criminality is much greater among foreign-born residents than among natives, but the statistics are absurdly misleading: the larger number of crimes are committed by persons between the ages of 20 and 45; and in this country 51 per cent. of the foreign-born are between those ages, as compared with 34 per cent. of the native-born. Then, too, the amount of criminality among males is from three to five times greater than among females, and the proportion of males among the foreign-born is very much higher than among the natives. When, therefore, the same sex and age classes are compared, it is found that the criminality of the foreign-born is only very slightly greater than among the natives.[2]

[1] Industrial Commission, *Report*, XV., 171, 245, 247; Hall, *Immigration*, 20–22.

[2] Industrial Commission, *Report*, XV., 287.

General Francis A. Walker, superintendent of the tenth and eleventh censuses, undertook to demonstrate that immigration, instead of reinforcing the population of the country, simply resulted in the replacement of native by foreign elements.   This may be true in so far as immigration has led to sharper competition and given rise to class distinctions, resulting in later marriages among native Americans in order to maintain their social superiority; but the decreasing birth-rate among native Americans cannot be attributed to this cause alone.[1]

The most serious social problem presented by the immigration of recent years is the tendency of the foreign-born to congregate in the slums of the larger cities: in 1900, while making up only a little over one-eighth of the total population of the United States, they formed one-fourth of the total population of the cities and a much larger proportion in many places; thus the foreign-born formed 47 per cent. of the population of Fall River, 39 per cent. of Duluth, 37 per cent. of New York, 35 per cent. of Boston, 34 per cent. of San Francisco and Chicago.[2] The tendency to congregate in the large cities is particularly marked among the Russians, Poles, Italians, and Irish.   This accumulation of colonies in the great cities is the principal obstacle to the assimilation of immigrants, which is the great desideratum. If they could be distributed more evenly throughout

[1] Industrial Commission, *Report*, **XV.**, 277.
[2] Hall, *Immigration*, 170.

the country, the process of Americanization would go on much faster.[1]

Various plans have been proposed for the distribution of immigrants on arrival, but with little or no success. The shiftlessness of the negro and the growing demand for farm laborers in the southern states have led certain states to solicit, through state agencies, the immigration of desirable persons, such action not being deemed a violation of the statute of 1885 prohibiting "any person, company, partnership, or corporation" from assisting or encouraging the importation of aliens under contract. This demand will hardly draw people out of the crowded cities, since the kind mainly wanted in the South are farm laborers with families. The Italian government and some of the steamship companies have expressed a desire, in which President Roosevelt has heartily acquiesced, to aid in the effort to divert Italian immigration from the northern cities to the southern states.[2]

As to the economic effects of immigration, there is great difference of opinion: it is claimed by some that immigrants add to the general productive force of the country, and that even the lower class of immigrants are desirable to do the rough work that has to be done. Others maintain that the rapid influx of foreigners of lower intelligence and lower standard of living tends to depress wages and to

[1] Cf. Hart, *National Ideals* (*Am. Nation*, XXVI.), chap. iii.
[2] *Foreign Relations*, 1905, pp. 567–571.

lessen the amount of employment available for American labor, and thus displaces higher by lower standards of living. The uneven distribution of immigrants in the several occupations and localities does undoubtedly work a hardship on those engaged in unskilled and unorganized occupations. In common labor—coal-mining, clothing and textile manufactures particularly — there have been overcrowding and displacement of native workmen, or of earlier immigrants, and consequent reduction of wages. The constant stream of immigrants going into these occupations has been one of the many disintegrating forces which organized labor in this country has had to encounter;[1] hence the restrictive legislation which Congress, through fear of the labor vote, has enacted in recent years.

After a careful study of the social and economic conditions surrounding the immigrants after settlement in America, Professor Mayo-Smith came to the conclusion that the tendency to assimilation was inevitable and dominant. As he put it: "Owing to the unorganized character of the immigration: to the lack of political and social connection between the immigrants and the home country; to the variety of elements which more or less neutralize one another; and to the powerful influence of the established institutions—assimilation to the one type is the natural and almost inevitable result. . . . It is not in unity of blood, but in unity of institutions

[1] Industrial Commission, *Report*, XIX., 966.

and social habits and ideals that we are to seek that which we call nationality." [1]

The restriction of immigration by legislative enactment presents many practical difficulties. The first restrictive measures, beginning in 1862, were directed against the trade in Chinese coolies. Successive acts passed during the next thirty years added to the excluded classes convicts, prostitutes, lunatics, idiots, paupers, contract laborers, persons suffering from a contagious or loathsome disease, and polygamists. An act of March 3, 1893, while not adding to the excluded classes, provided for a much more rigid and efficient system of inspection. In February, 1897, an act establishing an illiteracy test passed both houses of Congress, but was vetoed by President Cleveland. An act of March 3, 1903, imposed a head tax of two dollars on every alien passenger except from Canada, Cuba, Mexico, or Newfoundland, and attempted a complete codification of existing law: to the classes already excluded were added epileptics, persons previously insane, professional beggars, anarchists, procurers, and contract laborers who have been deported within a year. Severe penalties were imposed for violation of the provisions of this act, and a number of administrative details were added. [2]

By act of February 14, 1903, the bureau of immigration was transferred from the treasury depart-

---

[1] *Pol. Science Quart.*, IX., 669, 670.
[2] Bureau of Immigration and Naturalization, *Immigration Laws and Regulations of February, 1906.*

ment to the new department of commerce and labor; and the statutes have since been administered, in response to the demands of organized labor, with much greater strictness and severity, the head of the bureau from 1902 to 1907 having been at the time of his appointment chief of the Brotherhood of Locomotive Firemen. The number of persons debarred for various reasons in 1906 was 12,432.[1]

The recent act of February 20, 1907, carries out more fully the principle underlying the act of 1903—namely, the admission of aliens who are sound in mind, body, and morals, and the exclusion of those who are unfit for American citizenship. It raises the head tax from two to four dollars, and requires steamship companies to provide more air space for steerage passengers; it adds to the excluded classes imbeciles, feeble-minded persons, persons who have been insane within five years, persons afflicted with tuberculosis, or with any mental or physical defect which may affect their ability to earn a living, and children under sixteen years of age unaccompanied by one or both parents. The distinctive features of the bill are the provisions for a bureau of information to keep in touch with the proper state officials and furnish immigrants with information which will enable them to go to the places where they are most needed; for the appointment of a commission to investigate and report to Congress on the general subject of immigration; and for negotiations with

[1] Commissioner-General of Immigration, *Report*, 1906, p. 10.

foreign countries with a view to controlling immigration by treaty agreement.

Since the exclusion act of 1882 Chinese immigration has rested on an entirely different footing from that from other countries. This act suspended the admission of Chinese laborers for a period of ten years, the Chinese government having consented in the treaty of 1880 to the exclusion of laborers, provided that teachers, students, merchants, and travellers should be allowed to come and go of their own free will, and that return certificates should be issued to laborers already in the United States for the purpose of allowing them to visit China.[1] The fraudulent transference of these certificates to new immigrants led to the suspension of the privilege by an act of October 1, 1888, a measure which was not only harsh, but in violation of treaty stipulations. In 1892 a new act was passed continuing in force for another period of ten years all existing laws against Chinese immigration and requiring all Chinese laborers within the limits of the United States to procure from the collectors of internal revenue within a year certificates of residence, under penalty of deportation. By the new treaty of 1894 China again consented to the exclusion of laborers, provided that return certificates should be issued to any laborer wishing to visit China who had a wife, child, or parent in the United States, or property therein of the value of one thousand dollars.

[1] Cf. Sparks, *National Development (Am. Nation*, XXIII.), chap. xiv.

The acquisition of the Hawaiian and Philippine Islands brought more than 65,000 Chinese within the jurisdiction of the United States; 25,000 in the former group and 40,000 in the latter.[1] The joint resolution of July 7, 1898, stopped Chinese immigration to the Hawaiian Islands and prohibited Chinese from those islands from entering the United States. An act of April 29, 1902, which continued in force all laws against Chinese immigration and made them perpetual in duration, also prohibited the immigration of Chinese laborers, not citizens of the United States, from all the island territories of the United States to the mainland.[2] The treaty of 1894 with China was renounced by that country January 24, 1904, and is consequently no longer in force; while the treaty signed at Shanghai October 8, 1903, was commercial in character and did not deal directly with the question of immigration; we have, therefore, in 1907, no treaty arrangements with China on this important subject.[3]

Both the judicial interpretation and the administration of the various Chinese exclusion acts have been harsh in the extreme. In the first place, the word "laborer" as used in the various treaties and acts of Congress is not construed in the popular sense,

[1] U. S. Census Bureau, *Census of the Philippine Islands*, I., 14.
[2] *U. S. Statutes at Large*, XXXII., pt. i., p. 176.
[3] *Foreign Relations*, 1903, p. 91; 1904, p. 117. The Bureau of Immigration regards the renunciation of the treaty of 1894 as reviving that of 1880, though upon what theory it would be difficult to say.

but is held to include all Chinese persons except the four classes specifically enumerated in the treaty of 1880—namely, teachers, students, merchants, and travellers.   All others, such as traders, doctors, lawyers, farmers, engineers, priests, clerks, and the countless avocations bordering on manual labor, are excluded.[1]   In their zeal to exclude Chinese laborers our officials have heaped indignities upon Chinese gentlemen, merchants, scholars, officials, and professional classes.   As a writer on the subject says: "Our immigration and port officials have, as a rule, so construed the laws as to subject Oriental personages, with all their dignity and Old-World culture, to the sort of treatment that belonged in the worst period before the war to the administration of the fugitive-slave laws.   We have paused at nothing except the branding of these Chinese gentlemen with red-hot irons." [2]

The Chinese government does not resent the exclusion of coolies so much as the harshness of American laws against educated Chinamen of the professional and business classes.   This resentment was the main factor in producing a boycott of American goods in northern China in 1905.   The movement was organized on an extensive scale by Chinese chambers of commerce and guilds, which advised the people of the whole empire to boycott American

---

[1] Commissioner-General of Immigration, *Report*, 1905, p. 80; Attorney-General, *Opinions*, XXIII., 485.

[2] Albert Shaw, in *Review of Reviews*, XXXII., 143.

schools, goods, products, and ships, unless more
equitable treatment was accorded their countrymen
in the United States.[1]   Fortunately the Chinese government succeeded in checking the movement, but
not until it had caused heavy losses to Americans.
There was a strong suspicion throughout the United
States that this movement was instigated by Japanese agents with the object of supplanting American
by Japanese commerce.   Formerly numbers of Chinese came to the United States to be educated; they
are now going to Japan by the thousands, thus cutting off one of the greatest sources of influence commercially and politically in China.   Japan is making
a desperate effort to control the forces that are re-
shaping China, but it is doubtful whether she is equal
to the task.   Recent reports indicate that the Chinese are not satisfied with the kind of education they
are receiving from Japan: in the government exami-
nations of 1907 most of the students educated in
Japan failed, while most of those who stood near the
head of the list received their training in America.
If these reports are true, the United States still has
a chance to recover lost ground and to re-establish
its former prestige in China.

The great scarcity and poor character of labor
on the Pacific coast has brought about a perceptible
change of opinion on the Chinese question on the
part of employers, who are beginning to compare
the inferior substitutes with the Chinamen they used

[1] *Foreign Relations*, 1905, pp. 204–238.

to have. This is especially the case since the Japanese have been coming in in considerable numbers,
with all their aggressiveness and pride of race. But
California is too evenly divided between the two
great political parties for either side to venture to
incur the hostility of organized labor, and opposition
to the Chinaman will come in the future as in the
past from this source. No man who has dealings
with labor unions or who aspires to public office can
be pro-Chinese even in the slightest degree, for labor
is better organized and more powerful in California
than anywhere else in America. So far from admitting the Chinese again, the demand of the unions is
now for the exclusion of the Japanese.

During the latter part of October, 1906, the American public suddenly became aware of the fact that
an active anti-Japanese agitation was in progress in
California. The San Francisco board of education
passed a resolution October 11 directing all Chinese,
Japanese, and Korean children to be sent to an
Oriental public school specially provided for them.[1]
The Japanese government was quick to resent this
action, and its ambassador formally demanded that
Japanese residents of California be protected in the
full enjoyment of the rights guaranteed them by the
treaty of 1894. President Roosevelt asserted very
emphatically that he would have justice done them,

[1] Secretary Root, "The Real Questions under the Japanese
Treaty and the San Francisco School Board Resolution," in *Am.
Journal of Int. Law*, I., 273–286.

and directed the United States district attorney to assist them in the effort to have their rights vindicated by the courts.   The incident created intense excitement throughout the country, and the press was filled with discussions as to whether the United States had the constitutional power to make a treaty which should override the laws of a state.   While the old question of state - rights was thus being hotly debated, the really significant question as to whether the Japanese treaty conferred school privileges was almost ignored.   The treaty guarantees to Japanese subjects in the United States, in "whatever relates to rights of residence," the same privileges, liberties, and rights as native citizens, or citizens or subjects of the most favored nation.[1]   The question as to whether the right to attend the public schools is a right of residence is open to debate; there is authority and reason for the opinion that it is not; but even granting that it is, it seems preposterous for foreigners to claim in this country under the "most-favored-nation" clause greater rights and privileges than are enjoyed by native-born citizens, who in many states are subject to segregation by race in the public schools.   California did all that could have been justly demanded of her under the treaty when she furnished equal, not identical, school facilities.[2]

But the school question was not the real question

---

[1] *Treaties in Force,* 1904, pp. 474, 475.
[2] *Am. Pol. Science Rev.,* I., 329, 510; *Am. Journal of Int. Law,* I., 150, 449.

at issue: the San Francisco school authorities could
easily have excluded Japanese men from association
with little children in the lower grades, which was
the main ground of complaint, by the adoption of
an age limit which is usual in most city schools.
The real question was the exclusion of Japanese
laborers from competition with American laborers,
and the assignment of Japanese children to a separate school was merely an incident in a general
agitation against the Japanese begun by the labor
unions of California.

The question has been adjusted, temporarily at
least, without being pushed to a conclusion in the
courts. Japan does not wish her subjects to come
in large numbers to the United States, and for some
time past it has been the practice of the Japanese
government not to issue passports to laborers desir-
ing to come to the United States, though passports
are issued for Hawaii, Canada, and Mexico, the holders of which in many cases finally enter this country.
Relying upon a continuance of this policy, Congress
inserted in the immigration act of February 20, 1907,
a clause authorizing the president to exclude from
the continental territory of the United States holders
of passports issued by any foreign government to its
citizens to go to any country other than the United
States or to the insular possessions of the United
States or to the Canal Zone. March 14, 1907, the
president issued an executive order directing that
Japanese laborers coming from Mexico, Canada, or

Hawaii be refused permission to enter the continental territory of the United States.[1]   The San Francisco school board thereupon agreed to admit Japanese children to the ordinary schools under certain conditions of age and ability to use the English language.

In recent years Japanese have been coming to the Hawaiian Islands in such large numbers as to give rise to serious apprehensions as to the future control of that important group.   The whole subject of Japanese immigration calls for treaty regulation, and it is to be earnestly hoped that the two countries will soon reach a satisfactory agreement on a basis that will insure a continuance of the traditional friendship and good feeling.

[1] *Am. Journal of Int. Law*, I., 450.

CHAPTER XVIII

ECONOMIC TENDENCIES
(1895–1907)

IN any attempt to analyze the economic and industrial development of the present generation three movements at once arrest our attention: first, the organization of capital; second, the organization of labor; and third, governmental interference for the regulation of both in the interests of the general public. The concentration of capital in large-scale production, which is the most striking feature of modern industry, is due to the ever-extending application of machinery and to the growing complexity of the processes of production. The economic advantages of large business units are too familiar to need repetition: in certain lines of industry the tendency to concentration is inevitable and cannot be stayed by legislation. To state the problem philosophically, 'co-operation is the great law of social development.[1]

For three or four years following the Spanish War, the unprecedented prosperity of the country and the rapid accumulation of capital greatly accelerated

[1] Ely, *Evolution of Industrial Society*, chap. v.

industrial combinations.   Bankers, brokers, and lawyers became promoters of such organizations and
undertook to float the stock of the purchasing or
holding companies.   The most gigantic industrial
combination that the world has ever seen was the
United States Steel Corporation, organized in 1901
under a New Jersey charter.   This concern purchased the stock of eleven great companies which
had control of about three-fourths of the steel industry of the United States, thus bringing under one
management capital amounting to $1,100,000,000.
The extent to which other combinations control the
output of the various lines of industry is difficult to
determine, but in sugar about 90 per cent. is controlled by a single combination, and in petroleum
at least 82 per cent.[1]   As to the ultimate outcome
of all this combination, the Industrial Commission,
in its concluding report of 1902, says: "There is
reason to believe that the movement toward concentration of industry will go steadily on, but there is
no reason for thinking that within measurable time
the combinations will cover the entire field of industry.   There will still be left abundant opportunity for individual ownership and management." [2]
Since the date of this report the fever for organization has somewhat subsided, and it is not so easy
now for a promoter to get the capital to float new
schemes of consolidation.

In the case of railroads competition had in most

[1] Industrial Commission, *Report*, XIX., 604.   [2] *Ibid.*, 600.

cases ceased long before consolidation took place.[1]
Various aspects of this question were brought prominently before the public in 1903 by the Northern
Securities suit, a case which is important not on
account of any fundamental questions settled by the
decision, for there were none, but as illustrating the
difficulties of the problem of legal control and the
trend of public sentiment.   The Great Northern and
Northern Pacific railroad systems, built separately,
the former by James J. Hill, had for a number of
years been operated in harmony; the lines are parallel, running across the continent through the northern tier of states between the Great Lakes and the
Pacific, and forming what are known as the Hill
lines.   Neither of these roads had direct connection
with Chicago or St. Louis, and in order to improve
their eastern connections Hill negotiated, through the
directors of the Chicago, Burlington & Quincy, for
the purchase of $108,000,000 of the $112,000,000
capital stock of that road, giving in exchange for it
joint four-per-cent. bonds of the Great Northern and
Northern Pacific.[2]

In this purchase of the Burlington the two roads
had in mind the consolidation of their lines under
one board of directors; but this could not be accomplished under the laws of Minnesota and other northwestern states which had granted their charters.
The result was therefore brought about indirectly:

[1] Cf. Dewey, *National Problems* (*Am. Nation,* XXIV.), chap. vi.
[2] Meyer, *Hist. of the Northern Securities Case,* 230.

James J. Hill and associate stockholders of the Great Northern, and J. Pierpont Morgan and associate stockholders of the Northern Pacific, formed under the laws of New Jersey a holding corporation, known as the Northern Securities Company, with a capital stock of $400,000,000, which in due time acquired in exchange for its own capital stock, upon an agreed basis, nearly all the stock of the Great Northern and more than half of the stock of the Northern Pacific, though Harriman made a "raid" on the latter stock and tried to wrest control from Hill.[1]

The authorities of Minnesota and the other states concerned regarded the formation of this company as an evasion of their laws, but as it could not be reached by the state courts, they finally called on President Roosevelt to proceed against the new company under the Sherman anti-trust law of 1890.[2] Action was accordingly brought in the United States circuit court at St. Paul, and the four judges sitting at the trial decided unanimously against the legality of the Northern Securities Company. The case was then appealed to the Supreme Court of the United States, where the judgment of the circuit court was affirmed, but by a division, five justices concurring and four dissenting. The opinion of the court, delivered by Justice Harlan, March 14, 1904, held that the Northern Securities Company was not organized

[1] Meyer, *Hist. of the Northern Securities Case*, 233, 240.
[2] For which see Dewey, *National Problems* (*Am. Nation*, XXIV.), chap. xii.

in good faith to purchase and pay for the stock of the said railways; that it was a mere depositary, custodian, holder, or trustee of the stocks; and that it destroyed every motive for competition between two roads engaged in interstate traffic; it was therefore a violation of the Sherman law.[1]

This decision was hailed by the public as a vindication of law, but lawyers have doubted its correctness and students of economics have regarded it as futile, to say the least. The dissolution of the company did not restore competition between the roads affected; and it would be difficult to demonstrate that any public good resulted.[2] Railroad competition no longer affords adequate protection to the public interests, and governmental regulation of some kind is necessary. With over two hundred thousand miles of railroads in the United States, three-fourths of which has been constructed within the last thirty years, it is not strange that the adjustment of legal theories has failed to keep pace with the work of construction, and that the problem of control yet remains to be solved.

The concentration of capital in large-scale production and the formation of industrial combinations have forced the wage-earners to organize and have made the labor movement a national problem. The American Federation of Labor, which was formed in 1881, and which has almost completely supplanted

---

[1] Northern Securities Company *vs.* U. S., 193 U. S., 197.
[2] Meyer, *Hist. of the Northern Securities Case*, 360.

the older organization of the Knights of Labor, had in 1905 a membership of about 2,000,000.[1] In addition to the federation there are certain unaffiliated organizations, numbering about 600,000 men, the most important being the railroad brotherhoods of engineers and firemen. The organized workers in the United States thus number at least 2,600,000, and exercise an active influence both on politics and legislation.

In the effort to improve the condition of the laboring classes through direct legislation, Massachusetts has led the way, and her child-labor and factory laws have been followed by many of the other states. The doctrine of free contract as held by courts of law was at first a serious obstacle to labor legislation, but so strong has been the demand for the protection of the laboring classes that the interpretation of that doctrine has undergone many modifications.[2] A large number of states have passed employers' liability acts, modifying the common-law doctrine of fellow-servant, acts prohibiting blacklisting and the exaction of a pledge from workmen not to join unions,[3] and acts establishing the eight-hour day for public works. The growing influence of the laboring classes and the growing importance of labor problems are further attested by the establishment in 1903 of the depart-

[1] *World Almanac*, 1906, p. 92; cf. Dewey, *National Problems* (*Am. Nation*, XXIV.), chap. iii.

[2] Adams and Sumner, *Labor Problems*, chap. xii.

[3] Wisconsin Free Library Commission, *Comparative Legislation Reference Bulletin*, No. 10.

ment of commerce and labor with a cabinet officer at its head.

The laboring classes are not satisfied to depend upon legislation alone. The most familiar methods employed by them to improve their condition are the strike and the boycott. During the period 1881–1900 there were recorded 23,798 strikes and lockouts in the United States, involving 127,442 establishments and 6,610,001 employés. Of the total number of employés involved 35 per cent. were wholly successful, 17 per cent. partially successful, and 48 per cent. wholly unsuccessful.[1] Strikes are less frequent in England than in America, owing, it is said, to the greater progress collective bargaining has made there. Of this method of avoiding labor disputes a recent writer says: "The era of individual bargaining has passed away in transportation, and is very nearly a thing of the past in all large-scale production. We must adjust ourselves to collective bargains between organized labor on the one hand, and organized capital on the other. Not suppression of organization, but regulation of organization, must be our watchword."[2]

Industrial arbitration has made great progress in recent years in England, and still greater progress in some of her colonies. Compulsory arbitration has been adopted in New Zealand, West Australia, and

[1] Adams and Sumner, *Labor Problems*, 180; Industrial Commission, *Report*, XIX., 868.
[2] Ely, *Evolution of Industrial Society*, 390.

New South Wales; but there are constitutional ob-
stacles in the way of its being tried in the United
States, though voluntary arbitration has been resorted to with marked success.[1]

The most striking instance was the settlement of
an anthracite coal strike through the agency of
President Roosevelt. On May 12, 1902, the miners
in the anthracite coal region of Pennsylvania, members of the United Mine Workers of America, went
on a strike to secure an increase in wages, a decrease
in hours of work, the weighing of coal wherever practicable, and the recognition of their union. This
strike involved 147,000 workmen, lasted five months,
and caused a general coal famine throughout the
country. At the head of the United Mine Workers
stood John Mitchell, to be recognized before the
strike was over as the ablest labor leader America
had produced. Opposed to the miners were the presidents of a small group of coal-carrying railroads
which constituted the coal trust and held an absolute monopoly of the anthracite coal trade, headed
by George F. Baer, president of the Reading Company. By the beginning of October the situation
had become critical in the extreme and the public
was thoroughly aroused. Great indignation was felt
against the group of operators, who seemed determined to persevere with the purpose of crushing the
miners' union. Senator Hanna, representing the
Civic Federation, went to New York and tried to

[1] Adams and Sumner, *Labor Problems*, 319.

persuade the operators to submit the dispute to arbitration, but was not able to move them. Soft coal was being substituted for hard wherever possible, but the price advanced in some cases three or four times, and great suffering seemed in store for the multitudes in the eastern cities.

Under these circumstances President Roosevelt invited Mitchell and the presidents of the coal-carrying roads to a conference in Washington, October 3, 1902; he reminded them that they were not the only parties concerned; that the interests of a large part of the American people were at stake; and he urged concessions on both sides. Mitchell rose promptly and offered to submit the miners' claims to a board of arbitration appointed by the president, promising on behalf of the miners to abide by the decision, and to resume work as soon as his proposal was accepted and arbitration agreed on. This proposition was rejected by the operators, who denounced the strikers and called on the president to send federal troops to the coal-fields. Their position increased the indignation felt against them and aroused new sympathy for the miners. Governor Stone sent the national guard of Pennsylvania into the mining region, but instead of going to work when the soldiers arrived, as the operators had claimed would be the case, the miners replied by passing resolutions indorsing Mitchell's course.[1]

Meanwhile the president was placed in an exceed-

---

[1] Mitchell, *Organized Labor* 368–396.

ingly embarrassing position: acting in a matter
wholly outside his official functions, he had so far
met with failure; and there arose clamors that he
had simply encouraged the miners by recognizing
their union.   The president did not give the matter
up; he was working on it from a new quarter.   He
sent Elihu Root, secretary of war, to New York to
confer with J. Pierpont Morgan, the financial backer
of the coal trust, with the result that the latter called
for a special train and started hurriedly for Washington, October 13.   As the result of a conference
with the president he agreed to bring the operators
to terms, so far as to submit the dispute to a commission appointed by the president.[1]

The mere appointment of the commission was a
great victory for the miners' union, which had all
along declared itself willing to arbitrate, and at once
the men returned to the mines and relieved the
famine.   After five months of arduous labors, involving visits to the mines and the taking of testimony of over five hundred witnesses, the commission
made a report March 18, 1903, which was a decided
victory for the miners, though a compromise on certain points.   It provided for a shortening of the
hours of labor and for a general increase of wages
arranged according to a sliding scale and dependent
on the price of coal delivered at New York.[2]

Although the president went outside of the tradi-

[1] *Review of Reviews*, XXVI., 516 et seq.
[2] *Senate Docs.*, 58 Cong., Special Sess., No. 6.

tional sphere of his duties and took action wholly
without precedent from any previous administration,
yet when his efforts proved successful and a danger-
ous crisis was averted, the great majority of the
American people regarded his course with approval.
In the end it turned out to be one of the most popular steps ever taken by President Roosevelt.

With the growth of industrial combinations and
labor organizations, competition, which is the legal
basis on which the framework of our social and
industrial order has been built, is fast disappearing
from many of the most important fields of enterprise.[1]   Monopoly is undermining the foundations of
society.   What is to take the place of competition?
Socialism is one solution of the question, and the
strength of socialism is that it offers a definite theory
for a new social order.   In Belgium, France, Germany, and Austria socialism is a force to be reckoned
with.   In Switzerland and New Zealand, on the other
hand, social reform has sapped its strength.   While
Americans still hold to the doctrine of *laissez-faire*,
they have to a very large extent abandoned it in
practice, and the field of direct governmental activity
has been greatly enlarged.   The states have enacted
a large amount of social legislation; they have established labor bureaus and corporation commissions;
but so far they have signally failed to check the
growth of monopoly.

The growth of trusts and monopolistic combina-

[1] Ely, *Evolution of Industrial Society*, 97, 190.

tions has been far greater in America than in any other country. Owing to the overlapping of state and national authority corporations engaged in interstate business have developed without adequate legal control from either source. They have taken advantage of constitutional limitations and political prejudices to play the national government against the states and the states against the national government. When the failure of the states to deal successfully with the problem gave rise to wide-spread dissatisfaction and alarm, the public willingly accepted the leadership of President Roosevelt and turned to the federal government for relief. But the passage of a rate bill and the agitation by Bryan of the question of ultimate government ownership, have had the effect of arousing the state legislatures to feverish activity on the railroad problem and to the passage of a number of ill-considered measures. Wiser legislation will in time doubtless follow. At any rate the states have given an unexpected and overwhelming response to Secretary Root's challenge to exercise their powers or surrender them to the central government.

While the corporation problem is fundamentally economic, and no remedy will be successful which ignores economic tendencies, it is also political and legal, and a solution should be sought which will not require radical readjustment of the constitutional system. The Constitution gives the federal government the power to regulate interstate commerce; but the federal power has its limitations, and under the system of state charters the federal arm is not long enough to reach the root of the evil. The co-operation of both federal and state governments is necessary.[1]

Prominent among the new problems of direct governmental activity is the improvement of public lands by irrigation. The existence of a frontier in the past not only acted as a competing influence to keep up the wages of the working-man in the East, but it afforded a wide field for corporate enterprise. All the conditions of a new frontier are again being developed by the United States government through the irrigation of arid lands; and the movement is in all probability destined to have a great influence on the social and industrial development of the future. Few people, perhaps, are aware of the fact that the United States still holds nearly five hundred million acres of public lands, exclusive of Alaska and the insular possessions.[2] A great deal of this is forest and mineral land; and still more of it is suitable for grazing; but millions of acres may be reclaimed by irrigation for agricultural purposes. These lands were being fraudulently taken up by speculators and occupied by grazers when the national irrigation movement called attention to the frauds and the president secured remedial legislation by Congress.

[1] Cf. Hart, *National Ideals* (*Am. Nation*, XXVI.), chap. xiii.
[2] Public Lands Commission, *Report* (*Senate Docs.*, 58 Cong., 3 Sess., No. 154).

The history of the movement for national irrigation is full of interest.   It was conducted by George
H. Maxwell with the support and aid of six of the
large western railroads, which agreed to contribute
$5000 each annually for a period of ten years for a
campaign of education on the subject of irrigation;
and placed the entire sum of $30,000 a year thus
made available at his disposal.   Maxwell founded
magazines,[1] furnished articles to the daily press, distributed literature, organized the National Irrigation
Association, enlisted the support of business organizations East and West, and carried on one of the
most remarkable propagandas this generation has
seen.   After securing irrigation planks in the national
platforms of both parties, the movement culmi-
nated in the national irrigation act of June 17, 1902,
and the organization of the reclamation service.

The act provided that all moneys received from
the sale of public lands in sixteen states and territories west of the Mississippi, beginning with the fiscal
year ending June 30, 1901, be set aside as a special
fund in the treasury to be known as the "reclamation
fund," to be used for the construction and maintenance of irrigation works.[2]   In order to prevent
private appropriation of land and water rights in
localities suitable for works of irrigation, over 43,-
000,000 acres of land were withdrawn from public
entry and reserved for homesteads after the comple-

---

[1] *The Homemaker*, and *Maxwell's Talisman.*
[2] *U. S. Statutes at Large*, XXXII., 388.

tion of irrigation projects. Up to June 30, 1905, over $28,000,000 had accumulated under the act to the credit of the fund, and projects in the various states aggregating $37,000,000 were by that time outlined and the work of construction begun.[1] The most remarkable feature of the act of June 17, 1902, is that it is in a sense self-perpetuating: all the proceeds from the sales of irrigated lands go back into the fund to be used for irrigating other lands; so that the work will go on indefinitely without further legislation by Congress.

Irrigation affords the only strictly scientific basis for agriculture, for where the farmer is dependent on rains he must trust much to chance. But the cultivation of small tracts of land under foreknown conditions will doubtless develop a type of agricultural community life hitherto unknown in America. The irrigation village, with its modest homes, its public library, its social life and educational opportunities, its trolley line and electric lights operated possibly by power from the irrigation plant, presents an alluring picture easily within the realm of the possible. If the plan succeeds, millions of modest, substantial, independent homes will be added in time for the upbuilding of the nation.[2]

The problems that the American people have to

---

[1] Reclamation Service, *Fourth Annual Report* (*House Docs.*, 59 Cong., 1 Sess., No. 86,) pp. 34–36.

[2] Smythe, *Conquest of Arid America;* and the regular numbers of the *Talisman*.

solve are social, economic, and industrial, rather than political or constitutional in the old sense. They demand not only a lofty patriotism, but a large measure of constructive statesmanship. The American nation is still endowed with the priceless gift of youth; and whatever mistakes it may fall into, it has the energy, intelligence, resourcefulness, and optimism to win ultimate success.

In the sphere of international relations America is undoubtedly destined to play a larger part. The United States has always been a world power in a sense: as the great exponent of civil liberty its influence has gone out to the remotest bounds of the earth; in its dealings with other nations it has always been an upholder of legality and an advocate of arbitration; and the record of its achievements is one of which every American may well feel proud.[1] Speaking of its influence in moulding international opinion on certain questions, a leading English authority says: "The policy of the United States in 1793 constitutes an epoch in the development of the usages of neutrality. There can be no doubt that it was intended and believed to give effect to the obligations then incumbent upon neutrals. But it represented by far the most advanced existing opinions as to what those obligations were; and in some points

---

[1] For an admirable summary of what American diplomacy has accomplished, see Moore, *American Diplomacy: Its Spirit and Achievements*, passim; cf. Hart, *National Ideals* (*Am. Nation*, XXVI.), chap. xvii.

it even went further than authoritative international custom has up to the present time advanced. In the main, however, it is identical with the standard of conduct which is now adopted by the community of nations." [1]

In spite of the really great achievements of the past, it cannot be denied that the war with Spain was in a sense the parting of the ways, the end of the old and the beginning of a new era in American diplomacy. It brought new prestige and enlarged opportunities. The occupation of the Philippine Islands has placed the nation on an altogether different footing in the Orient; and it can no longer pose as a disinterested spectator of political changes in that quarter of the globe. Strained relations with Japan have already resulted, and the future doubtless has in store burdens and responsibilities from which it is not possible to shrink. In the reshaping of the Far East the United States has interests that it must protect and a well-formulated policy that it cannot afford to renounce.

In her rôle as a world power, armed with a mighty navy, which expansion in the Pacific and the cutting of a canal have made inevitable, it is to be hoped that America will not depart from her ancient ideals of peace or from that traditional frankness and fair dealing in diplomacy of which John Hay was one of the greatest exemplars. By no means the least significant of recent changes is the development of

[1] Hall, *International Law*, (5th ed.), p. 593.

cordial relations with England; and it seems now that the course of world politics is destined to lead to the further reknitting together of the two great branches of the Anglo-Saxon race in bonds of peace and international sympathy, in a union not cemented by any formal alliance, but based on community of interests and of aims, a union that will constitute the highest guarantee of the political stability and moral progress of the world.

CHAPTER XIX

CRITICAL ESSAY ON AUTHORITIES

BIBLIOGRAPHIES

THERE are no general bibliographies covering the entire period of this volume; but the Library of Congress has published a number of valuable bibliographies on special topics, compiled under the direction of A. P. C. Griffin, chief bibliographer, of which the more important are the following: *List of Books relating to Cuba (including references to collected works and periodicals), with Bibliography of Maps* (1898); *List of Books relating to Hawaii (including references to collected works and periodicals)* (1898); *List of Books (with references to periodicals) relating to the Theory of Colonization, Government of Dependencies, Protectorates, and Related Topics* (2d ed., 1900); *A List of Books (with references to periodicals) on Porto Rico* (1901); *List of Works relating to the American Occupation of the Philippine Islands, 1898–1903* (reprinted with additions to 1905); *Select List of References on Industrial Arbitration* (1903); *Select List of References on Government Ownership of Railroads* (1903); *List of References on Federal Control of Commerce and Corporations* (1904); *Select List of Books (with references to periodicals) relating to the Far East* (1904); *List of References on Recognition in International Law and Practice* (1904); *A List of Books (with references to periodicals) on Immigration* (1904); *Select List of References on Chinese Immigration* (1904); *Select List of References on Anglo-Saxon Interests* (1906).

Other bibliographies of a special character are J. B.

Moore, *Digest of International Law* (8 vols., Washington, 1906), which contains a list of authorities and very full foot-notes; A. B. Hart, *Manual of the History, Diplomacy, and Government of the United States* (Cambridge, 1908); A. B. Hart, *Foundations of American Foreign Policy, with a Working Bibliography* (New York, 1901). The *American Historical Review* (index to first ten volumes), the *American Political Science Review* (first issue, November, 1906), the *American Journal of International Law* (first issue, January, 1907), the *Archives Diplomatiques*, and the *Revue Générale de Droit International Public* are especially valuable for reviews of new books and lists of current magazine articles.

For general references the reader should consult the above bibliographies. The present chapter will be confined mainly to documentary sources, occasional reference being made to secondary works of special significance. The government publications on the period covered by this volume are unusually full; and while it is doubtless true that some important documents have been withheld or suppressed, it may be safely asserted that never before in the history of this or of any other country have the documents relating to a ten-year period of equal importance been given to the public so soon or so fully. In preparing this volume these documents have been interpreted in the light of magazine articles, newspaper reports and editorials, and oral discussions too numerous, and in many cases too ephemeral, to be recorded. It will take years to sift and digest the enormous amount of literature to which the Spanish War and subsequent events have given rise.

INTERVENTION IN CUBA

The most important single reference on this subject is the volume of *Foreign Relations of the United States* for 1898, the publication of which was delayed for reasons of state until 1901. This volume contains the more important correspondence on the political situation in Cuba and the various proposals of the United States for a permanent settlement of the Cuban question. The state department has also issued in the form of a translation *Spanish Diplomatic Correspondence and Documents, 1896–1900, Presented to the Cortes by the Minister of State* (1905), containing much of the same correspondence that is found in the *Foreign Relations*, with additional material including the instructions to the Spanish peace commissioners and their reports of the conferences with the American commissioners at Paris. *Compilation of Reports of the Committee on Foreign Relations, United States Senate* (1901), VII., is almost all devoted to reports on affairs in Cuba from 1896 to 1898. The report of the *Maine* court of inquiry is published in *Senate Documents*, 55 Cong., 2 Sess., No. 207. Moore, *Digest of International Law*, VI., 105–236, contains an excellent chronological summary of events leading to the war. Richardson, *Messages and Papers of the Presidents*, X., contains messages, proclamations, and executive orders relating to the war. Le Fur, *La Guerre Hispano-Américaine de 1898* (1899), and Flack, *Spanish-American Diplomatic Relations Preceding the War of 1898* (1906), discuss critically the grounds of intervention.

THE WAR WITH SPAIN

Naval operations are set forth in Secretary of the Navy, *Annual Report* (1898); and military operations in Secretary of War, *Annual Reports* for the same year; the more important reports are published in full in *Message and Documents, 1898–1899, Abridgment* (4 vols., 1899), which constitutes a valuable documentary history of the war. Much additional information is found in *Correspondence relating to the War with Spain* (2 vols., war dept., 1902). A. T. Mahan, *Lessons of the War with Spain* (1899), derives special value from the fact that the author was a member of the Naval Advisory Board during the war. J. D. Long, *New American Navy* (1903), although written in a rather popular vein and not without personal bias, is especially valuable for the administrative side of affairs during the author's term as secretary of the navy. W. S. Schley, *Forty-five Years Under the Flag* (1904), is important in connection with the dispute growing out of the naval battle of Santiago. H. C. Lodge, *The War with Spain* (1899), by a prominent member of the Senate committee on foreign relations, is popular, sketchy, and laudatory, but not discriminating. The *Report of the Commission Appointed by the President to Investigate the Conduct of the War Department in the War with Spain*, published in *Senate Documents*, 56 Cong., 1 Sess., No. 221 (8 vols.), contains some valuable testimony, but the report itself is strongly biased in favor of the war department. The *Record of Proceedings of a Court of Inquiry in the Case of Rear-Admiral Winfield Scott Schley, U.S.N.*, including the president's review of the case, is published in *House Documents*, 57 Cong., 1 Sess., No. 485. Information in regard to the losses sustained by the American army from all causes during the war is contained in *Senate Documents*, 56 Cong., 1 Sess., No. 426.

Papers relating to the Treaty with Spain, containing the instructions to the United States peace commissioners, were first published in *Senate Documents*, 56 Cong., 2 Sess., No. 148, and later in the *Foreign Relations* for 1898. The actual records or protocols of the conferences between the American and Spanish commissioners at Paris, and the text of the treaty, together with much miscellaneous information in regard to the Philippines presented to the American commissioners, will be found in *Senate Documents*, 55 Cong., 3 Sess., No. 62, parts i.–iii. The discussions that took place in the Senate on the acquisition of the Philippines will be found in the *Congressional Record* for December, 1898, and January and February, 1899. The proceedings of the Spanish Treaty Claims Commission will be found in *Senate Documents*, 58 Cong., 2 Sess., No. 25, and 59 Cong., 1 Sess., No. 308.

THE STATUS OF DEPENDENCIES

On the so-called issue of imperialism there was a flood of pamphlets, the more noteworthy being W. G. Sumner,

Conquest of the United States by Spain (1899); C. F. Adams, *Imperialism and the Tracks of Our Forefathers* (1899); Carl Schurz, *American Imperialism* (1899); G. F. Hoar, *No Power to Conquer Foreign Nations and Hold their People in Subjection against their Will* (1899); Edward Atkinson, *Cost of War and Warfare from 1898 to 1904* (1904); Moorfield Storey, *What Shall We Do with Our Dependencies?* (1905); various publications by Herbert Welsh, of Philadelphia, editor of *City and State;* publications of the Philippine Information Society and of the New England Anti-Imperialistic League.

The official publications relating to the insular possessions of the United States already form a large body of literature. The *Annual Reports* of the war and navy departments contain full information in regard to the occupation of Hawaii, Cuba, Porto Rico, Guam, and the Philippines. The reports of the secretary of war for the five years following the war with Spain have been reissued in a single volume, *Annual Reports of the Secretary of War, 1899–1903*, which gives a convenient summary of the administration of the insular possessions during those important years. For statistical information the best reference is *Porto Rico, Hawaii, Philippine Islands, Guam, Samoan Islands, and Cuba : Their Area, Population, Agriculture and Mineral Products; Imports and Exports by Countries; and the Commerce of the United States therewith* (Bureau of Statistics, treasury department, *Summary of Commerce and Finance*, July, 1901). The same bureau has published the *Territorial and Commercial Expansion of the United States, 1800–1900, the Additions to National Area and their Subdivisions into Territories and States, and Statistics of Growth in Population, Wealth, Commerce and Production* (*Summary of Commerce and Finance*, August, 1902). The Bureau of Insular Affairs of the war department has published a number of valuable reports: *Legal Status of the Territory and Inhabitants of the Islands Acquired by the United States during the War with Spain, Considered with Reference to the Territorial Boundaries, the Constitution, and the Laws of the United States*, by Charles

E. Magoon, Law Officer of the Bureau of Insular Affairs
(1900); *Reports on the Law of Civil Government in Territory
Subject to Military Occupation by the Military Forces of the
United States*, by Charles E. Magoon (1902); and *Compilation of the Acts of Congress, Treaties, and Proclamations relating to Insular and Military Affairs, 1897–1903* (1904). The
latter is a valuable reference book. The reports of Magoon
contain a large amount of valuable information, but they
bear too much the character of a brief for the government,
and should be used with caution. C. F. Randolph, *Law
and Policy of Annexation* (1901), discusses the constitutional
aspects of imperialism. W. F. Willoughby, *Territories and
Dependencies of the United States* (1905), gives a clear description of the measures that have been adopted in the
organization of the various insular governments; it is especially valuable for Porto Rico, its author having been
for several years treasurer of that island. The decisions in
the insular cases are published in 182 U. S. Reports, 1 and
244; 183 U. S. Reports, 176; 190 U. S. Reports, 197. Of
such far-reaching importance were these cases deemed that
the briefs, records, and arguments of counsel were collected and published in *House Documents*, 56 Cong., 2 Sess.,
No. 509.

THE PHILIPPINE ISLANDS

The most important documents of a general character
are the *Report of the* [First] *Philippine Commission* (4 vols.,
1900); Philippine Commission, *Annual Reports* (Bureau of
Insular Affairs, war department); same collected and republished with omission of exhibits in one volume as *Reports
of the Philippine Commission, 1900–1903*; Philippine Commission, *Acts* (Manila, 1902–1907); *The Municipal Code and
the Provincial Government Act* (Manila, 1905); *A Pronounc-
ing Gazetteer and Geographical Dictionary of the Philippine
Islands* (Bureau of Insular Affairs, war department, 1902),
a volume of over nine hundred pages, containing maps,
charts, illustrations, and information in regard to climate,
population, and products, together with the text of the law

of civil government of July 1, 1902; *Atlas of the Philippine Islands* (Coast and Geodetic Survey, 1900), prepared under the supervision of Rev. José Algué, S. J., director of the Manila Observatory; *Report on the Census of the Philippine Islands* (4 vols., Office of the Census, Department of Commerce and Labor, 1905). J. G. Schurman, *Philippine Affairs: A Retrospect and Outlook* (1902), attracted much attention when delivered as an address, on account of its plain statements that the Filipinos were dissatisfied with American rule and longed for independence, and has a special value from the fact that its author was chairman of the first Philippine commission.

On relations with Aguinaldo prior to the outbreak of hostilities, see *Senate Documents*, 55 Cong., 3 Sess., No. 62; 56 Cong., 1 Sess., No. 208; and 56 Cong., 2 Sess., No. 148. The progress of events during the Philippine insurrection is described in the reports of the military governors and the appended reports of officers in the field: Report of General Merritt, *House Documents*, 55 Cong., 3 Sess., III.; Reports of General Otis, *House Documents*, 56 Cong., 1 Sess., V., and 56 Cong., 2 Sess., V.; Reports of General MacArthur, *House Documents*, 56 Cong., 2 Sess., VI., and 57 Cong., 1 Sess., V.; Report of General Chaffee, *House Documents*, 57 Cong., 1 Sess., VIII. On charges of cruelty to the natives, see *Senate Documents*, 57 Cong., 1 Sess., Nos. 205, 347, 422. *Hearings before the Committee on the Philippines of the United States Senate* (*Senate Documents*, 57 Cong., 1 Sess., No. 331, parts i.–iii.) contains about three thousand pages of testimony given before the Senate committee in 1902, including the testimony of Governor Taft, General Hughes, General Otis, General MacArthur, Admiral Dewey, a number of non-commissioned officers and privates of the army, and a number of civilians, together with numerous documents. This is the most important single publication on affairs in the Philippines during the insurrection. For the expenses of the civil administration, see the statement by the secretary of war covering the period from the date of the American occupation to June

30, 1901, *Senate Documents*, 57 Cong., 1 Sess., No., 382.
The *American Historical Review*, X. (July, 1906), contains
an interesting document by Mabini, the ablest of the revolutionary leaders, on the *Failure of the Philippine Republic*.

PORTO RICO

·*Report on the Island of Porto Rico: Its Population, Civil
Government, Commerce, Industries, Products, Roads, Tariff
and Currency, with Recommendations*, by H. K. Carroll,
special commissioner of the United States to Porto Rico
(1899); *Report on the Census of Porto Rico* (U. S. Office of
the Census, 1899); *Report of the Commission to Revise and
Compile the Laws of Porto Rico* (*House Documents*, 57 Cong.,
1 Sess., No. 52); *Register of Porto Rico* (editions of 1901
and 1902).

THE REPUBLIC OF CUBA

Information in regard to the reorganization of the Cuban
government during the period of American occupation will
be found in the *Report of the Military Governor of Cuba*
(8 vols., 1901). Material relating to the organization of
the Cuban republic will also be found in *Senate Documents*,
58 Cong., 2 Sess., No. 312; *Foreign Relations*, 1902, pp.
320–364; and Secretary of War, *Report*, 1902, Appendix A.
On Cuban reciprocity, see *Senate Documents*, 57 Cong., 1
Sess., Nos. 405 and 434; 57 Cong., 2 Sess., No. 206. A. G.
Robinson, *Cuba and the Intervention* (New York, 1905), by
a correspondent of the New York *Evening Post*, presents
an unfavorable view of General Wood's administration.

INTERNATIONAL RELATIONS

Works of a general character are *Foreign Relations of the
United States*, one or more volumes of which are issued by
the state department each year; *Treaties in Force, 1904;
Compilation of Reports of Committee on Foreign Relations,
United States Senate, 1789–1901* (8 vols., 1901); and J. B.

Moore, *Digest of International Law* (8 vols., 1906), started as a revision of Wharton's *Digest*, but practically a new work, issued by the state department, indispensable to students of American foreign policy; while this work did not appear in time to be of much service in the preparation of this volume, numerous references to it have been inserted in the foot-notes for the benefit of students. The British *Parliamentary Papers*, especially the *Treaty Series*, contain a vast amount of material on world politics not published in the United States documents. There are a number of foreign journals, such as *Archives Diplomatiques; Questions Diplomatiques et Coloniales; Revue Générale de Droit International Public*, devoted to international and colonial questions, and containing many valuable documents. Until recently there was no American journal devoted exclusively to such subjects, but in November, 1906, the first number of the *American Political Science Review* appeared, with a section devoted to international law and diplomacy; and in January, 1907, the *American Journal of International Law* made its appearance. A special feature of this review is the documentary supplement issued with each number; American students can now secure promptly texts of treaties, statutes, and cases, both foreign and domestic, which formerly took months to reach them through the official channels of publication.

INTERNATIONAL ARBITRATION

The standard authority is J. B. Moore, *Digest of International Arbitrations to which the United States has been a Party* (6 vols., Washington, 1898). On the proposed arbitration treaty with Great Britain, signed January 11, 1897, see *Senate Documents*, 58 Cong., 3 Sess., No. 161. F. W. Holls, *Peace Conference at The Hague* (1899), is the standard work on the first conference. Andrew D. White, *Autobiography* (1905), chaps. xlv.–xlix., is a briefer account but equally important. J. W. Foster, *Arbitration and The Hague Court* (1904), is a popular account by a diplomat of wide experi-

ence. On the practical work of the Hague court reference
may be made to the Pious Fund case reported at length in
Foreign Relations, 1902, Appendix, and to the Venezuelan
case reported in *Senate Documents*, 58 Cong., 3 Sess., No. 119.
The *Proceedings* of the Alaskan Boundary Tribunal (7 vols.)
are published in *Senate Documents*, 58 Cong., 2 Sess., No.
162; accompanying them and as part of the same docu-
ment are three large folio volumes containing *Maps and
Charts accompanying the Case and Counter Case of the
United States, Maps and Charts accompanying the Case of
Great Britain*, and *Twenty-five Sectional Maps and Index
Map showing the Line Fixed by the Tribunal*.

THE MONROE DOCTRINE

On the Monroe Doctrine and Pan-American affairs, consult the volumes of the *Foreign Relations;* J. B. Moore,
Digest of International Law; President Roosevelt's messages;
and the Second International American Conference, *Proceedings* (*Senate Documents*, 57 Cong., 1 Sess., No. 330). W.
F. Johnson, *Four Centuries of the Panama Canal* (1906), contains a large amount of information on the recent period
(1900–1906). Discussions of the present status of the Monroe Doctrine will be found in A. B. Hart, *Foundations of
American Foreign Policy* (1901); J. W. Foster, *A Century of
American Diplomacy* (1901); J. H. Latané, *Diplomatic Relations of the United States and Spanish America* (1900); and
J. B. Moore, *American Diplomacy* (1905).

DIPLOMATIC SITUATION IN THE FAR EAST

Much material will be found in the volumes of the
Foreign Relations. Additional correspondence concerning
China at the time of the Boxer troubles will be found in
House Documents, 55 Cong., 3 Sess., No. 1, and in the
British *Parliamentary Papers*, 1900, *China*, No. 3. Events
during the siege of the legations at Peking are described at
length in *Parliamentary Papers*, 1900, *China*, No. 4. An

account of the part taken by American troops in the relief expedition is found in the *Report* of the secretary of war, 1900. W. W. Rockhill, *Report on Affairs in China*, published in *Foreign Relations*, 1901, Appendix, contains a full account of affairs from the relief of the legations until the conclusion of the final treaty of peace. The papers relating to Hay's proposals of September, 1899, in regard to the open-door policy, are published in *House Documents*, 56 Cong., 1 Sess., No. 547. The Bureau of Statistics has published: *Commercial China in 1904 : Area, Population, Production, Railways, Telegraphs, and Transportation Routes, and Foreign Commerce and Commerce of the United States with China* (*Summary of Commerce and Finance*, January, 1904); and *Commercial Japan in 1904 : Area, Population, Production, Railways, Telegraphs, and Transportation Routes, and Foreign Commerce of the United States with Japan* (*Summary of Commerce and Finance*, February, 1904). A large number of interesting volumes on the Orient have appeared: P. S. Reinsch, *World Politics at the End of the Nineteenth Century as Influenced by the Oriental Situation* (1900); C. A. Conant, *The United States in the Orient : The Nature of the Economic Problem* (1900); Brooks Adams, *America's Economic Supremacy* (1900); J. M. Callahan, *American Relations in the Pacific and the Far East* (1900); A. T. Mahan, *The Problem of Asia and Its Effect upon International Policies* (1900); Henry Norman, *All the Russias* (1902); A. J. Beveridge, *The Russian Advance* (1903); G. F. Wright, *Asiatic Russia* (1902); A. R. Colquhoun, *Greater America* (1904); B. L. P. Weale, *The Re-shaping of the Far East* (1905); A. Little, *The Far East* (1905); T. J. Lawrence, *War and Neutrality in the Far East* (1904); K. Asakawa, *The Russo-Japanese Conflict : Its Causes and Issues* (1904); Smith and Sibley, *International Law as Interpreted during the Russo-Japanese War* (1905); A. S. Hershey, *The International Law and Diplomacy of the Russo-Japanese War* (1906); L. Aubert, *Paix Japonaise* (1906); B. L. P. Weale, *The Truce in the East and its Aftermath* (1907.)

NATIONAL AFFAIRS

A mass of material is issued from the government print-ing-office each year: *Senate Reports, House Reports, Senate Documents, House Documents, Senate Journal, House Jour-nal, Congressional Record*, messages of the presidents, de-partmental reports, and *Statutes at Large*. Associated Press despatches and despatches of Washington correspondents give valuable and for the most part reliable information. Of weekly and monthly magazines, the most helpful are the *Review of Reviews, Nation, North American Review, Forum, Outlook, Atlantic Monthly, World's Work, Literary Digest, Independent, Harper's Weekly*, and *Collier's Weekly*. More special and technical in character are the *Political Science Quarterly, Annals of the American Academy of Social and Political Science, Yale Review, American Journal of Sociology*, and various college and university publications.

ECONOMIC QUESTIONS

The *Report of the Industrial Commission* (19 vols., 1900–1902), prepared in accordance with an act of Congress ap-proved June 18, 1898, contains valuable statistics and the testimony of experts, business men, laboring men, etc., on almost every subject connected with the economic and industrial conditions of the day. The work of the commis-sion was outlined by experts and carried on with great success. While the pages of testimony and the work of experts employed by the commission are invaluable, the conclusions formulated by the commission are not in all cases warranted by the facts on which they are supposed to be based. The report is a mine of information to be worked over by economists. The new department of commerce and labor publishes a vast amount of statis-tical information: *Consular Reports, Commercial Relations, Monthly Summaries of Commerce and Finance*, the *Census Reports*, and the *Reports of the Commissioner-General of Im-migration*. Recent volumes which embody the results of the investigations made by the Industrial Commission are Adams and Sumner, *Labor Problems* (1905); R. T. Ely, *Evolution of Industrial Society* (1906); Prescott F. Hall, *Immigration* (1906); J. R. Commons, *Races and Immigrants in America* (1907).

INDEX